Workshop on Language Technologies for Digital Humanities and Cultural Heritage 2011

(DigHum 2011)

Held with the 8th International Conference on Recent Advances in Natural Language Processing 2011 (RANLP 2011)

Hissar, Bulgaria
16 September 2011

Editors:

Cristina Vertan
Petya Osenova
Milena Slavcheva
Stelios Piperidis

ISBN: 978-1-62276-461-7

Printed from e-media with permission by:

Curran Associates, Inc.
57 Morehouse Lane
Red Hook, NY 12571

Some format issues inherent in the e-media version may also appear in this print version.

Printed by Curran Associates, Inc. (2012)

Association for Computational Linguistics
209 N. Eighth Street
Stroudsburg, Pennsylvania 18360

Phone: 1-570-476-8006
Fax: 1-570-476-0860

acl@aclweb.org

Additional copies of this publication are available from:

Curran Associates, Inc.
57 Morehouse Lane
Red Hook, NY 12571 USA
Phone: 845-758-0400
Fax: 845-758-2634
Email: curran@proceedings.com
Web: www.proceedings.com

DigHum 2011

Proceedings of the Workshop on Language Technologies for Digital Humanities and Cultural Heritage

associated with

The 8th International Conference on Recent Advances in Natural Language Processing (RANLP 2011)

Edited by

Cristina Vertan, Milena Slavcheva, Petya Osenova and Stelios Piperidis

16 September, 2011

Hissar, Bulgaria

Foreword

Following several digitization campaigns during the last years, a large number of printed books, manuscripts and archaeological digital objects have become available through web portals and associated infrastructures to a broader public. These infrastructures enable not only virtual research and easier access to materials independent of their physical place, but also play a major role in the long term preservation and exploration.

However, the access to digital materials opens new possibilities of textual research like: synchronous browsing of several materials, extraction of relevant passages for a certain event from different sources, rapid search through thousand pages, categorisation of sources, multilingual retrieval and support, etc.

Methods from Language Technology are therefore highly required in order to ensure extraction of content related semantic metadata, and analysis of textual materials. There are several initiatives in Europe aiming to foster the application of language technology in the humanities (CLARIN, DARIAH). Through initiatives like those, as well as many other research projects, the awareness of such methods for the humanities has risen considerably. However, there is still enough potential on both sides:

• on one hand, there are still research tracks in the humanities which do not sufficiently and effectively exploit language technology solutions;

• on the other hand, there are many languages, especially historical variants of languages, for which the available tools and resources still have to be developed or adapted to serve successfully humanities applications.

The current workshop brings together researchers from the Humanities, as well as from Language and Information Technologies, and thus fosters the above mentioned directions.

As a confirmation of the generated interest in the topic of our workshop, we received a large number of very good submissions. This fact allowed us to provide a programme covering the most important aspects within the area of digital humanities and cultural heritage. Following the workshop programme, the Proceedings of the workshop are thematically structured as follows: Electronic Archives, Language Technology and Resources, Computational Methods for Literary Analysis, Multimodal Aspects in Digital Humanities.

The workshop papers address a multitude of problems and suggest a wealth of developments and solutions related to the digital humanities and the preservation of cultural heritage. The papers represent a whole spectrum of relevant topics: utilizing interlinked semantic technologies for managing and accessing museum data; exploiting topic models in a query classification system for an art image archive; metadata and content-oriented search methods for a multilingual audio-and-video archive; maintaining a digital library of Polish and Poland-related old ephemeral prints; normalization of historical wordforms in German; developing a Bulgarian-Polish on-line dictionary as a technological tool for applications in the digital humanities; semantic annotation models based on ontological representation of knowledge concerning Bulgarian iconography; preparation of an electronic edition of the largest Old Church Slavonic manuscript, the Codex Suprasliensis; literary research support by creating and visualizing profiles of sentimental content in texts; profiling of literary characters in 19th century Swedish prose fiction by interpersonal relation extraction; investigation of diachronic stylistic changes in British and American varieties of 20th century written English language; speeding up the process of creating annotations of audio-visual data for humanities research; automatic transcription of ancient handwritten documents; OCR processing of Gothic-script documents.

We would like to thank the Organisers of the RANLP events, especially Galia Angelova and Kiril Simov, for their unceasing help in the organisation of the workshop.

We are indebted to the Programme Committee members who provided very detailed reviews in extremely short time.

Special thanks are addressed to Gábor Prószéky, who accepted to be our keynote speaker and additionally raised the interest in our workshop.

September 2011

Cristina Vertan, Milena Slavcheva, Petya Osenova and Stelios Piperidis

Workshop Organizers:

Cristina Vertan (University of Hamburg, Germany)
Milena Slavcheva (Bulgarian Academy of Sciences, Bulgaria)
Petya Osenova (Sofia University and Bulgarian Academy of Sciences, Bulgaria)
Stelios Piperidis (ILSP, Greece)

Programme Committee:

Galia Angelova (Bulgarian Academy of Sciences, Bulgaria)
David Baumann (Perseus, Tufts University, USA)
Núria Bel (University of Barcelona, Spain)
António Branco (University of Lisbon, Portugal)
Nicoletta Calzolari (University of Pisa, Italy)
Günther Görz (University of Erlangen, Germany)
Walther v. Hahn (University of Hamburg, Germany)
Fotis Jannidis (University of Würzburg, Germany)
Steven Krauwer (University of Utrecht, the Netherlands)
Éric Laporte (Université Paris-Est, Marne-la-Vallée, France)
Anke Lüdeling (Humboldt University, Berlin, Germany)
Adam Przepiórkowski (Polish Academy of Sciences, Poland)
Gábor Prószéky (MorphoLogic, Hungary)
Laurent Romary (LORIA-INRIA, Nancy, France)
Manfred Thaler (Cologne University, Germany)
Tamás Váradi (Hungarian Academy of Sciences, Hungary)
Martin Wynne (University of Oxford, UK)

Invited Speaker:

Gábor Prószéky (MorphoLogic & Pázmány University, Budapest, Hungary)
Endangered Uralic Languages and Language Technologies

Table of Contents

Multimodal Aspects in Digital Humanites

Workshop Programme

Friday, 16 September 2011

9:00–9:15 Opening

9:15–10:15 *Endangered Uralic Languages and Language Technologies*
Gábor Prószéky

10:15–10:45 Coffee Break

Electronic Archives

10:45–11:10 *A Framework for Improved Access to Museum Databases in the Semantic Web*
Dana Dannélls, Mariana Damova, Ramona Enache and Milen Chechev

11:10–11:35 *Query classification via Topic Models for an art image archive*
Dieu-Thu Le, Raffaella Bernardi and Ed Vald

11:35–12:00 *Unlocking Language Archives Using Search*
Herman Stehouwer and Eric Auer

12:00–12:25 *Digital Library of Poland-related Old Ephemeral Prints: Preserving Multilingual Cultural Heritage*
Maciej Ogrodniczuk and Włodzimierz Gruszczyński

12:25–14:00 Lunch

Language Technology and Resources

14:00–14:25 *Rule-Based Normalization of Historical Texts*
Marcel Bollmann, Florian Petran and Stefanie Dipper

14:25–14:50 *Survey on Current State of Bulgarian-Polish Online Dictionary*
Ludmila Dimitrova, Ralitsa Dutsova and Rumiana Panova

14:50–15:15 *Language Technology Support for Semantic Annotation of Icono-graphic Descriptions*
Kamenka Staykova, Gennady Agre, Kiril Simov and Petya Osenova

Friday, 16 September 2011 (continued)

15:15–15:40 *The Tenth-Century Cyrillic Manuscript Codex Suprasliensis: the creation of an electronic corpus. UNESCO project (2010–2011)*
Hanne Martine Eckhoff, David Birnbaum, Anissava Miltenova and Tsvetana Dimitrova

15:40–16:10 Coffee Break

Digital Methods in Literary Analysis

16:10–16:35 *SentiProfiler: Creating Comparable Visual Profiles of Sentimental Content in Texts*
Tuomo Kakkonen and Gordana Galic Kakkonen

16:35–17:00 *Character Profiling in 19th Century Fiction*
Dimitrios Kokkinakis and Mats Malm

17:00–17:25 *Diachronic Stylistic Changes in British and American Varieties of 20th Century Written English Language*
Sanja Štajner and Ruslan Mitkov

17:25–17:40 Short break

Multimodal Aspects in Digital Humanites

17:40–18:05 *AVATecH: Audio/Video Technology for Humanities Research*
Sebastian Tschöpel, Daniel Schneider, Rolf Bardeli, Oliver Schreer, Stefano Masneri, Peter Wittenburg, Han Sloetjes, Przemek Lenkiewicz and Eric Auer

18:05–18:30 *Handwritten Text Recognition for Historical Documents*
Veronica Romero, Nicolas Serrano, Alejandro H. Toselli, Joan Andreu Sanchez and Enrique Vidal

18:30–18:55 *Reducing OCR Errors in Gothic-Script Documents*
Lenz Furrer and Martin Volk

18:55–19:15 Conclusions and closing

Endangered Uralic Languages and Language Technologies

Gábor Prószéky
MorphoLogic & Pázmány University, Budapest, Hungary
proszeky@morphologic.hu

Language tools and resources for analysis of less-elaborated languages are in the focus of our workshop. There are still research tracks which still do not sufficiently and effectively exploit language technology solutions, and there are many languages for which the available tools and resources still have to be developed to serve as a basis of further applications.

The presentation introduces a set of morphological tools for small and endangered Uralic languages. Various Hungarian research groups specialized in Finno-Ugric linguistics and a Hungarian language technology company (MorphoLogic) have initiated a project with the goal of producing annotated electronic corpora and computational morphological tools for small Uralic languages, like Mordvin, Udmurt (Votyak), Komi (Zyryan), Mansi (Vogul), Khanty (Ostyak), Nenets (Yurak) and Nganasan (Tavgi). Altogether around a dozen Uralic languages totaling some 3.3 million live as scattered minorities in Russia, as shown by the map below:

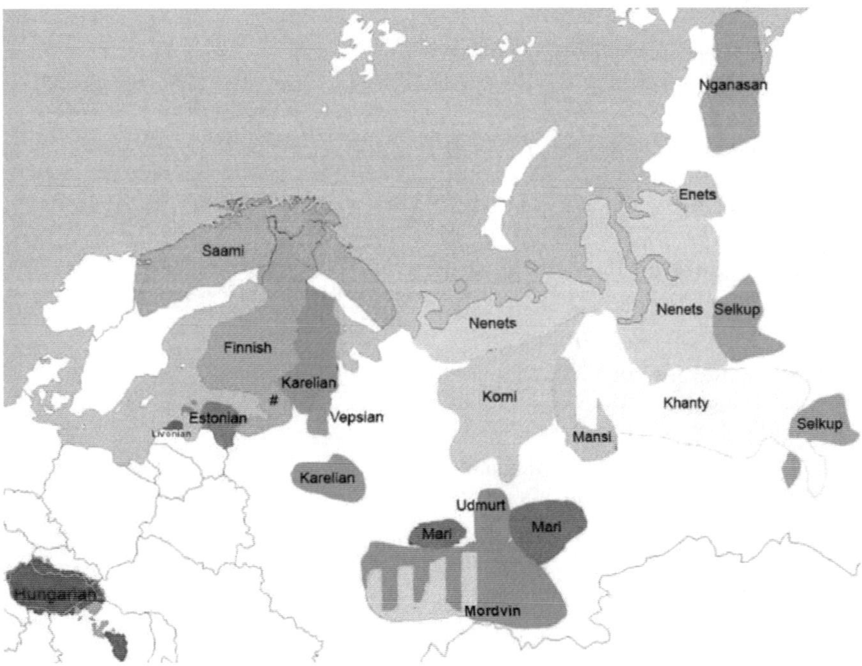

The morphologies of these languages are complex enough, thus the implementation of the morphological tools was a real challenge. The subprojects concerning the individual languages slightly differed, depending on the special problems these languages raise (how precisely the languages have been described so far, whether there is a standard dialect, what kinds of texts are available, etc.). In the project, we used the morphological analyzer engine called Humor ('High speed Unification MORphology') developed at MorphoLogic, which was first successfully applied to another Finno-Ugric language, Hungarian. We supplemented the analyzer with two additional tools: a lemmatizer and a morphological generator. Creating analyzers for the Samoyed languages involved in the project turned out to be a great challenge. Nganasan from the Northern Samoyed branch is a language on the verge of extinction (the number of native speakers is below 500 by now, most of them are middle-aged or old), so its documentation is an urgent scientific task. Nganasan morphology and especially its phonology is very complex and the available linguistic data and their linguistic descriptions proved to be incomplete and partly contradictory. Thus, using the Humor formalism, which we successfully applied to other languages involved in the project, was not to be feasible in the case of one of the chosen languages, Nganasan. The Humor formalism uses an 'item-and-arrangement' model of morphology where feature-based allomorph adjacency restrictions are the primary device for constraining word structure. Gradation in Nganasan is difficult to formalize as a set of allomorph adjacency restrictions because the segments involved in determining the outcome of the process may belong to non-adjacent morphemes. For Nganasan, we used therefore another tool (xfst of Xerox), mainly because gradation is just a small part of the complicated system of dozens of interacting productive and lexicalized morpho-phonological and phonological alternations.

Besides the annotated corpora and the morphological analyzers, a website was also developed where all of the tools described above are available for a wider public.

Acknowledgments

The projects have been funded by the Hungarian Scientific Research Fund (OTKA) and the National Research and Development Programme (NKFP): A Complex Uralic linguistic database (NKFP-5/135/01), Linguistic databases for Permic languages (OTKA T 048309), Development of a morphological analyzer for Nganasan (OTKA K 60807), Ob Ugric morphological analyzers and corpora (OTKA 71707).

A Framework for Improved Access to Museum Databases in the Semantic Web

Dana Dannélls
Department of Swedish Language
University of Gothenburg
SE-405 30 Gothenburg, Sweden
dana.dannells@svenska.gu.se

Mariana Damova
Ontotext
Sofia 1784, Bulgaria
mariana.damova@ontotext.com

Ramona Enache
Department of Computer Science and Engineering
GU and Chalmers University of Technology
SE-412 96 Gothenburg, Sweden
ramona.enache@chalmers.se

Milen Chechev
Ontotext
Sofia 1784, Bulgaria
milen.chechev@ontotext.com

Abstract

Digital museum databases have extremely heterogeneous data structures which require advanced mapping and vocabulary integration for them to benefit from the interoperability enabled by semantic technologies. In addition to establishing ways of extracting and manipulating digitally encoded cultural material, there exists a need to make this material available and accessible to human users in different forms and languages that are available to them. In this paper we describe a method to manage and access museum data by integrating it within a series of interlinked ontological models. The method allows querying and generation of query results in natural language. We report on the results of applying this method from experiments we have been pursuing.

1 Introduction

During the past few years several projects have been undertaken to digitize cultural heritage materials (Clough et al., 2008; Dekkers et al., 2009) through the use of Semantic Technologies such as RDF (Brickley and Guha, 2004) and OWL (Berners-Lee, 2004). Today there exist large number of digital collections and applications providing direct access to cultural heritage content.[1]

However, digitization is a labour intensive process and is long from being complete. Because of the heterogeneous data structures different museums have, digitally encoded cultural material stored in internal museum databases requires advanced mapping and vocabulary integration for it to be accessible for Semantic Web applications. In addition to establishing ways for managing various vocabularies, and for exploiting semantic alignments across them automatically (van der Meij et al., 2010), computer engineers also need to investigate automatic methods to make this information available to computer users in different forms and languages that are available to them.

Our work is a step towards this direction. It is about an automatic workflow of sharing data infrastructures that is explicitly targeted towards the Semantic Web. We have developed a method to manage and access museum data by integrating it within a series of interlinked ontological models. The method allows querying and generation of query results in natural language using the Grammatical Framework (GF). We have been experimenting with data collections from the Gothenburg City Museum that we made available for querying in the Museum Reason-able View loaded in the triple store OWLIM.

In the remainder of this paper we present the ontologies that were merged including CIDOC-CRM,[2] PROTON,[3], the Painting ontology and the data that we have been experimenting with (Section 2). We describe the creation of the Museum Reason-able View with structured query examples (Section 3). In Section 4, we introduce the Grammatical Framework and demonstrate the mechanisms of interfacing between the structured data and natural language. We provide an overview of related work (Section 5) and end with conclusions.

[1] http://www.europeana.eu/portal/

[2] The Conceptual Reference Model (CRM): http://cidoc.ics.forth.gr/

[3] http://proton.semanticweb.org/

2 The Ontologies and Museum Data

2.1 The CIDOC-CRM

The International Committee for Documentation Conceptual Reference Model (CIDOC CRM) that was accepted by ISO in 2006 as ISO21127 (Crofts et al., 2008), is one of a widely used standards that has been developed to facilitate the integration, mediation and interchange of heterogeneous cultural heritage information.

The CIDOC CRM, independent of any specific application, is primarily defined as an interchange model for integrating information in the cultural heritage sector. Although it declares rich common semantics of metadata elements, many of the concepts that are utilized for describing objects are not directly available in this model. To arrive at the point where information that is available in museum databases about paintings could be recorded using this model, we developed the painting ontology that integrates the CIDOC-CRM with more specific schemata.

2.2 The Swedish Open Cultural Heritage (SOCH)

The Swedish Open Cultural Heritage (SOCH) is a web service used to search and fetch data from any organization that holds information related to the Swedish cultural heritage.[4]

The idea behind SOCH is to harvest any data format and structure that is used in the museum sector in Sweden and map it into SOCH's categorization structure. The data model used by SOCH is an uniform data representation which is available in an RDF compatible form.

The schema provided by SOCH helps to intermediate data between museums in Sweden and the Europeana portal. More than 20 museums in Sweden have already made their collections available through this service. By integrating the SOCH data schema in the ontological framework we gain automatic access to these collections in a semantically interoperable way.

2.3 The Painting Ontology

The painting ontology is a domain specific ontology. It is designed to support integration and interoperability of the CIDOC-CRM ontology with other schemata. The main reference model of the painting ontology is the OWL 2 implementation of the CRM.[5] The additional models that are correctly integrated in the ontology are: SOCH, Time Ontology,[6] SUMO and Mid-Level-Ontology.[7] The painting ontology was constructed manually using the Protégé editing tool.[8]

Integration of the ontology concepts are accomplished by using the OWL construct: *intersectionOf* as specified below:

```
<owl:Class rdf:about="&painting;Painting">
 <owl:equivalentClass>
  <owl:Class>
    <owl:intersectionOf rdf:parseType="Collection">
      <rdf:Description rdf:about="&ksasok;item"/>
      <rdf:Description rdf:about="&milo;PaintedPicture"/>
     </owl:intersectionOf>
    </owl:Class>
   </owl:equivalentClass>
 <rdfs:subClassOf rdf:resource="&core;E22_Man-Made_Object"/>
</owl:Class>
```

The schemata that are stated in the above example are denoted with the following prefixes: painting ontology (&painting), SOCH (&ksamsok), Mid-Level-Ontology (&milo) and CIDOC-CRM ontology (&core). In this example, the class *Painting* is defined in the painting ontology as a subclass of *E22_Man-Made_Object* class from the CIDOC-CRM ontology and is an intersection of two classes, i.e. *item* from the SOCH schema and *PaintedPicture* from the Mid-Level Ontology.

The painting ontology contains 184 classes and 92 properties of which 24 classes are equivalent to classes from CIDOC-CRM and 17 properties are sub-properties of CIDOC-CRM properties.

2.4 Proton

PROTON (Terziev et al., 2005) is a light weight upper level ontology, which was originally built with a basic subsumption hierarchy comprising about 250 classes and 100 properties providing coverage of most of the upper-level concepts necessary for semantic annotation, indexing, and retrieval. Its modular architecture allows for great flexibility of usage, extension, integration and remodeling. It is domain independent and complies with the most popular metadata standards like DOLCE,[9] Cyc,[10] Dublin Core.[11]

PROTON is encoded in OWL Lite, and contains a minimal set of custom entailment rules (axioms). It is interlinked with CIDOC CRM, and is used in

[4] http://www.ksamsok.se/in-english/

[5] http://purl.org/NET/cidoc-crm/core

[6] http://www.w3.org/TR/owl-time/

[7] http://www.ontologyportal.org/

[8] http://protege.stanford.edu/

[9] http://www.loa-cnr.it/DOLCE.html

[10] http://www.ontotext.com/downloads/cycmdb

[11] http://www.cs.umd.edu/projects/plus/SHOE/onts/dublin.html

the data integration model to provide access to the Linked Open Data (LOD) for Cultural Heritage (Damova and Dannélls, 2011).

2.5 The Gothenburg City Museum Database

The Gothenburg City Museum (GCM) preserves 8900 museum objects described in two of the museum database tables. These two tables correspond to two of the museum collections, i.e. GSM and GIM. Each of these tables contains 39 properties for describing museum objects. Table 1 shows 20 of these properties, including the object type, its material, measurements, location, etc. All properties and object values stored in the database are given in Swedish.

Field name	Value
Field nr.	4063
Prefix	GIM
Object nr.	8364
Search word	painting
Class 1	353532
Class 2	Gothenburg portrait
Amount	1
Producer	E.Glud
Produced year	1984
Length cm	106
Width cm	78
Description	oilpainting represents a studio indoors
History	Up to 1986 belonged to Datema AB, Flöjelbergsg 8, Gbg
Material	oil colour
Current keeper	2
Location	Polstjärnegatan 4
Package nr.	299
Registration date	19930831
Signature	BI
Search field	BO:BU Bilder:TAVLOR PICT:GIM

Table 1: A painting object representation in the GCM database.

The Gothenburg City Museum's data that is used as our experimental data follows the structure of the CIDOC-CRM but it contains many concepts that are not available in CIDOC-CRM. So, in order to be able to fully integrate the Gothenburg City Museum data into a semantic view it was necessary to make use of concepts and relationships from the remaining ontologies.

Figure 1 shows how elements from the Goethenburg city museum are represented with elements from different schemata, e.g. CIDOC-CRM, PROTON, SOCH and the Painting ontology.

2.6 DBpedia

DBpedia (Auer et al., 2007) is the RDF-ized version of Wikipedia, comprising the information from Wikipedia infoboxes, designed and developed to provide as full as possible coverage of the factual knowledge that can be extracted from Wikipedia with a high level of precision. DBpedia describes more than 3.5 million things and covers 97 languages. 1.67 million of DBpedia things are classified in a consistent ontology, including 364,000 persons, 462,000 places, and 99,000 music albums. The DBpedia knowledge base has over 672 million RDF triples out of which 286 million extracted from the English edition of Wikipedia and 386 million extracted from other language editions.

DBpedia is used as an additional source of data, which can enrich the information about the Gothenburg museum data. For example, their location identified with the DBpedia resource referring to the city of Gothenburg.

3 Integrating and Accessing Museum Data

3.1 Integration for flexible computing

Integrating datasets into linked data in RDF usually takes place by indicating that two instances from two datasets are the same by using the built in OWL predicate: `owl:sameAs`.[12] However, recent research (Damova, 2011; Damova et al., 2011; Jain et al., 2011) has shown that interlinking the models according to which the datasets are described is a more powerful mechanism of dealing with large amounts of data in RDF, as it exploits inference and class assignment.

We have adopted this approach when creating the infrastructure for the museum linked data, including several layers of upper-level ontologies. They provide a connection to different sets of linked data, for example PROTON for the LOD cloud. They also provide an extended pool of concepts that can be referred to in museum linked data that do not directly pertain to the expert descriptions of the museum objects, and the strictly expert museum knowledge is left to CIDOC-CRM. This model of interlinked ontologies offers a flexible access to the data with different conceptual access points. This approach is implemented as a Reason-able View of the web of data (Kiryakov et al., 2009).

3.2 The Museum Reason-able View

Using linked data techniques (Berners-Lee, 2006) for data management is considered to have great potential in view of the transformation of the web of data into a giant global graph. Still there are challenges related to them that have to be handled

[12] `http://www.w3.org/TR/owl-ref/`

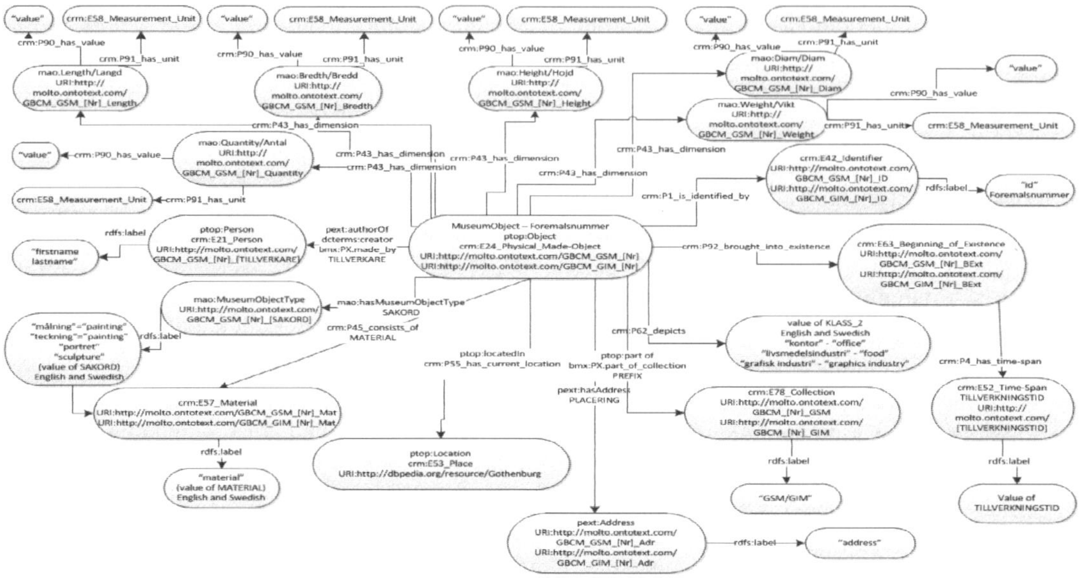

Figure 1: Dataset interconnectedness in the Museum Reason-able View.

to make this possible. Kiryakov et al. (2009) discuss these challenges and present an approach for reasoning with and management of linked data. In summary, a Reason-able View is an assembly of independent datasets, which can be used as a single body of knowledge with respect to reasoning and query evaluation. Each Reason-able View is aiming at lowering the cost and the risks of using specific linked datasets for specific purposes. We followed this approach when constructing the Museum Reason-able View with the data from the Gothenburg City Museum, DBpedia, Geonames and the ontologies listed in Section 2.[13]

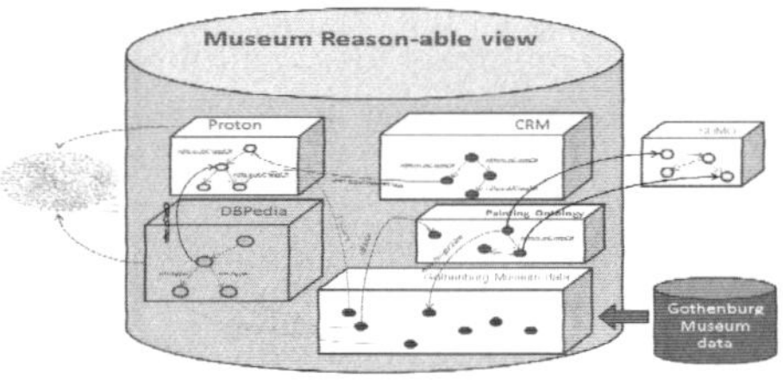

Figure 2: Integration of Gothenburg city museum data into the Museum Reason-able View.

The process of Gothenburg city museum data integration into the Museum Reason-able View consists in transforming the information from the museum database into RDF triples on the ontologies described in the previous section. Figure 2 shows the architecture of the Museum Reason-able View, which includes interconnected schemata and links to external to the Gothenburg museum data, such as DBpedia. The knowledge base contains close to 10K museum artifacts from the Gothenburg city museum, and the entire DBpedia.

3.3 Accessing Museum Linked Data

The Museum Reason-able View is loaded in OWLIM (Bishop et al., 2011) and its data are accessible via a SPARQL (Eric and Andy, 2008) end point and keywords.[14] The queries can be formulated by combining predicates from different datasets and ontologies in a single SPARQL query, retrieving results from all different datasets that are part of the Reason-able View.

A query example about the location, address, description and time of paintings by Carl Larsson is given below.

```
PREFIX crm: <http://purl.org/NET/cidoc-crm/core#>
PREFIX ptop: <http://proton.semanticweb.org/protontop#>
PREFIX painting:<http://spraakbanken.gu.se/rdf/owl/painting#>
PREFIX rdfs: <http://www.w3.org/2000/01/rdf-schema#>
PREFIX pext: <http://proton.semanticweb.org/protonext#>

select * where
{
?museumObject crm:P55_has_current_location  ?location .
?museumObject painting:hasCategory [rdfs:label "teckning"@sv].
?museumObject pext:authorOf  [rdfs:label "Carl Larsson"@sv].
?museumObject  crm:P55_has_current_location ?location .
OPTIONAL {
 ?museumObject pext:hasAddress [rdfs:label ?address].}
?museumObject  crm:P62_depicts  ?description .
?museumObject crm:P92_brought_into_existence
[ crm:P4_has_time-span [  rdfs:label  ?time ] ].
}
```

[13] Geonames website: http://www.geonames.org/

[14] The data is available at: http://museum.ontotext.com

SPARQL Query

Results for PREFIX crm: <http://purl... Download in JSON | SPARQL Results in XML | SPARQL Results in JSON

museumObject	location	collection	address	description	time
http://molto.ontotex...	http://dbpedia.org/r...	GIM@sv		glasindustri@sv	
http://molto.ontotex...	Göteborg@en	GIM@sv		glasindustri@sv	
http://molto.ontotex...	http://dbpedia.org/r...	GSM@sv	Huvudmagasinet Gårda@sv	1 göteborgsporträtt@sv	1889
http://molto.ontotex...	Göteborg@en	GSM@sv	Huvudmagasinet Gårda@sv	1 göteborgsporträtt@sv	1889
http://molto.ontotex...	http://dbpedia.org/r...	GSM@sv	Huvudmagasinet Gårda@sv	1 göteborgsporträtt@sv	1889
http://molto.ontotex...	Göteborg@en	GSM@sv	Huvudmagasinet Gårda@sv	1 göteborgsporträtt@sv	1889
http://molto.ontotex...	http://dbpedia.org/r...	GIM@sv		glasindustri@sv	
http://molto.ontotex...	Göteborg@en	GIM@sv		glasindustri@sv	
http://molto.ontotex...	http://dbpedia.org/r...	GSM@sv	Huvudmagasinet Gårda@sv	1 göteborgsporträtt@sv	1889

Figure 3: The results from a SPARQL query.

The above query returns the results that are depicted in Figure 3. Note that the returned location is the DBpedia resource about the city of Gothenburg. The results also show that museum items from the two collections – GIM and GSM – are harvested, which means that the data from the collections are integrated together and accessible from a single query point.

Other queries can be asked about the types of art work preserved in the museum, their material, or about artwork from a certain period of time, etc. Below follows another query example about the address, the time of paintings and the collection they are coming from.

```
select ?museumObject ?location ?collection
?address ?description ?time where
{
?museumObject crm:P55_has_current_location ?location ;
ptop:partOf [ rdfs:label ?collection ] ;
painting:hasCategory [ rdfs:label "teckning"@sv ] ;
crm:P62_depicts ?description .
OPTIONAL {?museumObject pext:hasAddress
[ rdfs:label ?address ] .}
OPTIONAL {?museumObject crm:P92_brought_into_existence
[ crm:P4_has_time-span [ rdfs:label ?time ] ] .}

}
```

The Reason-able View is accessible with SPARQL queries, which require intimate knowledge of the schemata describing the data, and technical expertise in SPARQL. Moreover, the results from SPARQL are not always easy to understand, in particular if the retrieved information is given in a language other than English. This is why the results are send forward to the NLP component to verbalize the ontology links.

4 Ontologies Verbalization

4.1 The Grammatical Framework (GF)

The Grammatical Framework GF (Ranta, 2004) is a grammar formalism, based on Martin-Löf's type theory (Martin-Löf, 1982). Its key feature is the division of a grammar in the abstract syntax-which acts as a semantic interlingua and the concrete syntaxes-representing verbalizations in various target languages (natural or formal).

GF comes with a resource library (Ranta, 2009), where the abstract syntax describes the most common grammatical constructions allowing text generation, which are further mapped to concrete syntaxes corresponding to 18 languages.[15] The resource library aids the development of new grammars for specific domains by providing the operations for basic grammatical constructions, and thus making it possible for users without linguistic background to generate syntactically correct natural language.

To verbalize the data that is stored in the Museum Reason-able View, we utilize GF. The advantages of using GF for verbalization is three fold: it provides mechanisms for type checking, by validating coercions between the basic class of an instance and the class required by the definition of the relation that uses it; the framework offers support of direct verbalization which makes it easier to generate text from the ontology and so to create natural language applications using it without the aid of external tools; GF has a resource library that cover the syntax for 18 languages.

4.2 Translation of the Museum Reason-able View to GF

The capabilities of GF as a host-language for ontologies were already investigated in Enache and Angelov (2010), where SUMO, the largest open-source ontology was translated to GF. It was shown that the type system provides a robust

[15] www.grammaticalframework.com

framework for encoding classes, instances and relations. The same basic implementation design that was used for encoding SUMO in GF is applied in this work for representing the Museum Reasonable View.

The classes form a hierarchy modelled by an inheritance relation, which is the reflexive-transitive closure of the subclass relation `rdfs:subClassOf` from the ontology, are encoded as functions in the GF grammar. Other information stated in the ontology, is encoded in GF as axioms, external to the grammar. These are used for verbalization as in the following example from the OWL entry corresponding to the painting *Big Garden*:

```
<owl:NamedIndividual
  rdf:about="&painting; BigGardenObj">
 <rdf:type
  rdf:resource="&painting;Painting"/>
 <isPaintedOn
  rdf:resource="&painting;Canvas"/>
 <createdBy
  rdf:resource="&painting;CarlLarsson"/>
 <hasCreationDate rdf:resource=
                 "&painting;Year1937"/>
</owl:NamedIndividual>
```

A representation of the instance *BigGardenObj* is defined as follows:

```
fun BigGardenObj : Ind Painting ;
```

Where the *Painting* was defined previously as a class. The remaining information about *Big Garden* from the ontology is encoded as a set of axioms with the following syntax:

```
isPaintedOn (el BigGradenObj) (el Canvas)

createdBy (el BigGardenObj)(el CarlLarsson)

hasCreationDate (el BigGardenObj) (el (year 1937))
```

A couple of clarifying remarks about the GF encoding are needed in order to understand better the representation of the ontology: the dependent type `Ind` is used to encode class information of instances, and the wrapper function `el` is used to make the above-mentioned coercion, where the two types, along with the inheritance object that represents the proof that the coercion is valid are not visible here, since GF features implicit arguments.

In GF, the natural language generation is based on composeable templates. We obtain the verbalization of classes and templates automatically, mainly based on their Camel-Case representation. For the relations, more work is needed, since a grammatically correct verbalization is not possible based only on the ontology information.

Below follow a few English sentence examples that we are able to generate:

- *B*ig Garden is a painting
- *B*ig Garden is painted on canvas
- *B*ig Garden is painted by Carl Larsson
- *B*ig Garden was created in 1937

Below we provide examples for ontology relations in the shape of *O1 is painted by O2* and feed these to the GF parser which will build an abstract syntax tree, from which we abstract over the placeholders *O1* and *O2*, replacing them with function arguments.

For example, the relation `hasCurrentLocation` and `hasCreationDate` have the following abstract syntax representation:

```
fun hasCurrentLocation : El Painting
 -> El Place -> Formula ;

fun  Painting_hasCreationDate :
 El Painting_Artwork
 -> El Painting_TimePeriod -> Formula ;
```

Their English representation in the concrete syntax is:

```
lin hasCurrentLocation o1 o2 =
 mkPolSent (mkCl o1
 (mkVP (passiveVP locate_V2)
      (mkAdv at_Prep o2))) ;

lin  Painting_hasCreationDate o1 o2 =
 mkPolSentPast (S.mkCl o1 (S.mkVP
   (S.passiveVP create_V2)
   (S.mkAdv in_Prep o2))) ;
```

Since the parser uses the resource library grammars, the result sentence will be syntactically correct, regardless of the arguments we use it with. Also, one does not need extensive knowledge of the GF library or GF programming in order to build verbalization. This might not make a difference for English, which is morphologically simple, but future work involves building such a representation for French, German, Finnish and Swedish, where it would be more difficult to achieve correct agreement, without grammatical tools.

Below follows an example of how the construct *owl:intersectionOf* is represented in the GF abstract syntax:

```
Equiv_TimePeriod =  Equivalent TimePeriod
 (both E52_TimeSpan Sumo.YearDuration) ;
```

Equivalent Class Class is a dependent type that encodes type equivalence.

5 Related Work

Museum Data Integration with semantic technologies as proposed in this paper is intended to enable efficient sharing of museum and cultural heritage information. Initiatives for developing such sharing museum data infrastructures have emerged in the recent years. Only a few of them rely on semantic technologies.

The Museum Data Exchange 2010 project has developed a metadata publishing tool to extract data in XML.[16] Brugman et al. (2008) have developed an Annotation Meta Model providing a way of defining annotation values and anchors in an annotation for multimedia resources. The difference between these approaches and our approach is that we chose to reuse many of the concepts and the relationships that are already defined in the standard model CIDOC-CRM.

Other related initiatives in the Web of structured data is the Amsterdam Museum Linked Open Data project,[17] aiming at producing Linked Data within the Europeana data model (Dekkers et al., 2009; Haslhofer and Isaac, 2011), and the National Database Project of Norwegian University Museums (Ore, 2001) who developed a unified interface for digitalizing cultural material.[18]

In Sweden, as well as other countries, semantic technologies enter the cultural heritage field increasingly and there have been some suggestions describing the tools and techniques that should be applied to digitalize the Swedish Union Catalogue (Malmsten, 2008). Following these ideas and experiences from experimenting with museum data (Bryne, 2009) who have shown that conversion of museum databases is best approached through integration of existing models, we decided to invest in a manual design step to built a framework that captures specific characteristics of museum databases.

[16] http://www.oclc.org/research/activities/museumdata/default.htm

[17] http://www.europeana.eu/portal/thoughtlab_linkedopendata.html

[18] http://www.muspro.uio.no/engelsk-omM.shtml

To our knowledge, we made the first attempt of using CIDOC-CRM to produce museum linked data with connections to external sources like DBpedia. Our attempt to generate natural language sentences from ontologies, and more precisely from the structured results of SPARQL queries are the novelty of the work presented in this paper.

6 Conclusions

We presented a framework for integrating and accessing museum linked data, and a method to present this data using natural language generation technology.

A series of upper-level and domain specific ontologies have been used to transform Gothenburg museum data from a relational database into RDF and build a Museum Reason-able View. We showed how federated results to SPARQL queries using predicates from multiple ontologies can be obtained. Consequently, we demonstrated how templates are automatically obtained in GF to generate the query results in natural language.

Future work includes extending the museum data in the Museum Reason-able View, running several queries, and increasing the coverage of the GF grammar. We intend to have a grammatical coverage for at least five languages. Other directions for future work, also include fluent discourse generation from the ontology axioms, as well as paraphrasing of the existing patterns for verbalization.

Acknowledgments

This work is supported by MOLTO European Union Seventh Framework Programme (FP7/2007-2013) under grant agreement FP7-ICT-247914.

References

Sören Auer, Christian Bizer, Georgi Kobilarov, Jens Lehmann, Richard Cyganiak, and Zachary Ives. 2007. DBpedia: A nucleus for a web of open data. In *Lecture Notes in Computer Science (LNCS)*, volume 4825, pages 722–735.

Tim Berners-Lee. 2004. OWL Web Ontology Language reference, February. W3C Recommendation.

T. Berners-Lee. 2006. Design issues: Linked data. Retrieved from http://www.w3.org/DesignIssues/LinkedData.html.

B. Bishop, A. Kiryakov, D. Ognyanoff, I. Peikov, Z. Tashev, and R. Velkov. 2011. OWLIM: A family of scalable semantic repositories. *Semantic Web Journal, Special Issue: Real-World Applications of OWL.*

Dan Brickley and R.V. Guha, 2004. *RDF Vocabulary Description Language 1.0: RDF Schema.* W3C. `http://www.w3.org/TR/rdf-schema/`.

Hennie Brugman, Véronique Malaisé, and Laura Hollink. 2008. A common multimedia annotation framework for cross linking cultural heritage digital collections. In *International Conference on Language Resources and Evaluation (LREC).*

Kate Bryne. 2009. Putting hybrid cultural data on the semantic web. *Journal of Digital Information (JoDI)*, 10(6). Eds. Martha Larson, Kate Fernie, John Oomen.

Paul Clough, Jennifer Marlow, and Neil Ireson. 2008. Enabling semantic access to cultural heritage: A case study of tate online. In *Proceedings of the ECDL. Workshop on Information Access to Cultural Heritage*, ISBN 978-90-813489-1-1, Aarhus, Denmark, September.

Nick Crofts, Martin Doerr, Tony Gill, Stephen Stead, and Matthew Stiff, 2008. *Definition of the CIDOC Conceptual Reference Model.*

Mariana Damova and Dana Dannélls. 2011. Reasonable view of linked data for cultural heritage. In *Proceedings of the third International Conference on Software, Services and Semantic Technologies (S3T).*

Mariana Damova, Atanas Kiryakov, Maurice Grinberg, Michael K. Bergman, Frederik Giasson, and Kiril Simov. 2011. Creation and integration of reference ontologies for efficient lod management. In *Semi-Automatic Ontology Development: Processes and Resources, IGI Global*, Hershey PA, USA.

Mariana Damova, 2011. *Data Models and Alignment*, May. Deliverable 4.2. MOLTO FP7-ICT-247914.

Makx Dekkers, Stefan Gradmann, and Carlo Meghini, 2009. *Europeana Outline Functional Specification For development of an operational European Digital Library*. Europeana Thematic Network Deliverable 2.5.

Ramona Enache and Krasimir Angelov. 2010. Typeful ontologies with direct multilingual verbalization. *Workshop on Controlled Natural Languages (CNL) 2010.*

Prud'hommeaux Eric and Seaborne Andy. 2008. SPARQL. the query language for RDF, January. W3C Recommendation.

Bernhard Haslhofer and Antoine Isaac. 2011. data.europeana.eu the europeana linked open data pilot. In *Proceedings of the Intl. Conf. on Dublin Core and Metadata Applications.*

Prateek Jain, Peter Z. Yeh, Kunal Verma, Reymonrod G., Mariana Damova, Vasquez Pascal Hitzler, and Amit P. Sheth. 2011. Contextual ontology alignment of lod with an upper ontology: A case study with proton. In *Proceedings of 8th ESWC, Extended Semantic Web Conference*, Heraklion, Greece, May.

A. Kiryakov, D. Ognyanoff, R. Velkov, Z. Tashev, and I. Peikov. 2009. LDSR: Materialized reason-able view to the web of linked data. In *Proceedings of OWL: Experiences and Directions (OWLED) 2009*, Chantilly, USA.

Martin Malmsten. 2008. Making a library catalogue part of the semantic web. In *Proceedings of the Intl. Conf. on Dublin Core and Metadata Applications*, Berlin, German.

Per Martin-Löf. 1982. Constructive mathematics and computer programming. In Cohen, Los, Pfeiffer, and Podewski, editors, *Logic, Methodology and Philosophy of Science VI*, pages 153–175. North-Holland, Amsterdam.

Christian-Emil Smith Ore. 2001. The norwegian museum project, access to and interconnection between various resources of cultural and natural history. In *European Conference on Research and Advanced Technology for Digital Libraries ECDL.*

Aarne Ranta. 2004. Grammatical framework, a type-theoretical grammar formalism. *Journal of Functional Programming*, 14(2):145–189.

Aarne Ranta. 2009. The GF resource grammar library. *Linguistic Issues in Language Technology*, 2(2).

I. Terziev, A. Kiryakov, , and D. Manov, 2005. *D.1.8.1 Base upper-level ontology (BULO) Guidance.* Deliverable of EU-IST Project IST.

Lourens van der Meij, Antoine Isaac, and Claus Zinn. 2010. A web-based repository service for vocabularies and alignments in the cultural heritage domain. In *Proceedings of the 7th Extended Semantic Web Conference, (ESWC 2010).*

Query classification via Topic Models for an art image archive

Dieu-Thu Le
DISI, University of Trento
dieuthu.le@disi.unitn.it

Raffaella Bernardi
DISI, University of Trento
bernardi@unitn.it

Edwin Vald
Bridgeman Art Library
ed.vald@bridgemanart.co.uk

Abstract

In recent years, there has been an increasing amount of literature on query classification. Click-through information has been shown to be a useful source for improving this task. However, far too little attention has been paid to queries in very specific domains such as art, culture and history. We propose an approach that exploits topic models built from a domain specific corpus as a mean to enrich both the query and the categories against which the query need to be classified. We take an Art Library as the case study and show that topic model enrichment improves over the enrichment via click-through considerably.

1 Introduction

In Information Science, transaction log analyses have been carried out since its early stages (Peters, 1993). Within this tradition, lately, Query Classification (QC) to detect user web search intent has obtained interesting results (Shen et al., 2006a; Shen et al., 2006b; Li et al., 2008; Cao et al., 2009). A QC system is required to automatically label a large propotion of user queries to a given target taxonomy. Successfully mapping a user query to target categories brings improvements in general web search and online advertising. Recently, most studies have focused on the mapping of user queries to a general target taxonomy. However, little has been discussed about learning to classify queries in a specific domain. In this paper, we focus on QC for queries in transaction logs of an image archive; we take the Bridgeman Art Library (BAL)[1], one of the world's top image libraries for art, culture and history, as our case study. Learning to classify queries in this domain is particularly challenging due to the specific vocabulary and the small amount of textual information associated with the images. Examples of user queries taken from BAL logs and categories from BAL taxonomy are:

Queries monster woman; messe; ribera crucifixion; woman perfume, etc.

Categories Religion and Belief; People and Science; etc.

Clearly, classifying these queries against these domain specific categories is a hard challenge and standard text classification techniques need to be tailored for the specific problem in hands.

Following the literature on web search classification (Cao et al., 2009), we enrich the queries by exploiting the click-through information, which provides us with titles of the images as well as keywords assigned by domain experts to the clicked images. Furthermore, we employ unsupervised Topic Models (Blei et al., 2003) to detect the topics of the queries as well as to enrich the target taxonomy. The novelty of our work is on the use of Topic Models for a domain specific application and in particular the proposal of using the metadata itself as a source to train the model.

We confirm the impact of the click-through information, which increased the number of correct categories found by 120%, and show that for closed domain image archive, Topic Models (TM) bring a valuable contribution when built out of a very domain specific data-set. In particular, we compare the results obtained by TM enrichment when the model is built out of (a) Wikipedia pages and (b) the Bridgeman Catalogue itself. The latter increased the number of correct categories found by 117% and resulted in a raise of 18% in F1-measure with respect to the classifier based on click-through information.

[1] http://www.bridgemanart.com/

2 Bridgeman Art Library (BAL)

Taxonomy In Bridgeman Art Library, images are classified with sub-categories from a two-level taxonomy. We use "top-category" and "sub-category" to refer to the first and second level, respectively. The taxonomy contains 289 top-categories and 1,148 sub-categories, with an average of ≈ 4 sub-categories for top-category. The top-categories can be divided into three main groups "topic", "object" and "material", we will come back to this with more details in Section 4. A sample of the taxonomy is given in Figure 1.

(-) Ancient and world cultures
Greek, roman and etruscan
Egyptian
Asia
Middle and near east
Pre-history and europe
Oceania
Africa
Americas

(-) Business and industry
Money
Banking
Industry
Shops and markets
Trades and professions
Agriculture
Portraits of people in business and industry

(-) Religion and Belief
Christianity old testament general
Christianity old testament personalities
Christianity new testament life of virgin
Christianity new testament nativity madonna & holy family
Christianity new testament life of christ
Christianity parables / sacraments
Islam / islamic / moslem / muslim
Hinduism / hindu
Buddhism / buddhist
...

Figure 1: Taxonomy

Catalogue The Catalogue contains 324,232 images. Their distribution by group of category is as following: "Topic" 79%, "Material" 18% and "Object" 3% (Figure 2). For each image the metadata contains the title, a description, keywords and a sub-category from the taxonomy above, besides other information we are not going to consider in this paper. The keyword field is for free-text terms (no controlled vocabulary is used), the terms provides physical description, aspects of the image, like the color, shape or the object described, dates, conceptual terms, etc. An example is given in Table 1.

Query Logs Query logs contain information about the queries (usually 1 to max. 5 words each)

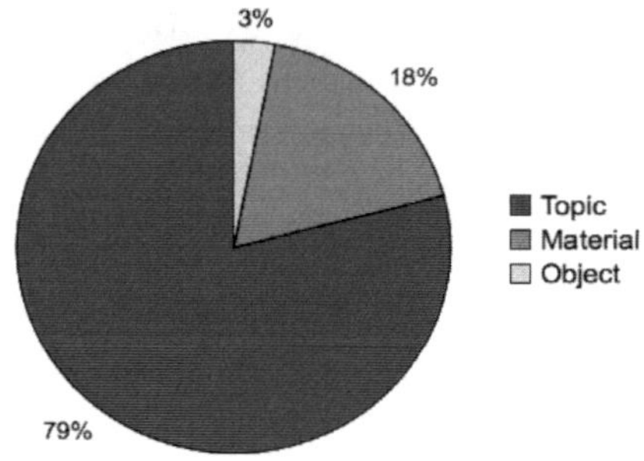

Figure 2: Distribution of images in the Bridgeman metadata among the three groups: topic, material, object

and the corresponding clicked images (i.e., the image that the user clicked after submitting the query). Via this clicked image, queries can be mapped to the information about the image provided in the metadata.

3 Data enrichment via Topic Models

Since a query can express different information needs and hence can be associated to different categories, we choose multiple classification and aim to classify a query by assigning to it three top-categories out of the BAL taxonomy.

To overcome the distance in the vocabulary between the queries and the categories, we enrich the query with the words from the title, description and keywords associated with the corresponding clicked image, and enrich the top-category with its sub-categories. We represent the enriched queries and enriched categories as vectors built using occurrence counts as values for these words. Still this enrichment does not cover the gap between the query and the top-categories, hence we exploit topic models (TMs) to reduce the distance and capture their semantic similarity. The full enrichment process is sketched in Figure 3.

Hidden Topic Models A topic model (Blei et al., 2003; Griffiths and Steyvers, 2004; Blei and Lafferty, 2007) is a semantic representation of text that discovers the abstract topics occurring in a collection of documents. Latent Dirichlet Allocation (LDA), first introduced by (Blei et al., 2003), is a type of topic model that performs the so-called latent semantic analysis (LSA). By analyzing similar patterns of documents and word use, LDA allows representing text on a *latent* semantic level,

Title	A Section of the Passaic Class Single-Turret Ironclad Monitor (engraving)
Keywords	design, battleship, weapon, armoured, boat, submarine, warship, naval, cannon, ship;
Description	Transverse section of pilot-house and turret;
	The Passaic class, single- turret monitors of the U.S. Navy were enlarged versions of the original Monitor ships;
	the first Passaic was commissioned 5 November 1863;
Sub-category	Sea Battles

Table 1: Meta-data: An example

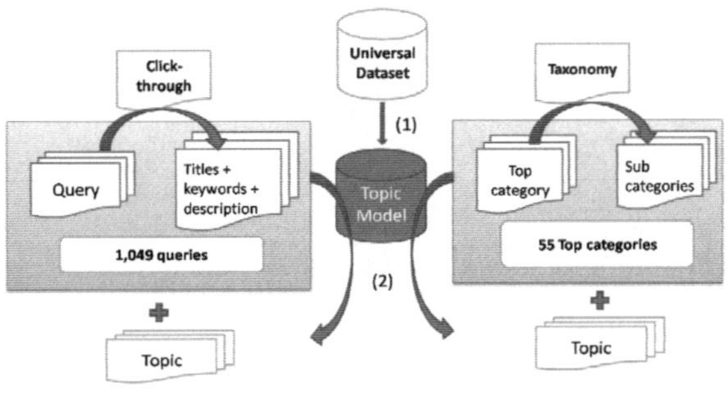

Figure 3: Enriching queries and categories: (1) Learning a TM from the universal data-set; (2) Enriching queries and categories with their topics

rather than by lexical occurrence. It has been used in many applications such as dimensionality reduction (Blei et al., 2003), text categorization, clustering, collaborative filtering and other tasks for textual documents as well as other kinds of discrete data.

The underlying idea of LDA is based upon a probabilistic procedure of generating new documents: First, each document d in the corpus is generated by sampling a distribution θ over topics from a Dirichlet distribution $(Dir(\alpha))$. After that, the topic assignment for each observed word w is performed by sampling a topic z from a multinomial distribution $(Mult(\theta))$. This process is repeated until all T topics have been generated for the whole corpus.

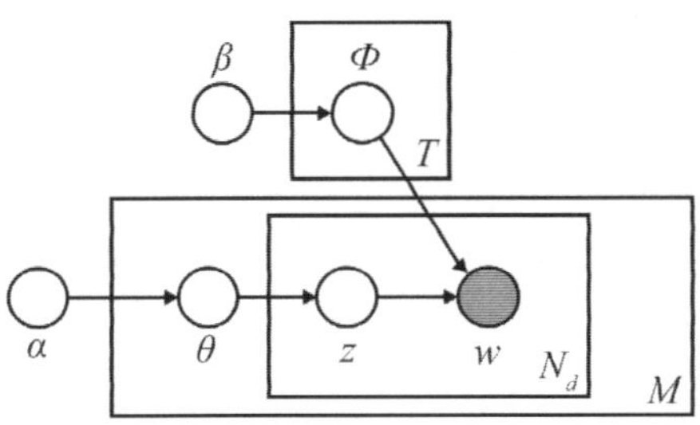

Figure 4: Latent Dirichlet Allocation

- α, β: Dirichlet prior
- M: number of documents
- N_d: number of words in document d
- z: latent topic
- w: observed word
- θ: distribution of topic in documents
- ϕ: distribution of words generated from topic z

Conversely, given a set of documents, we can discover a set of topics that are responsible for generating a document, and the distribution of words that belong to a topic. Estimating these parameters for LDA is intractable. Different solutions for approximating estimation such as Variational Methods (Blei et al., 2003) and Gibbs Sampling (Griffiths and Steyvers, 2004) can be used. Gibbs Sampling is an example of a Markov chain Monte Carlo with relatively simple algorithm for approximate inference in high dimensional models, with the first use for LDA reported in (Griffiths and Steyvers, 2004).

In our experiment, we have estimated the multinomial observations by unsupervised learning with GibbsLDA++ toolkit.[2] Following the data enrichment approach in (Phan et al., 2010), we have enriched the query and category with hidden topic. In particular, given a probability $\vartheta_{m,k}$ of document m over topic k, the corresponding weight $w_{\text{topic}_k,m}$ was determined by discretizing $\vartheta_{m,k}$ using two parameters *cut-off* and *scale*:

$$w_{\text{topic}_k,m} = \begin{cases} \mathit{round}\left(\mathit{scale} \times \vartheta_{m,k}\right), \text{if} \\ \vartheta_{m,k} \geq \mathit{cut\text{-}off} \\ 0, \text{if } \vartheta_{m,k} < \mathit{cut\text{-}off} \end{cases} \tag{1}$$

We chose *cut-off* = 0.01, *scale* = 20 as to ensure that the number of topics assigned to a query/category does not exceed the number of original terms of that query/category, i.e., to keep a balance weight between topics enriched and original terms.

To discover the set of topics and the distribution of words per topic, we need to choose a universal data set. Since we are interested in topics within

[2] http://gibbslda.sourceforge.net/

a rather specific domain, we need to choose a data set that provides an appropriate vocabulary. We have tried two options, a Topic Model built out of selected pages of Wikipedia and a Topic Model built out of BAL Catalogue.

Wikipedia Topic Model Wikipedia is a rich source of data that has been widely exploited to extract knowledge in many different domains. We have used a version of it, viz. WaCKypedia (Baroni et al., 2009),[3] that contains around 3 million articles from Wikipedia segmented, normalized, POS-tagged and parsed. In order to extract those pages that could provide a better model for our specific domain, we selected those pages that contain at least one content word of the BAL browse categories listed below.

The Arts and Entertainment, Ancient and World Cultures, Architecture, Business and Industry, Crafts and Design, Places, Science and Medicine History, Religion and Belief, Sport, People and Society, Travel and Transport, Plants and Animals Land and Sea, Emotions and Ideas

For our vocabulary, we considered only words in the selected WaCKypedia pages that are either Nouns (N.*) or Verbs (VV.*) or Adjectives (J.*) after being lemmatized. We obtain ≈ 14K documents, with a vocabulary of ≈ 200K words, out of which we computed 100 topics. Examples of random topics are illustrated in Figure 5.

Topic 0	Topic 4	Topic 19	Topic 33	Topic 45	Topic 89
business	ship	sport	design	japan	plant
company	military	team	designer	japanese	cell
travel	war	world	intelligent	manga	soil
management	force	football	industrial	tokyo	specie
market	army	league	product	ainu	flower
service	navy	play	graphic	shogi	grow
sell	sea	event	interior	textbook	seed
financial	weapon	win	creative	osaka	tree

Figure 5: Hidden topics derived from WaCKypedia

Bridgeman catalogue Topic Model The most straightforward way of choosing a close domain corpus is to use the Bridgeman catalogue itself. We group together images that share the same sub-categories and consider each group of sub-category as a document. We have 732 documents and ≈ 136K words, out of which we computed 100 topics. Examples of topics estimated from this dataset are given in Figure 6.

[3]WaCkypedia (`http://wacky.sslmit.unibo.it/doku.php`)

Topic 3	Topic 15	Topic 21	Topic 45	Topic 59	Topic 81
railway	bc	christ	portrait	cotton	wedding
train	century	jesus	king	design	valentine
car	marble	crucifixion	queen	silk	bride
railroad	stone	cross	engraving	tapestry	marriage
carriage	bronze	life	charles	textile	baptism
locomotive	photo	supper	henry	printed	cotract
express	depicting	lord	prince	carpet	mariee
pacific	statue	holy	duke	wool	groom

Figure 6: Hidden topics derived from the Bridgeman catalogue

4 Data Sets

Categories From a BAL six month log, we extracted all the top category connected to the queries via the click-through information and obtained the list of 55 categories given by group in Table 2.

Queries From the six month log we have extracted a sample of 1,049 queries by preserving the distribution of queries per top-category obtained via the click-through information and the taxonomy. We selected only queries with at least one clicked image. Not all image metadata contains title, keywords and a description: for around 60% of images the meta-data provides only the title and sub-category. For each query, we kept only one clicked image randomly selected. We leave for future study the impact the full set of clicked images per query could have on our query classifier.

Gold-standard: annotation by domain experts The 1,049 queries have been annotated by a domain expert who was asked to assign up to three categories per query out of the 55 categories in Table 2 and to mark the query as "unknown" if no category in the list was considered to be appropriate. The domain expert looked at the click-through information and the corresponding image to assign the categories to the query. The distribution of queries per group of categories obtained by this manual annotation is as following: 1395, 268, 87 queries have been annotated with a category out of the "topic", "object" and "material" group, respectively.

Out of this sample, 100 queries have been annotated by three annotators, BAL cataloguers, twice: (a) by looking at the click-through information and the image, and (b) by looking only at the query. The agreement between the annotators in both cases is moderate (kappa in average 0.60 for

Topics	Land and Sea; Places; Religion and Belief; Ancient and World Cultures; Mythology Mythological Myth; Allegory/Allegorical; People and Society; Sports and Leisure; History; Travel and Transport; Personalities; Business and Industry; Costume & Fashion; Plants and Animals; Botanical; Animals; The Arts and Entertainment; Emotions and Ideas; Science and Medicine; Science; Medicine; Architecture; Photography.
Materials	Metalwork; Silver, Gold & Silver Gilt; Lacquer & Japanning; Enamels; Semi-precious Stones; Bone, Ivory & Shellwork; Glass; Stained Glass; Textiles; Ceramics.
Objects	Crafts and Design; Manuscripts; Maps; Ephemera; Posters; Magazines; Choir Books; Cards & Postcards; Sculpture; Clocks, Watches, Barometers & Sundials; Oriental Miniatures; Furniture; Arms, Armour & Miltaria; Objects de Vertu; Trade Emblems, City Crests, Coats of Arms; Coins & Medals; Icons; Mosaics; Inventions; Jewellery; Juvenilia/Children's Toys & Games; Lighting;

Table 2: Categories used by the annotators

the annotation without click-through information and 0.64 for the annotation done using the click-through information), the agreement is higher for the categories within the "topic" group. For each annotator, using the click-through information and the image has not had a significant impact on the annotation of categories from the "topic" group (kappa in average 0.80), whereas it has increased and changed the annotation of categories from the other two groups, "object" (kappa 0.57) and "material" (kappa 0.62).

Gold-standard: automatic extraction from the meta-data of the clicked image The top-category associated in the taxonomy with the sub-categories of the image clicked after querying can be extracted automatically exploiting the click-through information. Hence, we created a second gold-standard using such automatic extraction. Though our extraction is automatic, the assignment of the categories to the images is the result of the manual annotation by BAL cataloguers through the years. This annotation was done, of course, by looking only at the images, differently from the previous one for which the domain experts was given both the query and the clicked image. This second gold-standard differs from the one created by domain experts. For instance, the query "mountain lake near piedmont" is classified to the category "Places" by the expert, while using the automatic mapping method, we obtain the category "Emotions & Ideas: Peace & Relaxation". The kappa agreement between the manual annotation and the automatic extraction is 0.52, 0.53, 0.6 for categories within the "material", "object" and "topic" group, respectively.

In our experiment, we will evaluate the classifier against the "manual" gold-standard and use the second one only to select the most challenging queries (those queries the classifiers fail classifying in either cases: when evaluated against the manual or the automatic gold-standard) and analyse them in further detail.

5 Experiments

Let $Q = \{q_1, q_2, \ldots, q_N\}$ be a set of N queries and $C = \{c_1, c_2, \ldots, c_M\}$ a set of M categories. We represent each query q_i and category c_j as the vectors $\overrightarrow{q_i} = \{w_{tq_i}\}_{t \in V}$ and $\overrightarrow{c_j} = \{w_{tc_j}\}_{t \in V}$ where V is the vocabulary that contains all terms in the corpus and w_{tq_i}, w_{tc_i} are the frequency in q_i and c_j, respectively, of each term t in the vocabulary.

We use the cosine similarity measure to assign categories to the queries. For each query q_i, the cosine similarity between every pair $\langle q_i, c_j \rangle_{j=1..M}$ is computed as:

$$cosin\_sim(q_i, c_j) = \frac{\overrightarrow{q_i}.\overrightarrow{c_j}}{|\overrightarrow{q_i}|.|\overrightarrow{c_j}|} =$$

$$= \frac{\sum_{t \in V} w_{tq_i}.w_{tc_j}}{\sqrt{\sum_{t \in V} w_{tq_i}^2}.\sqrt{\sum_{t \in V} w_{tc_j}^2}}$$

For each query, the top 3 categories with highest cosine similarities are returned.

The different query and category enrichment methods are spelled out in Table 3. To evaluate the effect of click-through information in query classification, we set up two different configurations: QR, where besides the terms contained in the top and sub-categories, V consists of terms appearing in the queries; $QR\text{-}CT$ for which V consists also of terms in the title, keywords, description fields of the clicked images' meta-data. In the case of the classifiers exploiting topic models, both vocabulary is extended with the hidden topics too and both queries and categories are enriched with them as explained in section 3. In particular, TM_{wiki} is the classifier based on the model built with the hidden topics extracted from WaCKpedia, and TM_{BAL} is the one based on the model built out of Bridgeman metadata.

Setting	Query enrichment	Category enrichment
QR	q	CAT + sCAT
QR-CT	$q + ct$	CAT + sCAT
TM_{wiki}	$q + ct \oplus HT_{wiki}$	CAT + sCAT $\oplus$ HT_{wiki}
TM_{BAL}	$q + ct \oplus HT_{BAL}$	CAT + sCAT $\oplus$ HT_{BAL}

- q: query
- ct: click-through information: title, keywords and description - if available
- CAT: top category
- sCAT: all sub categories of the corresponding CAT
- HT_{wiki}: hidden topics from WaCKpedia
- HT_{BAL}: hidden topics from Bridgeman Metadata

Table 3: Experimental Setting

5.1 Results

To evaluate the classifiers, first of all we compute Precision, Recall and F-measure as defined for KDD Cup competition and reported below.[4] The results obtained are given in Table 4.

$$P = \frac{\sum_i \# \, queries \; correctly \; tagged \; as \; c_i}{\sum_i \# \, queries \; tagged \; as \; c_i} \quad (2)$$

$$R = \frac{\sum_i \# \, queries \; correctly \; tagged \; as \; c_i}{\sum_i \# \, queries \; manually \; labeled \; as \; c_i} \quad (3)$$

$$F - measure = \frac{2 \times P \times R}{P + R} \quad (4)$$

The F-measure average at KDD Cup competition was 0.24, with the best performing system reaching the result of 0.44 F-measure. Differently from our scenario, the KDD Cup task was for web search query classification against 67 general domain categories (like shopping, companies, cars etc.) and classifiers could assign max. 5 categories.

In the following we report further studies of our results by considering the number of queries that are assigned the correct category in each of the three positions (Hits # 1, 2, 3). Furthermore,

[4] http://www.sigkdd.org/kddcup/index.php?section=2005\&method=task

	Precision	Recall	F-measure
QR-CT	0.11	0.17	0.13
TM_{BAL}	0.26	0.40	0.31

Table 4: P, R and F measures – Evaluation

we provide the total number of correct categories found in all position 1, 2 and 3 ($\sum_{Top\_3}$).

Setting	Hits			
	# 1	# 2	# 3	$\sum_{Top\_3}$
QR	92	38	26	156
QR-CT	183	97	62	342
TM_{wiki}	145	112	88	345
TM_{BAL}	340	257	144	741

Table 5: Results of query classification: number of correct categories found (for 1,049 queries)

As can be seen in Table 5, the performance of query classification using only terms in the queries (QR) is very poor. Already enriching the query with the words from the title, keywords and description (QR-CT) increases the $\sum_{Top\_3}$ by nearly 120%.

Topics derived from the TM estimated from Wikipedia (TM_{wiki}) did not help much in finding the right categories for a query. In comparison to QR-CT classifier, they decreased the number of correct categories in position 1 and they only slightly raised the number of correct categories when considering the three positions.

On the other hand, the TM built from the Bridgeman catalogue (TM_{BAL}) increased the results considerably for each of the three positions. Compared with QR-CT, 399 other correct categories were further found by using topics extracted from the catalogue, giving a raise of 117%.

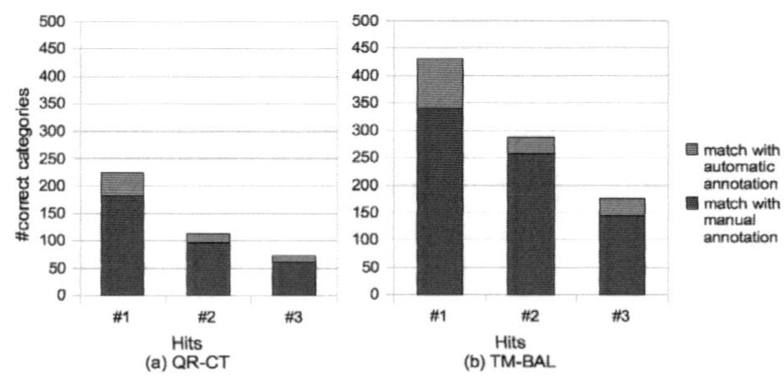

Figure 7: Matching QR-CT and TM_{BAL} correct categories against the manual and automatic gold-standards

Figure 7 reports the number of hits in each position 1, 2, 3 for the two settings QR-CT and TM_{BAL}. It clearly shows that TM_{BAL} outperforms QR-CT and matches more correct categories both when considering either of the two gold-standards. It is interesting to note that this holds in particular for categories in the first position of the ranked list (Hits #1): it results in a raise of 92% in the first position (from 224 correct categories to 431).

5.2 Analysis of wrong classification

To better understand the results obtained, we looked into the wrong classification. Figure 8 reports the number of queries for which $QR\text{-}CT$ and TM_{BAL} have not selected in the top three positions any correct category using either the manual gold-standard and the automatic classification.

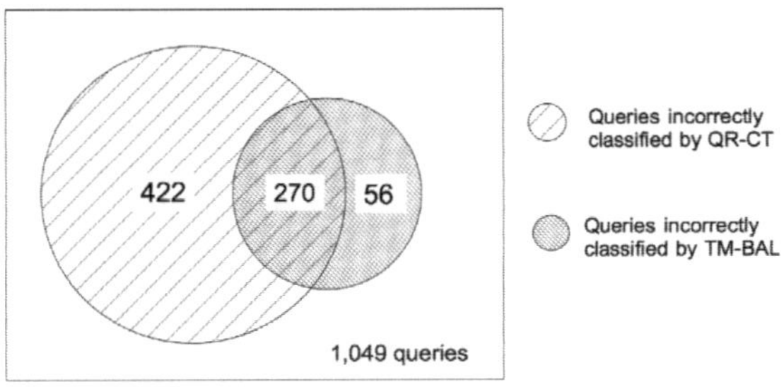

Figure 8: Queries incorrectly classified

We found that there were 692 queries (422+270) for which $QR\text{-}CT$ had not found any correct category in the top three positions; whereas 326 queries incorrectly classified by TM_{BAL}, of which 270 queries were in common with those wrongly classified by $QR\text{-}CT$.

We further analyzed the set of 270 queries of Figure 8 which we take to be the most difficult queries to classify since neither of the two classifiers have succeed with them considering either the manual or the automatic gold-standard. These queries and the categories assigned to them by the $QR\text{-}CT$ and TM_{BAL} classifier have been checked and evaluated again by the domain expert.

Figure 9 gives an example out of the 270 and the result of the second run evaluation by the domain expert. The top categories assigned to the query "mountain lake near piedmont" by the classifier $QR\text{-}CT$ and TM_{BAL} are "Ancient & World Cultures" and "Land & Sea", respectively. The two categories do not match either the correct category assigned by the expert ("Places") or the category assigned by the automatic method ("Emotions & Ideas"). However, after being checked by the expert, it was decided that the category proposed by the TM_{BAL} classifier ("Land & Sea") was also correct whereas the one assigned by $QR\text{-}CT$ was not. This query and click-through information do not share any common words with the category "Land & Sea" and its sub-categories, hence it was not possible for the $QR\text{-}CT$ classifier to spot their similarity. However, the enrichment with the hidden topics discovered the similarity between the query and the top-category: they share `topic 14` with high probability.

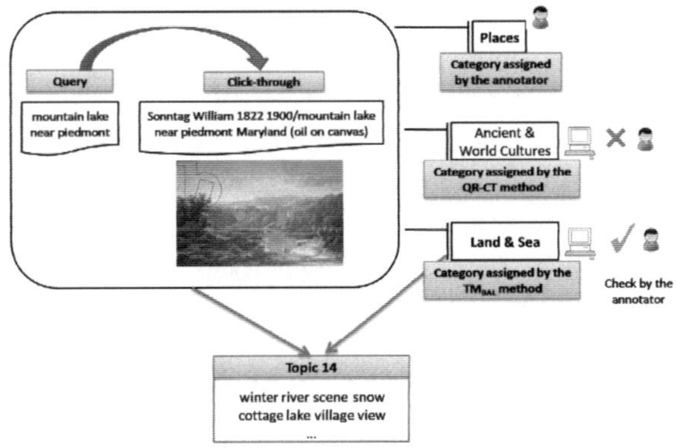

Figure 9: Effects of TM on the classification task

In total, the categories assigned to these 270 queries, were considered to be corrected in 123 cases for the TM_{BAL} classifier and in 45 cases for the $QR\text{-}CT$ (Table 6).

Setting	Hits			
	#1	#2	#3	$\sum_{Top\_3}$
$QR\text{-}CT$	31	7	7	45
TM_{BAL}	59	43	21	123

Table 6: Correct categories checked by the expert for the 270 queries (using the click-through information)

Finally, the numbers of queries with at least one correct label out of these 270 queries are 39 (14%) for the $QR\text{-}CT$ method and 115 (43%) for the TM_{BAL} method.

6 Related Work

(Cao et al., 2009) shows that context information is crucial for web search query classification. They consider the context to be both previous queries within the same session and pages of the clicked urls. In this paper, we focus on information similar to the latter and postpone the analysis of query session to further studies. (Cao et al., 2009) also shows that the taxonomy-based association between adjacent labels is useful for our task. Similarly, we exploit Bridgeman taxonomy to enrich the categories target of the classifier.

Finally, the use of a gold-standard automatically

created via click-through information is inspired by (Hofmann et al., 2010) where it has been shown that system rankings based on clicks are very close to those based on purchase decisions. There is strong evidence in favor of the relevance of click-through data to detect user's intention.

7 Conclusions

This paper shows the effect of the click-through information and the use of topic models in query classification in the art, history and culture closed domain. The main contribution of this study is the proposal of using the metadata as a source to train topic models for the query and category enrichment. In particular, we first enriched the queries with the click-through information including information associated with the image clicked by the user. Then, we used topic models built out of Wikipedia and the Bridgeman catalogue to analyze topics for both of the queries and the target categories. Experiments from the real dataset extracted from the query logs have shown the impact of the click-through information and topic models built from the catalogue in helping to find the correct categories for a given query.

In this paper, we have not considered more than one click-through image for each query. However, we expect that more click-through images can give a better understanding of user intent. Further research regarding this issue might be studied in more detail in future.

Acknowledgments

This work has been partially supported by the GALATEAS project (http://www.galateas.eu/ – CIP-ICT PSP-2009-3-25430) funded by the European Union under the ICT PSP program.

References

Marco Baroni, Silvia Bernardini, Adriano Ferraresi, and Eros Zanchetta. 2009. The WaCky wide web: a collection of very large linguistically processed web-crawled corpora. *Language Resources and Evaluation*.

David M. Blei and John D. Lafferty. 2007. A correlated topic model of science. *AAS*, 1(1):17–35.

David M. Blei, Andrew Y. Ng, and Michael I. Jordan. 2003. Latent dirichlet allocation. *J. Mach. Learn. Res.*, 3:993–1022, March.

Huanhuan Cao, Derek Hao Hu, Dou Shen, Daxi Jiang, Jian-Tao Sun, Enhong Chen, and Qiang Yang. 2009. Context-aware query classification. In *SIGIR'09, The 32nd Annual ACM SIGIR Conference*.

T. L. Griffiths and M. Steyvers. 2004. Finding scientific topics. *Proceedings of the National Academy of Sciences*, 101(Suppl. 1):5228–5235, April.

Katja Hofmann, Bouke Huurnink, Marc Bron, and Maarten de Rijke. 2010. Comparing click-through data to purchase decisions for retrieval evaluation. In *SIGIR'10*.

Xiao Li, Ye-Yi Wang, and Alex Acero. 2008. Learning query intent from regularized click graphs. In *SIGIR'08*.

Thomas Andrew Peters. 1993. The history and development of transaction log analysis. *Library Hi Tech*, 11(2):41–66.

Xuan-Hieu Phan, Cam-Tu Nguyen, Dieu-Thu Le, Le-Minh Nguyen, Susumu Horiguchi, and Quang-Thuy Ha. 2010. A hidden topic-based framework towards building applications with short web documents. *IEEE Transactions on Knowledge and Data Engineering*, 99(PrePrints).

Dou Shen, Rong Pan, Jian-Tao Sun, Jeffrey Junfeng Pan, Kangheng Wu, Jie Yin, and Giang Yang. 2006a. Query enrichment for web-query classification. *ACM Transactions on Information Systems*, 24(3):320–352.

Dou Shen, Jian-Tao Sun, Qiang Yang, and Zheng Chen. 2006b. Building bridges for web query classification. In *SIGIR'06*.

Unlocking Language Archives Using Search

Herman Stehouwer
MPI for Psycholinguistics
herman.stehouwer@mpi.nl

Eric Auer
MPI for Psycholinguistics
eric.auer@mpi.nl

Abstract

The Language Archive manages one of the largest and most varied sets of natural language data. This data consists of video and audio enriched with annotations. It is available for more than 250 languages, many of which are endangered.

Researchers have a need to access this data conveniently and efficiently. We provide several browse and search methods to cover this need, which have been developed and expanded over the years. Metadata and content-oriented search methods can be connected for a more focused search.

This article aims to provide a complete overview of the available search mechanisms, with a focus on annotation content search, including a benchmark.

1 Introduction

Digital preservation of cultural data has been an important topic in much recent research. Large amounts of cultural heritage data is still only available in paper form. Digitization and digital preservation is relatively affordable and provides a number of significant benefits. Digital data does not degrade in quality with use. In addition, dissemination, access, and analysis techniques are easier with digital data. Furthermore, digital data enables researchers to answer questions which were unfeasible to answer before. (Ordelman et al., 2009; Reynaert, 2010)

Some of these digitization and accessibility projects have focused specifically on access, i.e., by improving search methods for the domain. Only a powerful search tool allows researchers to quickly find their "needles in the haystack". (Auer et al., 2010; Kemps-Snijders et al., 2009; Kemps-Snijders et al., 2010; Ringersma et al., 2010; Skiba, 2009; Wittenburg and Trilsbeek, 2010; Wittenburg et al., 2010; Johnson, 2002)

In terms of preservation and access to cultural heritage data the MPI occupies a unique position. The uniqueness is captured by four aspects of the situation, (1) the cultural heritage data concerns mainly currently spoken linguistic data, (2) often the linguistic data is accompanied by video to capture non-verbal communication and cultural background, (3) the archive now hosts data from many linguistic preservation projects, linguistic studies and psycholinguistic experiments, and (4) there are a variety of methods offered to browse, search, and leverage the large archive of data.

This article is structured as follows. In Section 2 we provide an overview of the archive, in the form of a brief history and an overview of available data. In Section 3 we describe the current access methods, including our powerful combined metadata and content search. We will present some performance statistics for the content search in Section 4. We end this article in Section 5 with a summary.

2 The Archive

The archive stores a large variety of material in more than 250 different languages. It contains circa $160,000$ annotation files for more than $200,000$ audio or video recordings. The recordings include more than $4,300$ hours of SD quality[1] video and more than $3,500$ hours of CIF quality[2] video. The archived content is supported by almost $200,000$ metadata files and $50,000$ auxiliary information files.

[1]SD means Standard Definition (resolution). Circa $14,500$ videos, 78% are 720×576 pixels (resolutions from $640 \ldots 768 \times 480 \ldots 576$)

[2]CIF means Common Intermediate Format, which implies a specific (lower) resolution range. Circa $40,400$ videos, 78% are 352×288 pixels (resolutions from $320 \ldots 384 \times 240 \ldots 384$, plus $2,350$ double width videos merged from 2 CIF videos each)

The material in the archive occupies more than 40 terabyte of storage capacity, most of which for the media recordings. There are 22 gigabytes of annotation files, 2.5 gigabytes of metadata and 7 gigabytes of auxiliary files. In addition, there is currently more than 55 terabyte of "pre-archive" data in the pipeline on the way to the archive. Based our experience, the creation of one terabyte of archive-able data costs around 1.5 million €.

(Wittenburg et al., 2010) gives a recent description of the state of The Language Archive (TLA). They deal with three aspects pertaining to the archive: (1) replication of archived material, bitwise copies of the original material – each file is stored in six copies in two countries, (2) encoding and metadata standards, and how they apply to the archive itself, and (3) controlled access to archived materials. The article provides a good overview of the TLA resources and software used for managing the archive.

Access Methods

The archive itself is accessible in a number of ways, most of which can be reached from the www.clarin.eu Virtual Language Observatory (VLO) (Uytvanck et al., 2010). The classic access method is the IMDI[3] browser, which displays a tree view on the Directed Acyclic Graph (DAG) type archive structure graph.

When using the catalogue on the CLARIN VLO portal, the TLA archive and several external archives can be visited in one browser session. To enable central access, CLARIN exchanges and harvests metadata with other archives using the OAI protocol. We remark that the different archives are also accessible separately. For instance, the TLA data is accessible on the web at www.lat-mpi.eu/tools/browser. A faceted search (based on Apache SOLR) of the combined archives is available in the VLO language resource inventory described below. The researcher can also browse the virtual language world in the VLO. The virtual language world presents the available corpora on a world map. Faceted search and geographical browsing always present the combined archives, not just TLA data. The TLA archive is also accessible via a number of other search methods, which we outline below.

Quality Control

The whole archive is permanently under active quality control. Files can only be uploaded by authorized researchers using the web-based LAMUS[4] archive upload and editing tool which also applies format checks. Those checks ensure that only file formats for which free viewers (and preferably editors) are widely available are stored. Archive managers define format rules and make statistics about archived data, e.g. about video resolutions or audio sampling rates. They also run regular consistence checks on the archive, link structure and file formats.

For annotation file formats supported by the search methods, files are parsed to verify their syntactic validity. Parse logs are reviewed to find problematic files and adapt parsers for common syntax variants, for example for CHAT, ELAN and Toolbox[5]. The customized parser for example has heuristical parsing of CHAT participant lists, which in turn can be used to search.

3 Searching

We aim to help researchers answer their scientific questions. Often these questions may be answered by providing the right data. To help locate the right data we provide a variety of browse and search methods. In this section we aim to give a brief overview of each of the available methods. Any part or multiple parts of the DAG tree in the IMDI browser can be selected to perform any type of search on.

3.1 Metadata Search

Here we briefly describe the metadata search. The metadata search is available from within the IMDI browser. The metadata search contains two different search methods: (1) a keyword search, and (2) an advanced metadata search.

The first performs a quick search for a set of keywords in all available metadata fields. The second allows the researcher to define a set of constraints. These constraints are then used to select all matching records in the part of the archive that is searched on.

[3]Isle MetaData Initiative, an XML metadata standard.

[4]Language Archive Management and Upload System – www.lat-mpi.eu/tools/lamus

[5]CHILDES CHAT: Child Language Data Exchange System, Codes for the Human Analysis of Transcripts childes.psy.cmu.edu/clan/. ELAN EAF: EUDICO Linguistic Annotator www.lat-mpi.eu/tools/elan/. Toolbox, Shoebox: www.sil.org/computing/toolbox/.

We provide a telling example. To search for audio recordings of young speakers, we can use the following two constraints: (1) actor age is smaller than 10, and (2) the format of the resource is an audio file. The second constraint is entered with a user friendly choice list. Optionally, the researcher can see which choices would match how often. Using a fast Apache Digester index, results are presented without noticeable delay.

Once a researcher has performed a metadata search they can choose to use the results in three ways: (1) the results can be viewed and printed, (2) the results can be exported as links in an IMDI file for later use, and (3) the results can be used directly to specify the domain of a content search (described below).

3.2 Trova Annotation Content Search

Here we briefly describe Trova, the annotation content search. A Trova search always starts from a selection of elements in the archive, which are used as the search domain. Typically the search domain consists of a corpus, or of the domain selected using the metadata search. While all metadata is freely accessible, all access to annotation content including search is controlled by the access rules[6] for the individual corpora.

Trova supports three different search methods: (1) the simple search, (2) the single layer search, and (3) the multiple layer search. We describe them in order of complexity.

In all three search modes, the researcher can select which of the searchable file types should be considered: ELAN EAF, CHILDES CHAT, Shoebox, Toolbox, text, HTML, XML, PDF, SubRip, Praat TextGrid and CSV[7].

Usage Considerations

The Trova application is the main way to search the online archive. However, after excluding queries made for demonstration, teaching and testing purposes, it turned out that Trova was not used heavily in the past:

In the period from April 2008 to July 2010, there were more than 2000 user queries, about 80 per month, of which 75% unique. Most searches were in Dutch corpora such as CGN. Simple or single layer search were most common.

In the first half of the analyzed period, only 11 queries per month used structured multi layer search. Most structured search queries had a complexity of up to four keywords or constraints and were not in Dutch corpora. Half of the complex queries used a constraint that keywords in two tiers had to co-occur (same timing).

Two possible reasons for the infrequent use of Trova in the past are the steep learning curve of structured search and slow speed. To address this, we improve documentation and teaching. Also, Trova was slow compared to typical web search engines. Incremental processing already helped by showing the first results while the query was still running. However, overall processing time was still high and complete result lists are of more interest in linguistic context than in web searches.

Optimizations

To optimize search performance, searching is performed in three steps: First, when a researcher enters the search page, the properties of all tiers (a tier is a layer of annotation) in the selected search domain are processed. Second, as soon as a query is made, fingerprinting is used to limit searching to a small set of candidate tiers to improve query speed. Each tier is indexed with four different character n-gram fingerprints. The current fingerprints group all possible combinations of 1 to 4 characters into a limited number of slots. A tier can only contain a match for a given keyword when it fills at least all slots used by that keyword. For regular expression search, plain text is extracted from the query to still use partial fingerprinting. Third, the candidate tiers are processed in small groups, displaying hits as they come in.

While a query is still running, the researcher can already browse the first results. However, the hits will only be displayed in their final ordering when they all have been found. At that point, hits can also be viewed sorted by their most frequent concordances. Hits can be saved in CSV files using a user-selectable order and choice of columns. From each hit, the researcher can navigate to Annex (Berck and Russel, 2006), a browser based presentation of the parsed annotation file along with corresponding media files.

[6] The TLA AMS access management system (www.lat-mpi.eu/tools/ams) allows to define individual and group access rules on the level of corpora, sessions, filetypes and files.

[7] Our database contains circa $123,000,000$ annotations in $750,000$ tiers from $110,000$ parsed files. The most common annotation file types are CHAT ($48,600$ files), EAF ($28,100$ files) and plain text ($26,400$ files).

Simple Search

The simple search allows searching for keywords in the selected search domain. The search performed using these keywords performs a case-insensitive substring matching.

Single Layer Search

Single layer search gives the researcher more control over the search than when using the simple search. The researcher can select whether matching should use exact matching, substring matching, or regular expression matching. Furthermore the researcher can choose whether he wants the matching to be case sensitive. It is also possible to perform searches over n-grams of annotations. Both n-grams inside and across annotations can be searched. The n-gram search modes support single position wildcards (#) and per word negation, e.g., *the # NOT(green) house*. In the example, the phrase *I went to the big red house yesterday.* would match.

We remark that exact match means that one annotation has to match the keyword exactly. The researcher has to be aware that some annotation tiers annotate whole utterances as one annotation while others annotate word by word. In some cases, searching with a regular expression can be more appropriate.

A further option in single layer search is restricting the search to a subset of the available tiers. Annotation tiers can be selected by several properties, namely: name, type, participant, and annotator. The researcher can see how many tiers match which value and can sort the choice list by that. This allows to quickly see that a corpus contains more *type pho* tiers than *type Phonetic* tiers[8].

Multiple Layer Search

Multiple layer search is the most advanced search interface available on the archive. In multiple layer search, a grid of search terms can be entered, with constraints between them. Constraints on the X axis can be used to require a certain (or minimum or maximum) time or number of annotations between keyword hits. Constraints on the Y axis give the researcher fine grained control over whether and how keyword hits in different tiers have to overlap. In the grid, the X axis corresponds to the time axis, while the Y axis corresponds to different tiers within one file. Similar to the single layer search, the researcher can activate constraints about the properties of tiers, but now separately for each grid row. An example query could be *'pink' before 'elephant' in a text type tier, 'elephant' overlapping 'big' time-wise in a gesture type tier.* In Figure 1 we show an example of the multiple layer search, showing this example.

3.3 CQL Search Service

In the context of the European search infrastructure we make available a machine-accessible web-service for content search. This web-service provides a search-service on parts of the archive (as access rights permit) and is integrated in the European search infrastructure. The European search infrastructure provides a central location for researchers to perform searches in many different language resources. The web-service is based on SRU/CQL(Morgan, 2004; S.H. McCallum, 2006), where SRU is the communication protocol and CQL the search query language.

CQL search provides functionality based on the Trova single layer search through a REST[9] interface. More complex processing will be added in the future, as CQL allows to express fairly complex queries. These queries differ from the 2d grid paradigm of Trova. As stateless REST means processing whole queries in one single HTTP access, CQL search can cache intermediate results for later re-use. So when the same researcher makes multiple queries to the same corpus, hits will be returned faster. REST queries can optionally return as soon as some results have been found or wait until all results are ready.

3.4 Virtual Language Observatory

A separate way in which to browse the metadata is available in the Virtual Language Observatory (VLO). The VLO makes available a faceted browser on the metadata from several language sources, including our archive. To use the VLO, enter the *language resource inventory* on the www.clarin.eu/vlo virtual language observatory page. In faceted browsing, different IMDI and CMDI metadata fields can be used to zoom in on corpora. Supported facets include origin (e.g., MPI, Open Language Archives Community), con-

[8] Unfortunately, there are no widely used controlled vocabularies to classify tiers. We plan to use ISOcat / RELcat concept registries to allow a more semantic view on tier properties. This would allow selections such as *tier types with parent category DC-2641: phonetics.*

[9] Representational State Transfer, e.g. via HTTP.

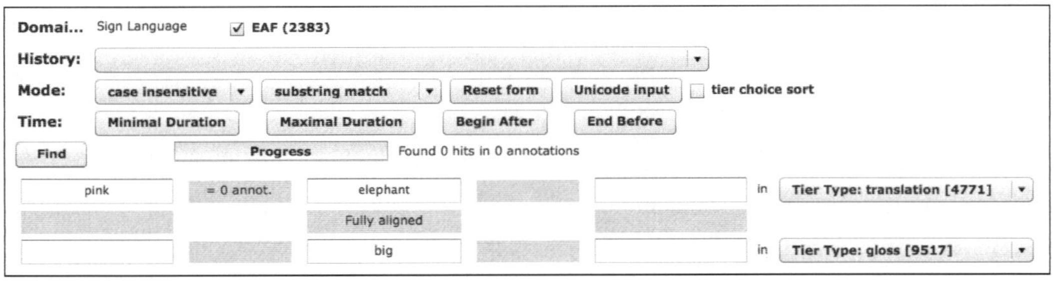

Figure 1: Partial screenshot of multiple layer search. Showing the *pink elephant* search example.

tinent, country, language, resource type (e.g., audio), subject, genre, and organization.

All facet lists are shown with counts of occurrences which are dynamically updated as the researcher makes selections. For example, after selecting Dutch (18,000 resources), the facet origin is updated, showing that most Dutch resources are from the CGN corpus. The researcher can then proceed to specify more facets, for example select the Dutch Bilingualism Database (DBD) corpus as origin, select a genre, and so on. Facets can be specified in any order and page updates are almost instantaneous, using a SOLR database.

At any moment, a keyword search on metadata descriptions can be used to narrow down the results. From the result list, metadata sets can be displayed as tables and the researcher can jump directly to resources such as audio recordings.

3.5 ELAN Structured Multiple File Search

A modified version of Trova is one of the search functions of ELAN annotation editor. This enables the researcher to search in (a group of) annotation files while they are still being worked on. Different from Trova, this search parses files on the fly. ELAN can import and export a number of other file formats and the search could parse some of them directly. In addition, ELAN supports list-of-constraints style search similar to metadata search. Not using a full corpus database means reduced speed compared to Trova, but all annotation updates are available in searches immediately.

4 Annotation Search Benchmark

4.1 Test Corpus and Hardware

The various metadata search methods provide results almost instantaneously. However, with almost 120,000,000 individual annotations in more than 100,000 annotation files in the archive, content search is a more demanding task. Thanks to various optimizations described above, such as fingerprinting of tiers and queries, response times are still reasonably fast.

To provide some benchmarks, we ran a number of searches on a large subset of the archive consisting of several sizable corpora: All of DoBeS[10], the Dutch Spoken Corpus CGN, the MoLL L2 acquisition corpus[11] as well as local mirrors of Talkbank and the CHILDES sub-corpora Biling, Japanese, Cantonese, Turkish, Spanish, French and German. The size of this search space is almost 55,000,000 annotations in 354,000 tiers in 43,000 files. The initial analysis of the search domain can take 20 seconds or more but then multiple queries can be done with low further overhead. Finding **all** occurrences of *elephant*, *needle* or *haystack* in more than 50 million annotations can then be done within 7 seconds and initial results are shown much sooner. Among other things, speed depends on narrowing down the search space by fingerprinting and on I/O caching at the Linux and PostgreSQL level. Searching in smaller corpora is much faster. For example searching only in the seven mentioned CHILDES sub-corpora, worth about 4,000,000 annotations, has a set-up time of less than 10 seconds and after that, searches take at most a few seconds.

All benchmarks were done on an older test server with two dual core 1.8 GHz AMD Opteron 265 CPUs, 16 GB of DDR400 RAM (8 modules) and a small SCSI 160 RAID with 120 MB/s read bandwidth. A modern desktop PC can have twice the speed, cores, RAM and disk bandwidth with one CPU and a consumer SSD. Trova used up to three database threads on our test server, PostgreSQL uses one core per thread. PostgreSQL is configured to use 3.5 GB of shared buffers, 1 GB of work memory per task and 6 GB of cache size.

[10] Dokumentation Bedrohter Sprachen

[11] Project "Modalität in Lernervarietäten im Längsschnitt"

4.2 Task Design

We searched for ten keywords each from a set of eight languages in our 55M annotation test domain. For German, English and Dutch, we used entries 991 to 1000 of the "top1000" lists of wortschatz.uni-leipzig.de; For French, Spanish and Turkish, we used entries 991 to 1000 of the word frequency lists on en.Wiktionary.org; For Russian, the masterrussian.com list of most common words was used. No frequency list was available for Japanese, so we used a selection of words from "1000 Japanese basic words" from Wiktionary. The Japanese selection contains nouns which are translations of words present in the selections of the other languages.

For this set of terms[12], we investigated three search paradigms in sequence: (1) keyword search with substring matching (i.e., the keyword can match any part of the annotation), (2) regular expression search, either for "word between word boundaries" (German, English, Dutch, French and Spanish), or for "word starts with..." (Turkish, Russian and Japanese)[13], and (3) keyword search with exact matching (i.e., the keyword must match the entire annotation).

All queries were done via the CQL REST interface three times in a row, requesting to wait until **all** results have arrived. We observe that repetitions of queries differ in average speed by less than 10%. In addition, we first searched for a bogus word (**start**), taking up to 20 seconds while CQL search caches domain properties before the timed queries start.

4.3 Results

Substring Search

In Table 1 we show the results for the substring matching. We observe that the query speed varies significantly with language: Our test corpus contains a large number of Dutch annotations, so this task takes the most time and finds the most hits.

Block **substr**	AM hits	AM	MD	Min	Max
		duration (in seconds)			
Dutch	9453	13.16	13.23	4.2	27.5
English	3532	8.26	6.44	4.2	20.0
French	3603	7.25	6.19	3.9	17.4
German	1634	6.57	4.75	2.7	23.0
Japanese	689	0.89	0.55	0.3	2.0
Russian	50	0.61	0.60	0.5	0.8
Spanish	1336	5.98	5.10	4.1	9.4
Turkish	113	6.80	6.75	2.1	23.1

Table 1: Benchmark results for substring queries. 30 queries per language, 60 for Japanese. AM = Arithmetic Mean, MD = Median.

Block **regexp**	AM hits	AM	MD	Min	Max
		duration (in seconds)			
Dutch	2834	11.55	10.86	4.7	25.8
English	2512	9.18	7.71	5.1	26.2
French	2134	7.68	7.60	3.7	21.6
German	371	5.85	4.77	2.8	11.6
Japanese	414	0.85	0.51	0.3	1.9
Russian	15	0.64	0.63	0.5	0.9
Spanish	882	5.55	4.81	3.8	8.1
Turkish	132	9.56	7.84	3.4	32.2

Table 2: Benchmark results for regexp queries. 30 queries per language, 60 for Japanese. AM = Arithmetic Mean, MD = Median.

Searching for English, French, German and Spanish already is twice as fast, as is Turkish. Turkish words tend to have fingerprints similar to those of words in other languages. Searching only in the Turkish sub-corpus would be a lot faster.

But why do we get all results within less than one second for Japanese and Russian, without explicitly searching only in relevant sub-corpora? This is again due to fingerprinting: Text in other languages will most likely not contain any cyrillic, kanji or hiragana characters at all. So even by looking only at unigrams, Trova and CQL search can quickly discard most tiers in other languages when searching for Japanese or Russian words.

Regular Expression Search

The second block of queries uses regular expression search, results are shown in Table 2. As expected, we observe fewer hits than with a plain substring search. This also explains small speed

[12] We replaced a number of word forms from the original lists to be more suitable for raw string search as follows: *pahnut'* (infinitive) to *pahnet*, *zavod'* (-' only in one form) to *zavod*, *querías* to *quería*, *hareket etmek* (inf.) to *hareket ettiler* and *istenmek* (inf.) to *istenem*. Of course we used cyrillic strings in the actual queries. The latin transliterations are only used for easier reading.

[13] Word boundaries ($\backslash b$*keyword*$\backslash b$) are ASCII-oriented, not covering accented characters, but do work with punctuation marks. The regular expression ($\backslash s|\backslash A$)*keyw* works in Unicode space, anchoring *keyw* to the start of the annotation or a space. However, e.g. opening parentheses or quotation marks before *keyw* will not match.

Block **exact**	AM hits	AM	MD	Min	Max
		duration (in seconds)			
Dutch	1756	10.25	9.18	3.4	26.8
English	64	7.02	5.44	3.6	18.7
French	45	5.91	5.12	3.5	12.7
German	3	5.66	3.88	2.4	22.9
Japanese	0	0.74	0.40	0.2	2.8
Russian	6	0.51	0.50	0.4	0.7
Spanish	26	4.87	4.26	3.5	7.0
Turkish	1	5.23	5.58	2.1	7.9

Table 3: Benchmark results for exact queries. 30 queries per language, 60 for Japanese. AM = Arithmetic Mean, MD = Median.

Block **all**	AM hits	AM	MD	Min	Max
		duration (in seconds)			
Dutch	4681	11.65	10.29	3.4	27.5
English	2036	8.15	6.61	3.6	26.2
French	1927	6.95	5.58	3.5	21.6
German	669	6.03	4.51	2.4	23.0
Japanese	368	0.83	0.52	0.2	2.8
Russian	24	0.58	0.59	0.4	0.9
Spanish	748	5.47	4.92	3.5	9.4
Turkish	82	7.19	6.43	2.1	32.2

Table 4: Benchmark results for all queries. 30 queries per language, 60 for Japanese. AM = Arithmetic Mean, MD = Median.

gains for Dutch and Spanish. For the other languages, in particular Turkish, a small speed loss can be seen. Here, two forces act on the processing load: Searching for (shorter) prefixes means that fewer tiers can be discarded based on n-gram fingerprints. More have to be considered, yet those contain fewer hits because specifying a regular expression is more restrictive than a substring. In addition, regular expressions take more CPU time to process. Note that the fingerprinting only considers the plain parts: For example, a search for $(\backslash s|\backslash A)$*yumurt* will consider all tiers which satisfy the n-grams of *yumurt*[14].

[14]The "stemming" of *yumurta* to *yumurt* is an artificial example and not meant to be linguistically correct. Using fingerprint tables up to n-gram size 4, from *y, u...*, *yu, um...* to *murt* have to be present in a tier to make it a candidate. To balance disk space usage against speed, not all possible combinations of 1 to 4 Unicode characters are fingerprinted separately. Instead, n-grams are hashed into bins – for example, all possible 4-grams share $2,000$ classes.

Exact String Search

Our third round of queries only considers exact matches. We show this round in Table 3. While there is some speed gain compared to substring matches, related to having fewer hits, it is much smaller than expected. Some time is saved because string inequality can often be detected without having to scan the whole string. However, the set of candidate tiers chosen by fingerprinting is as big as for substring search.

Adding specific indexes can improve exact match speed, but will only have an effect on this match mode. For example, such an index could bin whole-string hashes in slots. Another possibility would be an index of only the sets of string lengths occurring in each tier.

Substring searches are most used, especially because not all corpora have annotations at word granularity. Many corpora annotate larger units, such as phrases, sentences or utterances, but at higher quality, e.g., stating recording timestamps for them. Searching for annotations which are exactly *elephant* will not work in a corpus treating *I saw an elephant.* as one atomic annotation.

Overall Speed

Finally, Table 4 gives a summary of all queries in our benchmark task: The average and in particular median query durations in our 55M annotation test corpus are considerably below 10 seconds for most languages. For languages which can be readily identified from their writing system, waiting times below one second can be expected.

While it is not visible in this table, our experience shows that long waiting times relate to novel queries for hard to filter words. The slowest query is the regular expression search for words starting with *isten*. Searching for *isten*-after-space would be faster (37% fewer candidate tiers) but would not find annotation-initial occurrences of *isten*. Repeating the query later reduces waiting time from 32 to 28 seconds, showing the effects of disk caching.

5 Summary

In this article we have described the TLA language archive and possibilities to search in it. The archive contains a large and diverse collection of language data occupying over 40 terabytes of storage for more than 250 languages.

We presented a variety of browse and search methods available for our archive, developed over several years. We described the speed of our annotation content search on a small server, using a large test corpus. We have listed results from benchmarks, and analyzed them.

Furthermore, we have discussed several current and future optimizations that can improve search and browse speed. Of course, our implementation is also guided by the most common use cases.

References

[Auer et al., 2010] Auer, E., Wittenburg, P., Sloetjes, H., Schreer, O., Masneri, S., Schneider, D., and Tschöpel, S. (2010). Automatic annotation of media field recordings. In Sporleder, C. and Zervanou, K., editors, *Proceedings of the ECAI 2010 Workshop on Language Technology for Cultural Heritage, Social Sciences, and Humanities (LaTeCH 2010)*, pages 31–34, Lisbon. University de Lisbon.

[Berck and Russel, 2006] Berck, P. and Russel, A. (2006). Annex – a web-based framework for exploiting annotated media resources. In *LREC*.

[Johnson, 2002] Johnson, H. (2002). The archive of the indigenous languages of latin america: Goals and visions. In *Proceedings of the Language Resources and Engineering Conference*, Las Palmas, Spain.

[Kemps-Snijders et al., 2010] Kemps-Snijders, M., Koller, T., Sloetjes, H., and Verweij, H. (2010). Lat bridge: Bridging tools for annotation and exploration of rich linguistic data. In Calzolari, N., Maegaard, B., Mariani, J., Odijk, J., Choukri, K., Piperidis, S., Rosner, M., and Tapias, D., editors, *Proceedings of the Seventh conference on International Language Resources and Evaluation (LREC'10)*, pages 2648–2651. European Language Resources Association (ELRA).

[Kemps-Snijders et al., 2009] Kemps-Snijders, M., Windhouwer, M., and Wittenburg, P. (2009). Isocat: Remodeling metadata for language resources. In *International Journal of Metadata, Semantics and Ontologies (IJMSO)*, volume 4 (4), pages 261–276.

[Morgan, 2004] Morgan, E. (2004). An introduction to the Search/Retrieve URL Service (SRU). *Ariadne*.

[Ordelman et al., 2009] Ordelman, R. J. F., Heeren, W. F. L., de Jong, F. M. G., Huijbregts, M. A. H., and Hiemstra, D. (2009). Towards affordable disclosure of spoken heritage archives. *Journal of Digital Information*, 10(6):17.

[Reynaert, 2010] Reynaert, M. (2010). Character confusion versus focus word-based correction of spelling and ocr variants in corpora. *International Journal on Document Analysis and Recognition*, pages 1–15. 10.1007/s10032-010-0133-5.

[Ringersma et al., 2010] Ringersma, J., Zinn, C., and Koenig, A. (2010). Eureka! user friendly access to the mpi linguistic data archive. In *SDV - Sprache und Datenverarbeitung/International Journal for Language Data Processing*.

[S.H. McCallum, 2006] S.H. McCallum (2006). A look at new information retrieval protocols: Sru, opensearch/a9, cql, and xquery. In *WORLD LIBRARY AND INFORMATION CONGRESS: 72ND IFLA GENERAL CONFERENCE AND COUNCIL*, Seoul, Korea.

[Skiba, 2009] Skiba, R. (2009). Korpora in der Zweitspracherwerbsforschung: Internetzugang zu Daten des ungesteuerten Zweitspracherwerbs. In Ahrenholz, B., Bredel, U., Klein, W., Rost-Roth, M., and Skiba, R., editors, *Empirische Forschung und Theoriebildung: Beiträge aus Soziolinguistik, Gesprochene-Sprache- und Zweitspracherwerbsforschung: Festschrift für Norbert Dittmar*, pages 21–30.

[Uytvanck et al., 2010] Uytvanck, D. V., Zinn, C., Broeder, D., Wittenburg, P., and Gardelleni, M. (2010). Virtual language observatory: The portal to the language resources and technology universe. In Calzolari, N., Maegaard, B., Mariani, J., Odijk, J., Choukri, K., Piperidis, S., Rosner, M., and Tapias, D., editors, *Proceedings of the Seventh conference on International Language Resources and Evaluation (LREC'10)*, pages 900–903. European Language Resources Association (ELRA).

[Wittenburg and Trilsbeek, 2010] Wittenburg, P. and Trilsbeek, P. (2010). Digital archiving – a necessity in documentary linguistics. In Senft, G., editor, *Endangered Austronesian and Australian Aboriginal languages: Essays on language documentation, archiving and revitalization*, pages 111–136. Canberra: Pacific Linguistics.

[Wittenburg et al., 2010] Wittenburg, P., Trilsbeek, P., and Lenkiewicz, P. (2010). Large multimedia archive for world languages. In *Proceedings of the 2010 ACM Workshop on Searching Spontaneous Conversational Speech, Co-located with ACM Multimedia 2010*, pages 53–56. Association for Computing Machinery, Inc. (ACM).

Digital Library of Poland-related Old Ephemeral Prints: Preserving Multilingual Cultural Heritage

Maciej Ogrodniczuk
Institute of Computer Science
Polish Academy of Sciences
maciej.ogrodniczuk@gmail.com

Wlodzimierz Gruszczynski
Warsaw School of Social Sciences and Humanities
wgruszczynski@swps.edu.pl

Abstract

The article presents the results from the project of the thematic Digital Library of Polish and Poland-related Ephemeral Prints from the 16th, 17th and 18th Centuries, intending to preserve the unique multilingual material, make it available for education and extend it with the joint efforts of historians, philologists, librarians and computer scientists.

The paper also puts forward the idea of a living digital library, created with a closed set of resources which can form the basis for their further extension, thus turning traditional digital archives into collaboration platforms.

1 Introduction

Nowadays digital libraries most likely tend to mirror traditional libraries. They collect and display resources as traditional librarians would do, perfectly embracing the new archiving capabilities, but too often stopping at this border. The thematic Digital Library of Polish and Poland-related Ephemeral Prints from the 16th, 17th and 18th Centuries (PL. *Cyfrowa Biblioteka Drukow Ulotnych polskich i Polski dotyczacych z XVI, XVII i XVIII w.* – hence and from here: CBDU, `http://cbdu.id.uw.edu.pl`) offers a new approach to the idea of a modern digital library by extending the conventional paradigm with using consistent sets of materials as an object pool for new collaboration tasks. In our case the prints digitized in the first step of the project were further analyzed and enhanced by experts co-operating on a digital content platform.

The work had been carried out within the project financed by the Polish state with intention to provide public online access to all preserved and described in the literature pre-press documents. Some of them have been preserved in the single copy, so their availability had been evidently restricted. In the course of the project the resources were gathered basing on the list of 2,000 bibliographical entries from Konrad Zawadzki's publication (Zawadzki, 1990) extended with objects described or discovered after its issue. Selected prints have been commented by historians, media experts and linguists to explain less known background details or presently unintelligible metaphors or symbols. Links have been created between related documents (e.g. translations and their alleged sources or derivates) to facilitate comparisons of similar materials. For 70% of the prints their images were obtained and made available in DjVu format. At the end of the project the revised edition of Zawadzki's work was published in electronic form.

Apart from this particular work plan, the ulterior idea was to test the concept of using the digital library as a collaboration platform for experts from different backgrounds basing on the assumption that real opening resources to the public means not just providing them for viewing and download, but preparing the environment to extend them in the immediate or more distant future. The technical challenge was to select the computer system which could serve this purpose best by mostly configuration and without too much tedious low-level programming. This goal was achieved with EPrints free repository software.

At present the library is actively used by historians and linguists (not to mention the students) who seem to benefit the most from the cooperation and further development of the resources. Their recent interests include adding transliterations (which already started with a new project based on the library materials) and using the print texts as source data for the searchable text corpus. Multilinguality of texts should also be shortly addressed since the first stage of work concentrated mostly on Polish and German documents.

The aspect of making the digital library a collaboration platform seems the most important in our study, putting less light into other important issues of creating thematic libraries, commenting historical content or digital library-based teaching. As such, creation of a digital library may be in most cases turned into a development project, being of benefit to the scientific community.

2 Origin, scope and limitations of the project

The project has been initiated in response to the need of permanent access to ephemeral prints from 16th-18th centuries by researchers coming from the academic teams preparing the historical dictionaries of Polish (Institute of Polish Language and Institute of Literary Research at Polish Academy of Sciences) as well as journalism and translation historians (Institute of Journalism, Institute of Applied Linguistics and Institute of German Studies at the Warsaw University) and students of journalism.

Temporal range of selected materials results from the long history of Polish journalism with three significant dates: 1501 – when the first known press materials in Polish appeared in print (the report on the anti-Turkish treaty signed by the Holy See and several European countries, including Poland, in Buda), 1661 – when the first regularly issued Polish newspaper "Merkuriusz Polski Ordynaryjny" came out, and 1729 – when "Nowiny Polskie" (Polish news) started regular circulation. The period in between was filled by ephemeral prints – disposable and occasional informative publications, playing an important part in the development of Polish writing, serving as a the most influential media for important news.

The scope of the materials is Poland-related, which combines the Polish sources with prints published abroad, concerning the Republic of Poland, political, religious and military issues (e.g. the reports on the famous relief of Vienna in 1683), but also sensational facts or canards. The materials were prepared "live", mostly by participants or observers of the reported events and as such they are valuable sociological source of information on mechanisms of spreading information at that time, its reception, propaganda and readers' interests.

The list of bibliographical data of prints complying with all above-mentioned requirements has been collated by Konrad Zawadzki in the 1970s and 1980s and was published as a three-volume work with the first volume issued in 1979 and the last one in 1990. It covers 1967 prints dating from 1501 to 1725, each described with the title (in modern transcription), issue date and place, printer name, format, volume size, information on bibliographical sources and an exact description of the title page (with line breaks, font names, illustrations etc.).

The originals of prints remain in various libraries over Europe, but at the period of preparing the bibliography many were successfully borrowed from their mother institutions to produce microfilmed copies to be included into the resources of The Polish National Library (Zawadzki's place of employment). As microfilmed resources are not the most comfortable ones to operate on a daily basis, usually their photocopies were used for research and teaching. The online era created a new possibility to interact with such resources (e.g. broaden the scope of materials showed to students) and resulted in applying for funds to create a digital library of metadata and images of prints enhanced with information useful for understanding the context of a given object.

The priority of making prints available for the daily work (disparate with the need of preservation of original objects) resulted in the assumption of building on the quality of microfilms rather than archiving originals scattered over many libraries in many countries. This also helped minimize costs and speed up the overall process, mostly also thanks to the presence of vast majority of materials at the National Library.

The source of funding was constrained to national (ministry) level and not to the consortium of libraries (owners of microfilmed print copies) knowing the three contradictory factors:

1. vast resources of large libraries, such as the Polish National Library,
2. their limited funds for digitization,
3. a policy (telling the truth, a reasonable one) of digitizing the most valuable resources first.

This combination can make many interesting materials wait for years to be made available at their owner's institution. Providentially, in March 2009 the 12-month project obtained the support

Figure 1: A sample bibliographical entry

1012. A letter from the king of Poland to his queen, in which is inserted many particulars relating to the victories obtained against the Turks. London, R. Baldwin [po 19 X] 1683. 2°. K. 1, sygn. A.

E. — Hos. 497. Sturm. 1920.

[Tytuł nagł., ant.:] A || LETTER || FROM THE || King of Poland || TO HIS QUEEN. || In which is Incerted || [kurs.:] Many Particulars Relateing to the Victories obtained || against the Turks. With a Prayer of the [ant.:] Turks [kurs.:] against || the [ant.:] Christians. || [linia] || Translated from the [kurs.:] Colonne [ant.:] Gazette, Octobr. 19. 1683. [kurs.:] Numb. 84. || [linia] ||

[Kolofon na k. A v., kurs.:] London, [ant.:] Printed for [kurs.:] R. Baldwin, [ant.:] in the [kurs.:] Old-Bailey. 1683. ||

List króla Jana III Sobieskiego do królowej Marii Kazimiery o zwycięstwie wojsk sojuszniczych nad armią turecką pod Wiedniem 12 IX 1683.

Tekst polski zob. poz. 1005-1007, 1659.

Egz.: WStBibl. Wien
Mikrofilm: BN Mf. 62115

from the Ministry of Culture and National Heritage and the Foundation for the Development of Journalism Education.

3 Towards the thematic digital library

The project team was headed by Wlodzimierz Gruszczynski and joined forces of computer scientists (Maciej Ogrodniczuk, Jakub Wilk), historians (Adam Kozuchowski), philologists (Ewa Gruszczynska, Anna Just, Dorota Lewandowska-Jaros, Katarzyna Jasinska-Zdun) and librarians (the team of Maria Piber), coordinated by Grazyna Oblas.

The process started with scanning Zawadzki's bibliography in the format sufficient to automated OCR processing of the text (200 dpi, greyscale, lossless compression of the result files, see Fig. 1). The images have been read with ABBYY FineReader 9 with support for several modern languages turned on (French, German, Latin, Polish) since texts could contain transcriptions of names in various (modern) languages.

As a result, a recognized plain text of the bibliography has been obtained, covering not only full bibliographical entries (with additional comments, location information etc.), but also all front and back matter data (volume introductions, errata, foreign-language abstracts etc.) to be reused in the electronic edition of the bibliography. Plain text version was used to expedite the task of extraction of individual fields of each entry regardless of its initial inconsistent formatting (which was easily introduced at a later stage, basing on the entry structure). The text has been saved in UTF-8 character encoding to seamlessly represent all diacritics.

Perl scripts have been implemented to split bibliographical entries into individual data records according to the description of fields retrieved from the bibliography introduction (full and short title, information about author, publisher, format etc.) In fact, the field list was designed to be more specific than the original to support verification of content (e.g. the model of a list of copies with subfields storing library name and a catalogue number was introduced against the original composite string value). The field set has been later used as a basis of the target model for the computer system storing the library data with new fields describing the project-specific properties going beyond the traditional bibliographical entry (e.g. commentaries of an object). The records were then verified with regular expression patterns testing their contents (e.g. publication date standard format) and content of fields used in further steps (e.g. microfilm catalogue numbers) extracted separately and additionally verified.

As the majority of microfilms were available at the National Library, the preparation of scans has been commissioned mainly to this institution, after obtaining formal permission to use the resulting electronic documents on the project site, ultimately available to the general public. Since the project duration was relatively short, the scans were produced in batches to let contributors start work on the previous portion when the following one was still in preparation (which sometimes required cleaning the microfilm plates or seeking improperly catalogued collection). Similarly, all other project phases (metadata proofreading, import and conversion of scanned materials, preparation of commentaries and dictionaries etc.) were also being carried out simultaneously.

Among many available repository systems for digital libraries, including a prominent (in Poland) dLibra (dLibra, 2010), EPrints has been selected as the target storage and publication framework. EPrints (EPrints, 2010) is a free, GPL-licensed multiplatform repository software developed since 2000 at the University of Southampton. Its open source origin presents a major benefit for projects intending not only to deploy it "as is", but seeking possibilities to extend it with new solution-specific functionalities. The system has been installed, configured and in most respects translated into Polish (with translations made available to the community), setting up the print repository.

As already stated above, an important organizational assumption made at the beginning of the project was to use EPrints also as a collaboration platform, starting from the very first phases of the work. Following this statement, the bibliographical entries (henceforth, metadata descriptions) were imported into EPrints even before they were finally proofread. This stage has been carried out already in the system, using the workflow defined for the project. After metadata has been revised against the image (or paper) version of the bibliography, the scanned images of prints were converted into DjVu format and uploaded into the library (each object corresponding to one file).

Versions of objects (most likely translations or alterations of the base text) have been linked basing on information available in the bibliography or detected by the experts. For materials only reported in literature, when the original is unknown or not preserved, the information on the base language has been provided.

Going beyond simply making the objects available as electronic versions of the bibliographic entries with scanned copies, the repository model has been extended with new fields storing the new value created by the project: historical commentaries relating to facts and people described in the material, media-historical or language-historical observations, translations of then common Latin interjections and translations of foreign texts into Polish or local dictionaries. Such approach seems novel in the design of digital libraries. What is more, the system creates possibility to form a living thematic information exchange environment around the library site, making it possible to store expert comments, versions of materials etc.

To make the scope of description complete and up-to-date, a survey of the library holdings has been carried out. The annual volumes of library professional journals published by ten major scientific libraries in Poland has been investigated and 80 new objects (not included in Zawadzki's bibliography) discovered. Since the project was short of funds to generate their scanned versions, only their metadata were added to the library.

The last phase of the project was preparation of the supplemented electronic edition of Zawadzki's bibliography which illustrates how digital content can help maintain traditional publications. The electronic version was intended to be published, but cuts in the initial project budget forced the team to leave this additional step to future projects.

The new publication layout has been created in LateX. To facilitate usage, in contrast to the original work, separation into three volumes was not preserved and a single volume was produced. Introductions, lists of printers and print shops as well as back matter illustrations were taken over from the OCR-ed source and collated. All materials transferred to the digital library have been exported into XML format and were included in the final edition. This means that all supplements and errata which were merged with the library objects were automatically corrected. Back matter content such as lists of titles, people names and geographical names were not transferred from the original work but were regenerated from the library.

All scripts and transformations created throughout the project were preserved to facilitate generation of new electronic editions of the bibliography in case new errors are reported by the library users or new materials included. This also demonstrates new collaborative approach to preparation of electronic publications

4 Library interface, statistics and usage

The repository is located on the server of the Institute of Journalism of the University of Warsaw and

Figure 2: Library homepage

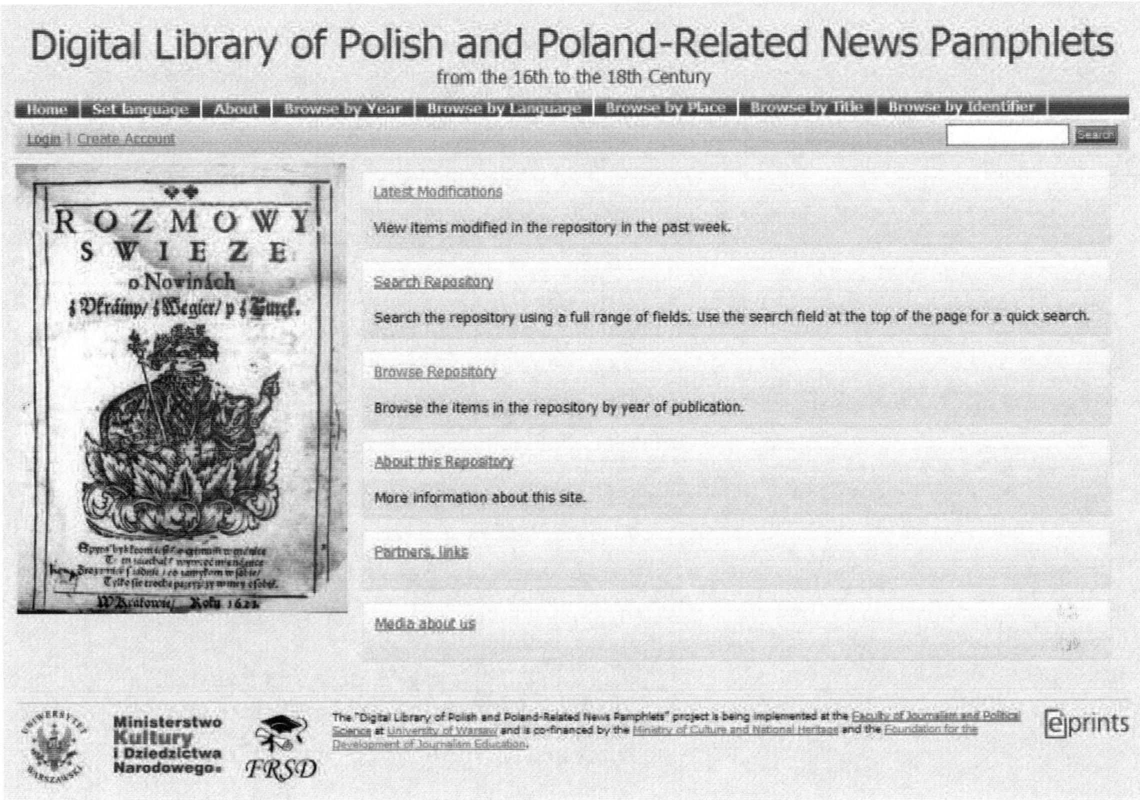

the library has been made available at `http://cbdu.id.uw.edu.pl`[1]. The site (see homepage on Fig. 2) allows typical browse and search interfaces in Polish or English. Objects can be browsed according to multiple criteria, including those normally used in bibliographical descriptions (mostly borrowed from Zawadzki), as well as those less typical: thematic, genre-related and other. The native EPrints advanced search is supplemented with a recently customized simple search with a Google-like single text field.

Prints relating to the same facts are hyperlinked, especially those that are most likely or certainly translations from other texts available in the library. Taking into account the number of identified dependencies and benefits resulting from possibility of their visual comparison, the system offers a function to open related documents in a split window. Moreover, the new implementations include enhanced inter-metadata linking capabilities, new facets for repository browsing and a list of recently revised objects replacing the standard list of recently added.

Currently the library holds 2009 objects. 1404 objects have scans attached (with 11 585 pages in total). 11 languages are represented. The languages with widest coverage (over 50 objects) are: German (797 objects), Polish (325 objects – see Fig. 3), Italian (180) and Latin (69); the remaining ones are Swedish, French, Spanish, English, Dutch, Czech and Danish. Around 200 prints in Polish and 50 in German have attached dictionaries explaining currently unused words or phrases (giving explanations in contemporary Polish or German). Latin dictionaries are also included.

The final version of the library has been made official early 2010, so it has been more than half a year since its resources can be used for interested parties and some initial findings from observed usage of the library resources can be obtained. Data from March-November 2010 show that the library hosted 34 unique visitors daily (47 visits) and is stabilizing; approx. 40% of the open pages are DjVu files (not indexed by popular search engines which should imply human visitors).

[1] The default language of the interface is Polish; it can be changed to English by selecting the second menu option ("Ustaw jezyk") and then the first entry on the language list (English – "angielski").

Figure 3: A sample object

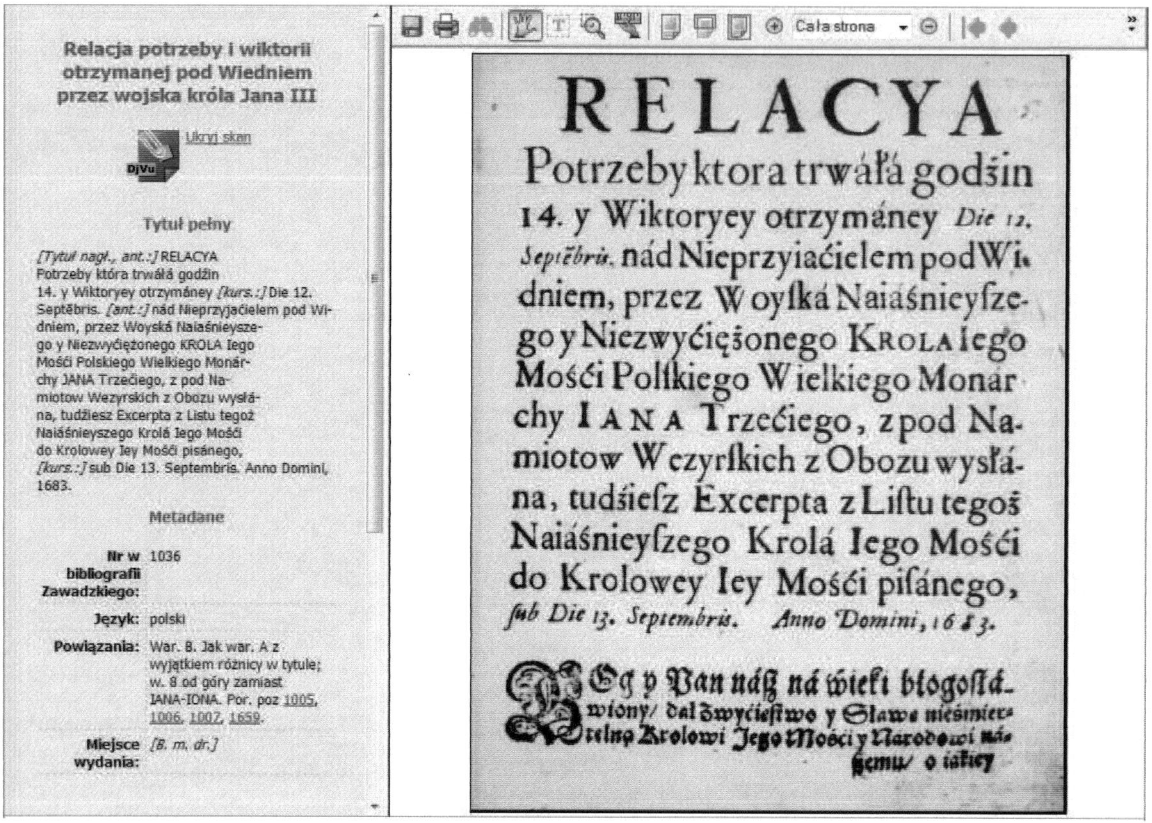

The library has been included into the network of Polish Digital Libraries Federation by means of The Open Archives Initiative Protocol for Metadata Harvesting (OAI-PMH, 2002) with metadata represented in Dublin Core (ISO, 2009). OAI-PMH is natively supported by EPrints, so no additional implementation was necessary.

To advertise the library among the general public a series of dissemination events have been organized. They included radio broadcasts (university radio Kampus, Polish news radio TOK FM), newspaper articles and historical portal news.

5 Further steps and conclusions

Recently the library contents found new applications: it is currently used in the EU-co-funded IMPACT project for training Gothic script OCR software by ABBYY (the producer of FineReader with XIX module for recognition of Fraktur or "black letter" texts). Simultaneously the transcribed versions are being prepared and are planned to be included in the library (respective metadata fields were defined in the project, but only one transcription was filled in since it exceeded the scope of the project). Other project which can benefit from the library resources, currently being carried out by the Institute of Polish Language at the Polish Academy of Sciences is the dictionary of the historical Polish from 17th and the first half of 18th century (see SXVII, 2010).

Another interesting direction is broadening of the scope of materials the library covers. Since the project has been closely related to the resources of The Polish National Library, it can be extended to cover materials coming from other libraries, most likely from abroad, both preserving originals and storing their microfilmed copies. With the possibility of preparation of copies on site, the costs should not significantly differ from the costs of the national project. Starting with Zawadzki's bibliography, there are still around 200-300 objects to be acquired this way. The geographical key seems an important factor here: the limitations imposed on Zawadzki before 1989 resulted in underrepresentation of resources from the libraries of the countries belonging to the former Soviet Union. Last but not least, Vatican archives can prove to be one of the most important source of materials of the described type, with so far limited availability.

Apart from obvious development ideas such as widening the scope of description of gathered objects or deepening the analysis, the idea of creating a collaboration platform of the digital library site can be followed. For instance, the system can be extended with new functionalities provided to the library users (not just experts with editing rights) such as adding comments to materials or an integrated forum. Such add-ons can prove similarly efficient in development of the materials and in related projects.

Despite its small scale, we trust that our library will prove equally useful for old-Polish researchers as much larger heritage accessibility projects such as Europeana (see `http://www.europeana.eu`) or ENRICH (European Networking Resources and Information concerning Cultural Heritage, see `http://enrich.manuscriptorium.com/`).

References

dLibra (2010). *Digital Library Framework.* Poznan Supercomputing and Networking Center affiliated to the Institute of Bioorganic Chemistry of the Polish Academy of Sciences.

EPrints (2010). *EPrints free software.* Southampton: School of Electronics and Computer Science at the University of Southampton.

Gruszczynski W., Ogrodniczuk M. (2010). *Cyfrowa Biblioteka Drukow Ulotnych Polskich i Polski dotyczacych z XVI, XVII i XVIII w. w nauce i dydaktyce (Digital Library of Poland-related Old Ephemeral Prints in research and teaching*, in Polish). In Proceedings of "Polskie Biblioteki Cyfrowe 2010" (*Polish Digital Libraries 2010*) conference, Poznan, 18-22 October 2010.

ISO 2009: *ISO 15836:2009. Information and documentation – The Dublin Core metadata element set.*

OAI-PMH (2002). *The Open Archives Initiative Protocol for Metadata Harvesting.* Protocol Version 2.0 of 2002-06-14, Document Version 2008-12-07. http://www.openarchives.org/OAI/openarchivesprotocol.html.

SVXI (1987). *Slownik polszczyzny XVI w. (Dictionary of 16 century Polish*, in Polish). Krakow: Instytut Badan Literackich PAN.

SVXII (2010). *Slownik jezyka polskiego XVII i 1. polowy XVIII w. (Dictionary of 17 century and 1st half of 18 century Polish*, in Polish). Warszawa: Polska Akademia Nauk, Instytut Jezyka Polskiego.

Zawadzki, K. (1990). *Gazety ulotne polskie i Polski dotyczace z XVI, XVII i XVIII wieku (Polish and Poland-related Ephemeral Prints from the 16th-18th Centuries*, in Polish). Wroclaw: Zaklad Narodowy im. Ossolinskich, Wydawnictwo Polskiej Akademii Nauk.

Rule-Based Normalization of Historical Texts

Marcel Bollmann **Florian Petran** **Stefanie Dipper**
Ruhr-University Bochum
bollmann,petran,dipper@linguistics.rub.de

Abstract

This paper deals with normalization of language data from Early New High German. We describe an unsupervised, rule-based approach which maps historical wordforms to modern wordforms. Rules are specified in the form of context-aware rewrite rules that apply to sequences of characters. They are derived from two aligned versions of the Luther bible and weighted according to their frequency. The evaluation shows that our approach (83%–91% exact matches) clearly outperforms the baseline (65%).

1 Introduction[1]

Historical language data differs from modern data in that there are no agreed-upon, standardized writing conventions. Instead, characters and symbols used by the writer of some manuscript in parts reflect impacts as different as spatial constraints or dialect influences. This often leads to inconsistent spellings, even within one text written up by one writer.

The goal of our research is an automatic mapping from wordforms from Early New High German (ENHG, 14th–16th centuries) to the corresponding modern wordforms from New High German (NHG). Enriching the data with modern wordform annotations facilitates further processing of the data, e.g. by POS taggers.

In this paper, we present a rule-based approach. Given an input wordform, (sequences of) characters are replaced by other characters according to rules that have been derived from two word-aligned corpora. The results show that our approach clearly outperforms the baseline. However, there is still room for some improvement.

The paper is organized as follows. Sec. 2 discusses related work; in Sec. 3, we introduce our data. Sec. 4 addresses the way we derive rewrite rules from the data, while Sec. 5 deals with the application of the rules to generate modern wordforms. Sec. 6 presents the evaluation, Sec. 7 the conclusion.

2 Related Work

Baron et al. (2009) present two tools for normalization of historical wordforms. VARD consists of a lexicon and user-defined replacement rules, and offers an interface to edit and correct automatically normalized wordforms. DICER[2] is a tool that derives weighted context-aware character edit rules from normalized texts. The algorithm that creates these rules is not described in their paper, though.

Jurish (2010) compares different methods to normalize German wordforms from 1780–1880. The methods include mappings based on phonetic representations and manually created rewrite rules. The highest F-score (99.4%) is achieved by an HMM (Hidden Markov Model) that selects one of the candidates proposed by the other methods.

Research on normalizing historical language data has also been done in the field of Information Retrieval, applied to historical documents. They address the task reverse to ours: mapping modern wordforms to historical (or dialectal) wordforms.

Ernst-Gerlach and Fuhr (2006) run a spellchecker on their data (19th century German) to detect wordforms that differ from NHG wordforms, and to generate normalized wordform candidates. Context-aware rules that rewrite character sequences are derived from the pairs. They achieve an F-score of 60%.

[1] We would like to thank the anonymous reviewers for helpful comments. The research reported here was financed by Deutsche Forschungsgemeinschaft (DFG), Grant DI 1558/4-1.

[2] http://corpora.lancs.ac.uk/dicer/

ENHG	AM	anfang	schuff	Gott	Himel	vnd	Erden	[...]	VND	Gott	schuff	den	Menschen	jm	zum	Bilde /
NHG	Am	Anfang	schuf	Gott	Himmel	und	Erde	[...]	Und	Gott	schuf	den	Menschen	ihm	zum	Bilde ,
EN	In_the	beginning	created	God	heavens	and	earth		and	God	created	the	man	him	in_the	image

ENHG	zum	Bilde	Gottes	schuff	er	jn	/	Vnd	schuff	sie	ein	Menlin	vnd	Frewlin .
NHG	zum	Bilde	Gottes	schuf	er	ihn	;	und	schuf	sie	ein	Männlein	und	Fräulein .
EN	in_the	image	of_God	created	he	him		and	created	them	a	male	and	female

Table 1: The original ENHG and the modernized NHG version of Genesis 1:1 and 1:27, along with an English interlinear translation.

Hauser and Schulz (2007) use a corpus from ENHG and a dictionary from NHG to derive replacement rules of (sequences of) characters. To this end, they first assign ENHG wordforms to NHG dictionary entries, using Levenshtein distance to pick suitable candidate entries; wordforms with ambiguous assignments are excluded. The rule frequencies are used as weights for the rule applications. For generating ENHG lemmas from NHG lemmas, they achieve F-Scores between 56.9% (without weights), 66.2% (with weights derived from lexicon mappings), and 71.2% (with perfect training pairs).

Strunk (2003) uses weighted Levenshtein distance to generate dialectal wordform variants for IR of Low Saxon texts. Weights are manually defined and encode phonetic similarity.

Our approach is similar to Ernst-Gerlach and Fuhr (2006) and Hauser and Schulz (2007) in that we derive replacement rules of character sequences from aligned pairs. The algorithms to learn rules differ, though. Ernst-Gerlach and Fuhr (2006) specify recursive definitions that take into account rewrite sequences and contexts of varying sizes; rules can refer to characters or to the underspecified classes 'vowel' and 'consonant'. Hauser and Schulz (2007) extract n-gram sequences of varying size from the aligned wordforms, and learn n-gram mapping rules. Furthermore, our approach differs from theirs in that our training pairs stem from aligned corpora.

The evaluations cannot be easily compared because it is not clear to what extent the language data base is comparable with regard to its variation. The data from Jurish (2010) contains 59.2% identical word pairs (types), the data from Ernst-Gerlach and Fuhr (2006) 94%. In our data, only 51% of the pair types align identical words.

Furthermore, in our task, a historical form is most often mapped to one modern equivalent form; in the reverse task, a modern form is mapped to multiple historical variants.

3 The Corpus

In our approach, replacement rules are derived from word-aligned parallel corpora. A source that provides a parallel corpus in many languages, including historical ones, is the bible.

The collected works of Martin Luther are freely available from the web.[3] They include several versions of his bible translation, modernized to varying degrees. We chose the original ENHG version of the 1545 bible (which has been enriched with modern punctuation) as well as a revised NHG version of it, which uses modern spelling and replaces extinct words by modern ones.[4]

Table 1 shows text fragments in both versions. Differences concern capitalization (*AM – Am, anfang – Anfang*), character reduplication (*schuff – schuf, Himel – Himmel*), deletion (*Erden – Erde*), insertion, or replacement (*Frewlin – Fräulein*).

Compared to other texts from that time, the language of Luther's 1545 bible is rather close to NHG, since the evolution of NHG was heavily influenced by Luther's bible translation (Besch, 2000). Furthermore, printed texts in general show more consistent spelling than manuscripts, and use abbreviations to a lesser extent than manuscripts (Wolf, 2000); no abbreviations occur in Luther's 1545 bible. Hence, we expect that our approach can be transferred and applied to other printed texts more easily than to manuscripts.

Alignment The files contain one bible verse per line. A verse usually corresponds to one sentence; some verses, however, consist of more than one sentence. Sometimes the assignment of sentences or phrases to verses had been changed from the original to the modernized version to an assignment that is presumably closer to the original

[3]For instance: `http://www.sermon-online.de`.

[4]The original 1545 version is incorrectly called "Altdeutsch" ('Old German') in the archive. Our NHG text (which is possibly the 1892 revision) is a rather conservative version, while the 1912 and 1984 revised versions also contain corrections of mistranslations by Luther and, hence, deviate from the original ENHG text to a greater extent.

Greek version. The verses were rectified manually so that each version had the same number of verses. A few OCR mistakes were also manually corrected (e.g. *3ott* was replaced by *Gott* 'god'). The entire corpus was then tokenized using the tokenizer script supplied with the Europarl corpus (Koehn, 2005), and afterwards downcased.

Since there were still asymmetries in the assignment of phrases and sentences to the verses between the versions, the resulting corpus was not yet properly aligned. We applied a sentence aligner to our data, the Gargantua toolkit (Braune and Fraser, 2010). Next, the words of each aligned verse pair were aligned using the GIZA++ toolkit (Och and Ney, 2003).

The modernization often involves transforming words into phrases and vice versa, such as *soltu – sollst du* 'should you', or *on gefehr – ohngefähr* 'approximately' (literally: 'without danger (of saying so)'). Hence, it is crucial that the word aligner can handle 1:n/n:1 alignments. Upon manual inspection, we found a lot of misalignments with rarer tokens, many of which involve numbers, such as *zweiundzwanzig* 'twenty-two', which would actually correspond to the multi-word token *zwey vnd zwenzig* in the original 1545 version. These were probably misaligned because their frequency in the corpus is not high enough to train a translation model.

To minimize noise in our system's input, alignment pairs with a length difference of more than five characters were excluded from further processing. Since the two texts are highly similar—around 65% of the pairs align identical wordforms—a length difference of that magnitude rarely leads to meaningful alignments.

Some corpus statistics To assess the quality of the resulting word pairs, we had a small sample of 1,000 pairs of aligned non-identical wordforms from the evaluation corpus manually inspected by a student assistant. We identified six types of alignments, listed in Table 2.[5] Instances that were difficult to classify are assigned to a special class.

For deriving replacement rules, type 1 alignments are the perfect input. Pairs of type 2 and 3 are still useful, to a certain extent: correct rules can be derived from the word roots; mapping of differing inflection and affixes, however, should probably not be learned. Type 4 and 5 pairs (which occur very rarely) could be used to derive mappings of entire words rather than character sequences. Type 6 alignments clearly constitute noise.

[5]Throughout the paper, the examples are taken from the development corpus while the figures are calculated based on the evaluation corpus.

Type	Example	Freq	Eval
1. Unproblematic	*vnd – und* 'and'	609	77%
2. Differing inflection	*truncken – trunkenen* 'drunken'	261	18%
3. Differing affixes	*oben – obenan* 'on top'	40	5%
4. Closer modern form exists	*noch – weder* 'neither/nor'	0	–
5. Extinct form	*stündlin - an dem Tage* 'on that day'	1	–
6. Incorrect	*zwey* 'two' – *für* 'for'	25	0%
7. Unclear cases	*fur* 'for' (?) – *für* 'for'	64	19%

Table 2: Alignment types: types 1–5 are correct to various degrees, type 6 is incorrect. For each type, its frequency in the sample and evaluation results for the more frequent types are given (see Sec. 6).

We further computed the number of target types a source word maps to. The pie chart in Fig. 1 shows that the vast majority of source types map to only one target type, with a significant minority mapping to two forms. The proportion of source types mapping to 4–8 target types was so negligible that they were merged in the pie chart. The quantity of source *tokens* that map to more than one target type on the other hand is pretty large. Even though the majority still has 1–2 mappings, about 20–30% of source tokens map to more than 5 target types, as the central bar plot of Fig. 1 shows. However, if we exclude targets that occur only five times or less, the graph shows a more balanced picture (right bar plot). Since the application of rules is based on their frequencies, it is highly likely that the impact of the infrequent rules is balanced out by the dominant ones.

Procedure The resulting corpus consists of 550,000 aligned pairs of words or phrases. We randomly picked 20% of the alignment pairs for a development corpus, which was used for the development of the rule extraction and application processes described below. Another 40% were afterwards used to extract the replacement rules for the following experiments (= training corpus), and a final 20% were picked for an evaluation corpus.

4 Normalization Rules

We used a modified algorithm for Levenshtein distance which not only calculates the numerical edit

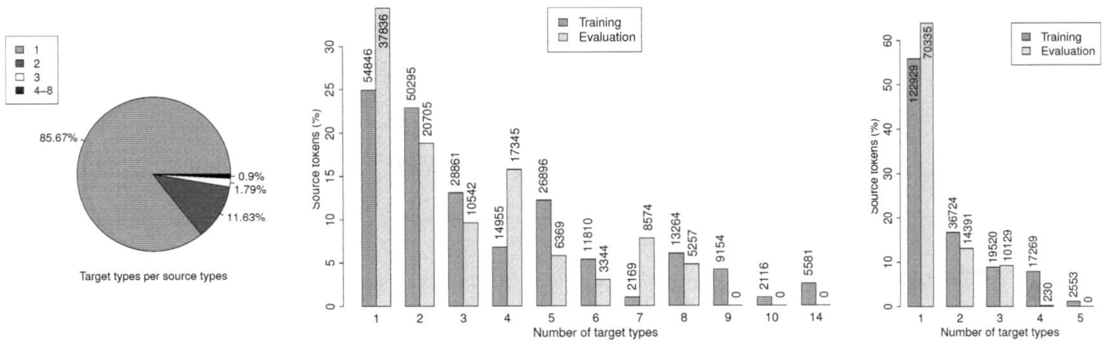

Figure 1: Target types per source type/token. The pie chart shows the result for source types (evaluation corpus), the central bar plot shows the results for all source tokens, the right bar plot only considers tokens with a frequency > 5 (training and evaluation corpus). The columns are labeled by absolute frequencies.

distance, but also outputs the respective edit operations (substitution, insertion, and deletion of single characters) that map the strings to each other. The record of edit operations was enriched with information about the immediate context of the edited character. Ex. (1) shows two sample edit operations, using the notation of phonological rewrite rules.

(1) a. `ε → h / j _ r`
('h' is inserted between 'j' and 'r')

b. `v → u / # _ n`
('v' is replaced by 'u' between the left word boundary ('#') and 'n')

Determining the context for these edit operations is not straightforward, because applying one rule can change the context for other rules. Since the Levenshtein implementation applies the rules from left to right, we decided to use the (new) target word for the left context and the (unaltered) source word for the right context (see also Fig. 2).

Identity rules In addition to canonical replacement rules, our rule induction algorithm also produces identity rules, i.e. rewrite rules that map a character to itself. Identity rules reflect the fact that the majority of words remain unaltered when mapped to their modernized forms, and many words are modified by few characters only. Identity rules and actual rewrite rules are intended to compete with each other during the process of rewriting.

Multiple optimal paths Since the dynamic programming algorithm works by determining a least-cost path through a matrix, we are faced with the problem that there may be multiple optimal paths. In fact, this situation arises quite often. Ex. (2) shows two optimal paths/alignments for the pair *jrem* – *ihrem* 'their'.[6]

(2) a.

Input	*j*		*r*	*e*	*m*
Operations	s	+	=	=	=
Output	*i*	*h*	*r*	*e*	*m*

b.

Input		*j*	*r*	*e*	*m*
Operations	+	s	=	=	=
Output	*i*	*h*	*r*	*e*	*m*

The ambiguity is obviously of no consequence for the numerical distance, which is two for both cases, but it makes a big difference for the rules. In particular, it is usually very clear that one of the alignments is the "correct" one (reflecting facts about language change, here: Ex. (2a)), while the other one is an implementation artifact (Ex. (2b)).

Rule sets and sequence-based rules To solve the ambiguity problem, we first pick a random path by preferring substitution over deletion over addition on the cell level in the matrix. The rules derived this way are combined to rule *sets* afterwards. This is done by inspecting the positions in the source and target word where the edits are made. Whenever a series of edits occurs at the same target or source position, we assume that this is actually an insertion or deletion of a *sequence* of characters, such as an affix. Whenever edits occur at adjacent positions, we assume that it is a substitution of a character sequence by another. By merging substitutions with adjacent deletions/additions, we account for character sequences of variable length on each side of the rule.

[6] Operations: '+' means insertion, '–' deletion, 's' substitution, '=' identity.

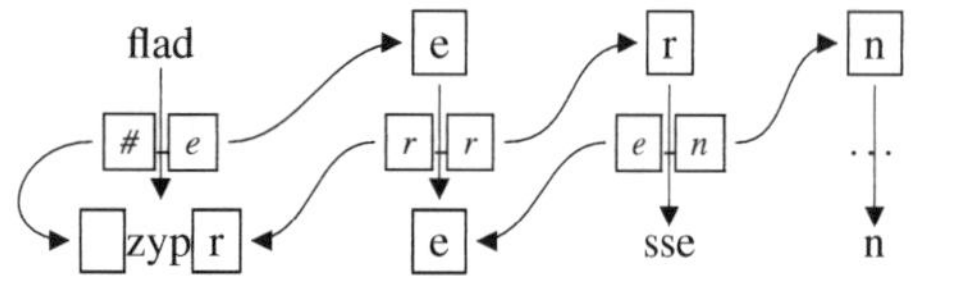

Figure 2: The graph illustrates the actual mappings derived from *fladernholtz – zypressenholz* 'cypress wood'. The central row shows the rule contexts and how they are determined.

In the example *jrem – ihrem* above (Ex. (2)), the first two rules would be merged since they are derived from adjacent non-identity edit operations. This leads to the correct solution to the multi-path problem, shown in Ex. (3).

(3)

Input	*j*	*r*	*e*	*m*
Operations	s	=	=	=
Output	*ih*	*r*	*e*	*m*

Note however that the rule merging does not always come up with entirely correct alignments. For the word pair *fladernholtz – zypressenholz* 'cypress wood', optimal alignment would map `flader→zypresse/#_n` whereas the actual algorithm outputs smaller mappings, see Fig. 2. Indiscriminate merging of identity rules would result in highly specific mappings of entire words rather than character sequences—hence, identity rules are never merged.

Epsilon identity rules In the system developed so far, insertion rules are rather difficult to handle. In generating modern wordforms by means of the rewrite rules (see Sec. 5), they tend to apply in an uncontrollable way, garbling the words in the process. This is due to the fact that the conditions for the application of insertion rules are less specific: while substitutions and deletions require the left hand side (LHS) *and* the context to match in the source word, insertions are constrained by their two context characters only, since the LHS of the rule is empty. At word boundaries, the problem gets even worse, since only one context side is specified here. Furthermore, substitution and deletion rules compete against the identity rules for their LHS, which reflects the fact that the majority of characters are not changed in a mapping to the modernized form—but no similar competitor exists so far to curb the application of insertion rules.

We therefore introduced epsilon identity rules: after all replacement rules for an alignment pair have been generated, an epsilon identity rule is inserted between each pair of non-insertion rules, i.e. at each position where no insertion has taken place. The epsilon identity rules are taken to mean that no insertion should be performed in the respective context, thereby restricting the actual insertion of characters.

	Rank	Frequency	Rule
=	1	24,867	ε → ε / n _ #
=	2	18,213	ε → ε / e _ r
=	3	18,200	ε → ε / e _ n
=	4	17,772	ε → ε / # _ d
=	5	14,871	ε → ε / r _ #
=	6	14,853	n → n / e _ #
s	20	8,448	v → u / # _ n
-	176	1,288	f → ε / u _ f
+	239	932	ε → l / o _ l
	156	1,443	j → ih / # _ r
	272	796	j → ih / # _ n
	329	601	j → ih / # _ m
	605	263	ε → ␣d / t _ u
	879	142	ss → ß / o _ e

Table 3: Sample rankings and rules

Ranking of the rules Applying the rule induction algorithm to the development corpus yielded about 1.1 million rule instances (training corpus: 2.2 million) of about 6,500 different types (training: 7,902). These were sorted and ranked according to their frequency. Table 3 lists sample instances of rules. Not surprisingly, none of the top-ranked rules modifies the input word. Rank 6 is taken by the first rule that maps some real character rather than ε to itself (identity rules, '='). Rank 20 features the first substitution rule ('s'), etc. The bottom part of the table lists frequent sequence-based rules. The rule ranked 605th maps the empty string to a whitespace followed by 'd'. This rule applies in mappings such as *soltu – sollst du* 'should you'.

5 Generating Normalized Wordforms

Normalizing ENHG texts is done on a word-by-word basis, i.e. the input of the normalizing process is always a single wordform. Words are processed from left to right; for each position within a word, applicable edit rules are determined. As with the rule extraction process, the left context is taken from the output already generated up to that point, while the right context is always taken from the input word. If a rule is applied, its right-hand side is appended to the output string, and the next character from the input word is processed. The process continues until the end of the word has been reached.

Rules with sequences of characters on the left-hand side (LHS) are applicable at the position of their first LHS character. In that case, if the rule is applied, processing continues with the next character that is not part of the LHS.

Epsilon rules Epsilon rules, and epsilon identities in particular, require special consideration to work within this system. If an epsilon identity is applied, no other epsilon rules should be allowed for the same context, otherwise insertions would not be blocked. To achieve this, epsilon is treated like an ordinary letter with regard to the LHS, and words are preprocessed so that exactly one epsilon is placed between each character and at word boundaries. For example, if the input word is *jrem* 'theirs', it is converted internally to the following form:

(4) # ε j ε r ε e ε m ε #

Now, if an epsilon rule is applied, the read/write head moves to the next character, thereby ensuring that no other epsilon rule can be applied at the same time in the same position. This also prevents application of multiple insertion rules but at the same time still permits insertion of multiple characters, since those are merged into sets during rule extraction. Of course, epsilon characters have to be ignored for all purposes except for the LHS of replacement rules; in particular, they do never influence rule contexts or prevent the recognition of character sequences on the LHS.

Ranking methods For each character and its context within a word, there will usually be a number of applicable rules to choose from. As our aim is to generate exactly one (modernized) form for each input word, a decision has to be made about which rule to apply. Two approaches were tested: (i) selecting the rule which had the highest frequency during rule acquisition ('best-rule'); and (ii) selecting the word with the highest probability score ('best-probability'), which is calculated based on rule frequencies.

(i) 'Best-rule': In the first approach, if more than one rule application is possible at a given position, we simply select the rule with the highest frequency. The evaluation shows that this method already works quite well, however, it also has a disadvantage: as the left context for a rule depends on the output of the previous one, applying one rule can result in different rules being applicable at later positions in the word. If we always apply the most frequent rule, this can create situations in which only very low-frequent rules are applicable later, indicating that the resulting wordform is unlikely to be correct. Also, when applying a rule with a sequence of characters on the LHS, replacement rules that modify any but the first character of that sequence are never even considered.

	Original bible words		Generated words	
	Old	Modernized	Best-rule	Best-prob.
1.	vnd	und	✓	✓
	jrem	ihrem	✓	✓
	vmbher	umher	✓	✓
2.	wetter	wetter	✓	*dieuetter
	krefftige	kräftige	✓	*krefftige
	vrteil	urteil	✓	*urteill
3.	fewr	feuer	*feur	✓
	soltu	sollst du	*soltu	✓
4.	ermanen	ermahnen	*ermanen	*ermannen
	zween	zwei	*zween	*zwen

Table 4: Example mappings (prior to the dictionary lookup) from the development corpus. '✓' means that the word is generated correctly by the respective method, '*' marks incorrectly generated wordforms. Words listed under 1. are generated correctly by both methods, words under 4. by neither of them, the rest by one of the methodes.

For this reason, we came up with another method that takes into account the frequencies of all applied rules across the whole word.

(ii) 'Best-probability': In the second approach, each generated variant is assigned a probability score. We define the probability of a replacement rule as its frequency divided by the sum of all rule frequencies. The word probability is calculated from the probabilities of the rules that were used to generate it; for this, we used the weighted harmonic mean, with the length of the LHS as weights. If the LHS contains a sequence, length is counted including additional epsilons between each character. This way, all variants generated from the same input word have the same total weight, regardless of whether sequence-based rules were used or not.

Table 4 lists sample mappings as they result from both methods.

Dictionary lookup Quite often, the highest-ranked rules generate non-existing words. This

		Total	Identical Tokens		NLD
		Count	Count	Ratio	Mean ± SD
Old bible text (Baseline)	All	109,972	71,163	64.71%	0.1019 ± 0.1630
	Identical	71,163	71,163	**100.00%**	**0.0000** ± 0.0000
	Non-identical	38,809	0	0.00%	0.2889 ± 0.1460
	Unknowns	2,911	1,190	40.88%	0.1215 ± 0.1359
Best-rule method	All	109,972	91,620	83.31%	0.0408 ± 0.1039
	Identical	71,163	70,467	99.02%	0.0018 ± 0.0198
	Non-identical	38,809	21,153	54.51%	0.1122 ± 0.1483
	Unknowns	2,911	1,390	***47.75%***	***0.1081*** ± 0.1357
Best-probability method	All	109,972	92,172	***83.81%***	***0.0396*** ± 0.1041
	Identical	71,163	69,358	97.46%	0.0042 ± 0.0279
	Non-identical	38,809	22,814	***58.79%***	***0.1046*** ± 0.1509
	Unknowns	2,911	1,255	43.11%	0.1201 ± 0.1407
Best-probability + dictionary method	All	109,972	100,074	**91.00%**	**0.0251** ± 0.0913
	Identical	71,163	70,854	***99.57%***	***0.0008*** ± 0.0126
	Non-identical	38,809	29,220	**75.29%**	**0.0697** ± 0.1423
	Unknowns	2,911	2,238	**76.88%**	**0.0646** ± 0.1428

Table 5: Evaluation of exact matches and normalized Levenshtein distance (NLD) compared to the modernized bible text; separately for all tokens (All), tokens that are or are not identical in both old and modernized version (Identical/Non-identical), and tokens that were not seen in the training corpus (Unknowns). The best result for each class is indicated in bold, the second-best in bold italics.

can be avoided by combining the methods described above with a dictionary lookup. For this, all variants are generated and then matched against a dictionary. From all variants that are covered by the dictionary, the one with the highest score (best-rule or best-probability) is selected as the output form. If no variant can be generated in this way, the input word is left unchanged. The dictionary used here consists of all wordforms from the modernized NHG Luther bible.[7]

6 Evaluation

For evaluation, we generated normalized forms of all words in the evaluation corpus and compared them to their aligned forms in the modernized bible text. Two methods of comparison were applied: (i) counting the number of identical wordforms; and (ii) calculating the average normalized Levenshtein distance (NLD). Full evaluation results are shown in Table 5. Results for the dictionary method are only reported in combination with the best-probability method, which clearly outperform the combination with the best-rule method.

Exact matches As our aim is to generate modernized wordforms from historical ones, the logical first step of an evaluation is to check how many words from the ENHG text from 1545, when processed with our algorithms, exactly match their modernized NHG counterparts. Before normalization, the ratio of identical tokens in the historical and the modernized text is about 65%, i.e., only a third of all wordforms even differ at all. This is the baseline for our algorithm; any normalizing process that results in less than 65% exact matches has likely done more harm than good, and it would be better to leave all words unchanged. Table 5 shows that both ranking methods we employed, best-rule and best-probability, achieve match ratios above 83% (lines 'All', column 'Ratio'), which is a significant increase from the baseline; combining the best-probability method with the dictionary lookup even yields 91% exact matches. Our normalization approach is not only successful in changing historical forms to modern ones, but also in correctly leaving most of the wordforms unchanged that do not need to be changed (97.46–99.57%; lines 'Identical', column 'Ratio').

Results from evaluating the dictionary method on the annotated sample set of non-identical word pairs are shown in Table 2. Although the sample size is very small, the numbers suggest that our approach is mostly suitable for pairs of type 1 (besides identical word pairs); in particular, it can only 'repair' some inflection or affixes (types 2–3). Incorrect mappings (type 6) are not produced.

[7]Using a dictionary with wordforms from current newspaper texts turned out problematic, since modern abbreviations, typos, etc., result in too many false positives with the dictionary lookup. Moreover, the vocabulary of newspaper texts differs considerably from religious texts.

	Total	Identical Tokens		NLD
	Count	Count	Ratio	Mean ± SD
Best-rule	18,352	696	3.79%	0.2483 ± 0.1368
	18,352	0	0.00%	**0.2443** ± 0.1226
Best-prob.	17,800	1,805	10.14%	**0.2372** ± 0.1495
	17,800	0	0.00%	0.2447 ± 0.1297
Dict.	9,898	309	3.12%	0.2876 ± 0.1528
	9,898	0	0.00%	0.2789 ± 0.1479

Table 6: NLD evaluation of word pairs that do not match their aligned word after normalization. The first line of each method shows the NLD before rule application, the second line afterwards.

Normalized Levenshtein distance However, simply counting correct guesses does not take into account near-misses, where the algorithm edited only a part of the word correctly, and is also not a very fine-grained way of evaluation. Therefore, we chose to use normalized Levenshtein distance (Beijering et al., 2008) to assess whether our normalized variants are 'closer' to the correct modern version than the (non-normalized) source words. The NLD of a word pair is defined as the Levenshtein distance divided by the length of the longest possible alignment of the two words.[8] To evaluate a set of word pairs, we calculate the average NLD of all word pairs in that set. This measure is not ideal for our task, since short words are unduly penalized for being wrong, but it has the advantage of being relatively intuitive; e.g., a NLD of 0.5 indicates that roughly every second character in a word was altered.

Comparing the old and the modernized bible text yields an average NLD of 0.1019; as two thirds of all words are already identical, this number is quite low. The three normalization methods reduce that number to 0.0408–0.0251; this reduction stems, in parts, from the higher match ratio. To evaluate whether the normalization improved the wordforms even if they do not exactly match the aligned form, we re-evaluated average NLD on the sets of words that did not result in an exact match. The results, given in Table 6,[9] show only a slight improvement for the best-rule method, while the best-probability method has even increased the average NLD. With the latter method, a high percentage of mismatches (10.14%) results from source words that did not need to be changed. Combined with the dictionary lookup, the ratio of such cases is considerably reduced (to 3.12%). Even the dictionary method is not able to completely avoid superfluous modifications. The reason is that there are ambiguous words such as *waren*, which can either be mapped to *wahren* 'true' or left unchanged: *waren* 'were'. This means that at the type level it cannot be decided which of the two mappings is correct. Instead, we would need context information at the token level, which is beyond our word-based approach.[10]

Method comparison Even though the results for both ranking methods are quite close when evaluated on all word pairs (83.31% versus 83.81%), the difference is statistically significant within a confidence level of 99.9%, i.e., the best-probability method results in better normalizations on average. This is especially reflected in the numbers for the non-identical word pairs, where the difference between the two methods is even greater. On the other hand, the best-rule method performs better on 'unknowns', i.e. words which were not already part of the training set (see Table 5). This seems to indicate that a combination of both methods could be favorable.

The overlap of the word lists generated by the two methods is 93.13%, showing that there is a noticeable percentage of words (around 3%) which is modernized correctly with one method but not the other. One crucial difference is the normalization of second person verb forms ending in *–tu*, e.g. *soltu* 'should you', which should be modernized to *sollst du*. These forms show a contraction of verb and pronoun and are quite common in the original ENHG bible text. With the best-rule method, they do not get changed at all, as the epsilon identity rules are ranked higher than the ones that would perform the necessary insertions. The best-probability method, on the other hand, outputs the correctly modernized form; rules that process the letter *u* appearing word-final after *t* have a very low probability, thus decreasing the total probability of the unmodified wordform.

Finally, combining the methods with a dictionary lookup results in remarkable improvements.

[8] As a side effect of our rules induction process, we can easily calculate the number of alignment slots, since it equals the total number of edit and (non-epsilon) identity rules.

[9] Words considered here include (i) words from identical word pairs that unnecessarily have been modified (this, e.g., concerns 696 words with the best-rule method) and (ii) words from non-identical word pairs that have not been normalized successfully (best-rule: 18,352–696 = 17,656 words).

[10] Jurish (2010) takes context information into account.

The number of exact matches increases from 83.31% to 88.66% (best-rule), and from 83.81% to 91.00% (best-probability). As can be seen from Table 5, the dictionary lookup on the one hand helps to avoid superfluous normalization (with identical word pairs). On the other hand, it also improves on rule application, by filtering out rules (or combinations of rules) that do not result in sensible words. In contrast to rules, which operate locally, the dictionary lookup has access to the entire wordform and thus serves as a complementary "guide" for suitable rule selection.

Since we use the complete modernized Luther bible as the source of our dictionary, all correctly normalized wordforms are guaranteed to be listed in the dictionary. In this sense, the results represent an upper bound of this method. However, the larger a dictionary is, the higher will be the chance of "false friends", i.e. wordforms that accidentally match a generated wordform.

7 Conclusion

We showed that using only unsupervised learning, a minimum of knowledge engineering, and freely available resources, it is possible to map historical wordforms to their modern counterparts with a high success rate. Even the simplest implementation of the process performs far better than the baseline, a success that we were able to further improve upon.

Open issues include the multi-path problem, which is still not entirely solved, despite the introduction of sequence-based rules (see Section 4 and especially Fig. 2). There are a number of potential solutions that we could pursue. The rule extraction process could be modified to output all possible paths from the source to the target word. This would require some means to decide on the most plausible path, such as the total number of rules after the single-character rules have been merged to sets. Phonetic or even graphemic similarity (such as the common substitutions of *u* and *v*) could also be taken into account.

Another issue would be to replace our simple heuristic of sequence determination by the use of an association measure, such as the log-likelihood ratio or the Fisher-Yates test, to determine which rules are merged to sequences. This could include identity rules in the sequences, which might solve problems such as the one presented in Fig. 2.

Association measures could be further used to determine the significance of the association between a rule and its context, and to potentially abstract the rules from their specific contexts.

Another open question is the handling of multi-tokens as source words. Since currently the rule application operates on single words, multiple source tokens can never be merged to a single target token, even though that happens quite frequently in our texts.

References

Alistair Baron, Paul Rayson, and Dawn Archer. 2009. Automatic standardization of spelling for historical text mining. In *Proceedings of Digital Humanities*.

Karin Beijering, Charlotte Gooskens, and Wilbert Heeringa. 2008. Predicting intelligibility and perceived linguistic distances by means of the Levenshtein algorithm. *Linguistics in the Netherlands*, pages 13–24.

Werner Besch. 2000. Die Rolle Luthers für die deutsche Sprachgeschichte. In Werner Besch et al., editor, *Sprachgeschichte. Ein Handbuch zur Geschichte der deutschen Sprache und ihrer Erforschung*, pages 1713–1745. de Gruyter, 2nd edition.

Fabienne Braune and Alexander Fraser. 2010. Improved unsupervised sentence alignment for symmetrical and asymmetrical parallel corpora. In *Proceedings of COLING, Poster Volume*, pages 81–89.

Andrea Ernst-Gerlach and Norbert Fuhr. 2006. Generating search term variants for text collections with historic spellings. In *Proceedings of the 28th European Conference on Information Retrieval Research (ECIR 2006)*. Springer.

Andreas W. Hauser and Klaus U. Schulz. 2007. Unsupervised learning of edit distance weights for retrieving historical spelling variations. In *Proceedings of the First Workshop on Finite-State Techniques and Approximate Search*, pages 1–6.

Bryan Jurish. 2010. More than words: Using token context to improve canonicalization of historical German. *Journal for Language Technology and Computational Linguistics*, 25(1):23–39.

Philipp Koehn. 2005. Europarl: A parallel corpus for statistical machine translation. In *Proceedings of MT Summit*.

Franz Josef Och and Hermann Ney. 2003. A systematic comparison of various statistical alignment models. *Computational Linguistics*, 29(1):19–51.

Jan Strunk. 2003. Information retrieval for languages that lack a fixed orthography. Seminar Paper, Stanford University. `http://www.linguistics.rub.de/~strunk/LSreport.pdf`.

Norbert Richard Wolf. 2000. Handschrift und Druck. In Werner Besch et al., editor, *Sprachgeschichte. Ein Handbuch zur Geschichte der deutschen Sprache und ihrer Erforschung*, pages 1705–1713. de Gruyter, 2nd edition.

Survey on Current State of Bulgarian-Polish Online Dictionary

Ludmila Dimitrova
IMI-BAS
Acad. G. Bonchev St bl. 8
1113 Sofia, Bulgaria
ludmila@cc.bas.bg

Ralitsa Dutsova
Veliko Tărnovo University and
IMI-BAS Master Program
Sofia, Bulgaria
r.dutsova@yahoo.com

Rumiana Panova
Veliko Tărnovo University and
IMI-BAS Master Program
Sofia, Bulgaria
rumiana.panova@gmail.com

Abstract

The dictionaries are among the well-known tools for applications in everyday life, education, sciences, humanities, and human communication. The recent developments of information technologies contribute to the design and creation of new software tools with a wide range of applications, especially for natural language processing. The paper presents an online bilingual dictionary as a technological tool for applications in digital humanities, and describes the structure and content of the bilingual Lexical Database supporting a Bulgarian-Polish online dictionary. It focuses especially on the presentation of verbs, which form the richest from a specific characteristics viewpoint linguistic category in Bulgarian. The main software modules for web-presentation of this digital dictionary are also shortly described.

1 Introduction

Recent developments in information technology have been successfully implemented in natural language processing, producing numerous tools with a wide range of applications. Digital dictionaries, being large-scale data repositories, are a popular tool for applications in everyday life, education, social sciences and digital humanities. Actually, every dictionary contains a large amount of language data, but a digital one contains incomparably more because it is a dynamic collection of dictionary entries and has the potential for infinite growth: new entries can be added without limitation.

All kinds of digital data are now accessible from remote computers via the Net. Online dictionaries freely published in Internet are accessible to every user through a URL-address. In order to use this kind of dictionary, the user does not need any necessary hardware on the local computer or any installation of necessary software. The only condition is that the user's computer be equipped with a web browser. This is why online dictionaries are so easy to distribute and use. A programmer of such software can easily and promptly correct any potential shortcoming that arises, since the application is installed on a web-server. Another advantage of online dictionaries is the possibility of changes in their content such as deletion or addition of new dictionary entries.

The first Bulgarian-Polish online dictionary was designed to be a general purpose dictionary oriented to the casual user and be available by open access via the Net. Authorized users can be provided with the ability to include within entries links to other entries, and to update or edit easily online (through the correction of eventual mistakes, or the addition of new entries or new information about headwords).

For the realization of these purposes a bilingual lexical database (LDB) supporting such a web-based dictionary and ensuring a good search system has to be developed. Besides, whenever possible the LDB should automatically generate a new (whether a single or multiple) structure/s of entries for the Polish-Bulgarian dictionary using the appropriate information from a Bulgarian-Polish entry.

The building of bilingual digital dictionaries is a complex and difficult process, due to the scarcity of formal models that adequately reflect the specific linguistic features of a given natural language. The lexical database has been chosen as a technological platform to support the Bulgarian-Polish online dictionary for free presentation and open access in the Internet.

The design of the Bulgarian-Polish LDB follows the CONCEDE model for dictionary encoding with some extensions and modifications. The project CONCEDE[1] has built lexical databases

[1] CONCEDE INCO-Copernicus project no. PL96-1142 Consortium for Central European Dictionary Encoding

in a general-purpose document-interchange format, for the six Central and East European languages: Bulgarian, Czech, Estonian, Hungarian, Romanian, and Slovene.

The project has produced lexical resources that respect the guidelines for encoding dictionaries (Ide and Véronis, 1995) and so are compatible with other TEI-conformant resources.

The LDB model offers a standardized hierarchical tree-structure of a dictionary entry with a understandable semantics. It is formally described in (Erjavec et al., 2000, 2003).

The first LDB for Bulgarian was developed under the CONCEDE project. It contains more than 2700 lexical entries (Dimitrova et al., 2002) prepared in accordance with encoding standards established by the TEI (Text Encoding Initiative). The Bulgarian LDB is based on the Bulgarian Explanatory Dictionary (Andreychin et al. 1994).

2 Bulgarian-Polish Lexical Database

The monolingual CONCEDE LDBs used two types of tags encoded according to the TEI: structural tags and content tags.

The bilingual dictionary needs a bilingual LDB. To meet the set goal, the CONCEDE model had to modified first and the monolingual LDB had to be extended to a bilingual one. Second, new tags were added to the bilingual LDS to cover more of the specific features of Bulgarian and Polish aiming more adequate presentation of both Slavic languages.

The brief description of the Bulgarian-Polish LDB tag set follows.

2.1 The structural tags of the Bulgarian-Polish LDB

Just like the CONCEDE LDB, the Bulgarian-Polish LDB uses three structural tags: **entry, struc, alt.** Each structural tag plays a corresponding role as follows:

alt: shows an alternation, nevertheless generally used in quite different contexts

entry: indicates main units of the BDB – dictionary entry

struc: indicates separate independent part (structure) in the dictionary entry. The type of this part is determined by the sub-tag **type**. The values of the **type** are modified "**Sense**" or a new one "**Function**".

The structure of a new type "**Function**" is introduced in order to represent different grammatical functions of some Bulgarian words, because the translation correspondences in Polish are different. The index of type "**Function**" counts the groups of grammatical functions that correspond to a particular part of speech of the specified Bulgarian word.

For example, for the following entry

приятелски *adi.* przyjacielski; *adv.* po przyjacielsku

two structures of type "**Function**" are created. The first structure (index n="1") represents the grammatical function *adjective* of a headword "приятелски"/*friendly*/ (part of speech is *adjective*), and the second structure (index n="2") represents the grammatical function *adverb* (part of speech is *adverb*):

```
<entry>
<hw>приятелски</hw>
<struc type ="Function" n="1">
        <pos>adi</pos>
        <struc type="Sense" n="1">
        <trans>przyjacielski</trans>
        </struc>
</struc>
<struc type ="Function" n="2">
        <pos>adv</pos>
        <struc type="Sense" n="1">
        <trans>po przyjacielsku</trans>
        </struc>
</struc>
</entry>
```

Note: Latin abbreviations **adi** /*adiectivum*/ for *adjective* and **adv** /*adverbium*/ for *adverb* are used.

2.2 The content tags of the Bulgarian-Polish LDB

The set of content tags includes the following elements:
case: contains grammatical case information given by a dictionary for a given form
conjugation: a new tag, contains information about the conjugation of the Bulgarian verbs
def: directly contains the text of the definition
domain: domain
eg: a structure, contains an example, as given in a dictionary, and allows the tags **source** and **q**
etym: a structure, contains etymological information and allows the tags **lang** and **m**, as given in a dictionary
gen: identifies the morphological gender of a lexical item, as given in the dictionary
geo: geographic area
gram: contains grammatical information relating to a word other than gender, number, case, per-

son, tense, mood, itype, as these all have their own element; for example, for aspect – perfect aspect (p.) and progressive aspect (i.)
hw: the headword; used for alphabetization and indexing
itype: indicates the inflectional class associated with a lexical item, as given in a dictionary
lang: language; for use in etymologies (in **etym**)
m: indicates a grammatical morpheme in the context of etymology
mood: contains information about the grammatical mood of verbs, as given in a dictionary
number: indicates grammatical number associated with a form, as given in a dictionary
orth: gives the orthographic form of a dictionary headword
person: indicates grammatical person associated with a form, as given in a dictionary
pos: indicates the part of speech assigned to a dictionary headword (noun, verb, adjective, etc.)
q: contains a quotation or apparent quotation
register: register, for type attribute on **usg** tag
semantic: a new tag, containing the active indication of the verb action (event or state)
source: bibliographic source for a quotation
subc: contains sub-categorization information (for ***verbs***: transitive/intransitive, for ***numerals***: countable/non-count, etc.)
time: temporal, historical era, for example, "archaic", "old", etc.
tns: indicates the grammatical tense associated with a given inflected form in a dictionary
trans: new tag contains translation text and related information, so may contain any of the basetags; the principle is that everything under **trans** relates to the target language
usg: contains usage information in a dictionary entry, other than **time**, **domain**, **register** (as these all have their own element), like "dialect", "folk", "colloquialism", etc.
xr: uses to indicate a cross reference with the pointer.

For each group of synonym Polish translations of a given Bulgarian word, a corresponding structure of type "**Sense**" is created.

The Polish translation of Bulgarian headword appears in the entry in structures of type "**Sense**" indexing by the numbers of synonymous group of translations:

```
<entry>
<hw>гале'ри|я</hw>
    ...
<struc type="Sense" n="1">
        <trans>galeria</trans/
                <gen>f</gen>
        <eg>
        <q>карт'инна ~я</q>
        <trans>galeria obrazów</trans>
        </eg>
</struc>
<struc type="Sense" n="2">
        <usg type="register">górn.</usg>
                <trans>chodnik</trans/
                <gen>m</gen>
</struc>
</entry>
```

3 Digital Presentation of Some Specific Features of Bulgarian

The structure and content tags of the designed structural unit should fully meet international standards so that the LDB and the electronic dictionaries are compatible with language resources created in other projects and for other languages.

Let us introduce some notation used in the lexical database. The symbol " ' " is used to mark the accent of the Bulgarian words, and the symbol " | " is used to separate the variable part of the word from the main part.

Structure of a dictionary entry:

- Headword
- Formal Features – phonetics, grammar, morphology, syntax, etymology, style
- Semantic information
- Quotations
- Additional information:

1. Derivatives
2. Phrases
3. Examples - phrasal and sentence usages, illustrations

Realization of homonyms:

The meanings of homonyms are entered in the dictionary as different database records. On the word-entry page, there is a field where the user must specify a homonym index - a number which shows the order of the meanings. For the representation of the homonym it is necessary to fill in the value of the attribute **n** (homonym index) in the tag <entry>:

<entry n="1">
<entry n="2">

Presentation of Bulgarian Verbs:

As expected, the richest from the viewpoint of specific characteristics is the Bulgarian verb. Traditional printed dictionaries, however, have the shortcoming that not all characteristics are coded and presented by respective classifiers (Dimitrova et al., 2009a).

To represent the Bulgarian verbs more adequately, in Bulgarian-Polish LDB ***new content tags*** were added:

- to represent the conjugation of verbs - the <**conjugation**> tag and the <**type**> tag (for the three types of conjugation),
- to represent semantic information - the <**semantic**> tag and the <**type**> tag (**1** for verbs expressing "**state**" and **2** for verbs expressing "**event**").

New information for the **aspect** of verbs in the tag <**gram**> (for perfect aspect and progressive aspect) is also added.

The content tag **subc** that contains subcategorization information is very useful for presentation of specific information of Bulgarian verbs, namely information about their transitivity/intransitivity.

The next example shows the presentation of the entry with headword ***повярвам*** */believe/* in paper Bulgarian-Polish dictionary (Sławski, 1987):

повя'рва|м, -ш *vp.* uwierzyć; **не мо'га да ~м на очи'те си** *pot.* nie mogę uwierzyć swoim oczom, nie wierzę swoim oczom

and corresponding presentation of this headword as an entry in Bulgarian-Polish LDB:

```
<entry>
  <hw>повя'рва|м</hw>
<conjugation>
  <orth>-ш</orth>
  <type>3</type>
  </conjugation>
<semantic>
  <orth>state</orth>
  <type>1</type>
 </semantic>
 <subc>transitive</subc>
  <pos>v</pos>
  <gram>p</gram>
<struc type="Sense" n="1">
  <trans>uwierzyć</trans>
  </struc>
<eg>
  <q>не мо'га да ~м на очи'те си</q>
  <usg type="register">pot</usg>
  <trans>nie mogę uwierzyć swoim oczom, nie
wierzę swoim oczom</trans>
  </eg>
</entry>
```

4 Relational Database of the Bulgarian-Polish Online Dictionary

The lexical database serves as the basis for designing the relational database which is the initial point for developing the Bulgarian-Polish online dictionary. Its main use is to store and search the dictionary entries.

The model of the relational database (RDB) of the Bulgarian-Polish online dictionary is based on the validated lexical entries. As the number of these lexical entries is limited, it is natural to assume that the relational database is experimental and could be improved with the increasing number of examined lexical entries.

In the design of the relational database an opportunity for translating from Polish to Bulgarian language is also provided. That translation will be made from the main senses of the Bulgarian headwords. The phrases and examples cannot provide synonymous meanings, so they will not be used for translating from Polish to Bulgarian language.

Therefore, the corresponding data for the Polish words (examples of usage, phraseology, etc.) have to be entered in the empty field in the Polish-Bulgarian dictionary entry.

The current model of the relational database is represented on Figure 1 and detailed information on it can be found in Tables 1 - 6 (see Appendix).

5 Transformation of the LDB into RDB

An XML parser is created to transform the lexical database into the relational database. The aim of the syntactic analyzer is to initialize the relational database, serving as a basis of the dictionary. The saved entries in the RDB can then be edited trough the administrative module of the web-based application of the dictionary.

The parser implementation uses the DOM technology (Document Object Model: http://www.w3.org/DOM/DOMTR). With this technology the whole document is read and a DOM tree is constructed. This tree represents a hierarchy of nodes and each node is an object in the XML document. A random access to the nodes of the DOM tree is possible. All embedded tags and attributes of the current node can also be accessed at random.

For that reason the DOM technology is chosen instead of the alternative SAX (**S**imple **API** for **XML**) technology which cannot process complex and embedded searches. The disadvantage of the DOM technology is the higher amount of memory required when reading large XML documents compared to the SAX technology.

The DOM parser for transforming the LDB of the Bulgarian–Polish dictionary into RDB is programmed in Java. In this way it can be run on different platforms independent of the architecture or the operating system.

6 Online dictionary – Brief Description

The Bulgarian–Polish online dictionary is realized by the web-based application supporting by the Bulgarian-Polish LDB and RDB. This web-based application is experimental, and the structure of the text fields is not permanently determined.

The implementation of the web-based application is based on the following technologies: Apache, MySQL, PHP and JavaScript. These are free technologies originally designed for developing dynamic web pages with greater functionality.

The web-based application consists of two main software tools: administrator and end-user module (Dimitrova et al., 2009b). The administrator module serves to create the database and update the dictionary. Access to the administrative module is restricted to authorized users (so called administrators) (Table 7 in Appendix). After logging onto the system the administrator has possibilities to access the database and to enter new entries, headwords, classifications, or to edit/delete existing ones.

The web-based end-user interface is bilingual. The user can choose the input language (Bulgarian or Polish) with possibilities to search for translation in both directions Bulgarian-to-Polish, or Polish-to-Bulgarian. The Bulgarian-to-Polish translation will display the whole information existing in the dictionary entry but the opposite translation will be made only from the main senses of the Bulgarian headwords (Figure 4).

Next, an example shows how the Bulgarian verb **повярвам** */believe/* is inserted in the data base through the administrative module of the web application (Figure 2) (especially the information about its transitivity, semantic features and conjugation type), and further, how this information is displayed on the screen to the end-user (Figure 3). (The Figures 2 – 4 are shown in the Appendix.)

7 Conclusion and Future works

The paper presents briefly the Bulgarian-Polish LDB that supports the first Bulgarian-Polish online dictionary. The dictionary is at an experimental stage and intended for research purposes, but it will also be widely applicable to the contrastive studies of Bulgarian and Polish, in a system for human and machine translation, as well as in education.

Future implementation will include some "search" functions with a query, where the search parameters are fixed and which as a result will extract and show to the user the relevant information from the Bulgarian-Polish LDB – dictionary entry (entries), for example, to show transitive Bulgarian verbs, or Bulgarian adjectives that serve also as adverbs.

References

Andreychin et al. 1994. *Bulgarian Explanatory Dictionary* /Dictionary of the Bulgarian Language. 4th revised edition, prepared by D. G. Popov/ Nauka i Izkuvstvo Publishing House, Sofia, 1994 (In Bulgarian)

Dimitrova, L., Pavlov, R., Simov, K. 2002. The Bulgarian Dictionary in Multilungual Data Bases. *Journal Cybernetics and Information Technologies*. 2 (2): 12-15, 2002

Dimitrova, L., Koseska-Toszewa, V., Satoła-Staśkowiak, J. 2009a. Towards a Unification of the Classifiers in Dictionary Entry. In Garabík (Ed.), *Metalanguage and Encoding Scheme Design for Digital Lexicography*. Bratislava, 48-58, 2009

Dimitrova, L., Panova, R., Dutsova, R. 2009b: Lexical Database of the Experimental Bulgarian-Polish online Dictionary. In Garabík (Ed.), *Metalanguage and Encoding scheme Design for Digital Lexicography*. Bratislava, 36-47, 2009

Erjavec, T., Evans, R., Ide, N., Kilgarriff, A. 2000. The Concede model for lexical databases. In *Proceedings of the 2nd International Conference on Language Resources and Evaluation, LREC'00*, Athens, ELRA, 2000

Erjavec, T., Evans, R., Ide, N. Kilgarriff, A. 2003. From Machine Readable Dictionaries to Lexical Databases: the Concede Experience. In *Proceedings of the 7th International Conference on Computational Lexicography, COMPLEX'03*, Budapest, Hungary, 2003

Ide, N., Véronis, J. 1995. *Encoding dictionaries*. In Ide, N., Veronis, J. (Eds.) The Text Encoding Initiative: Background and Context. Dordrecht: Kluwer Academic Publishers, 167-179, 1995

Sławski, F. 1987. *Podręczny słownik Bułgarsko-Polski z suplementem*. PW „Wiedza Powszechna", Warszawa, 1987

Appendix:

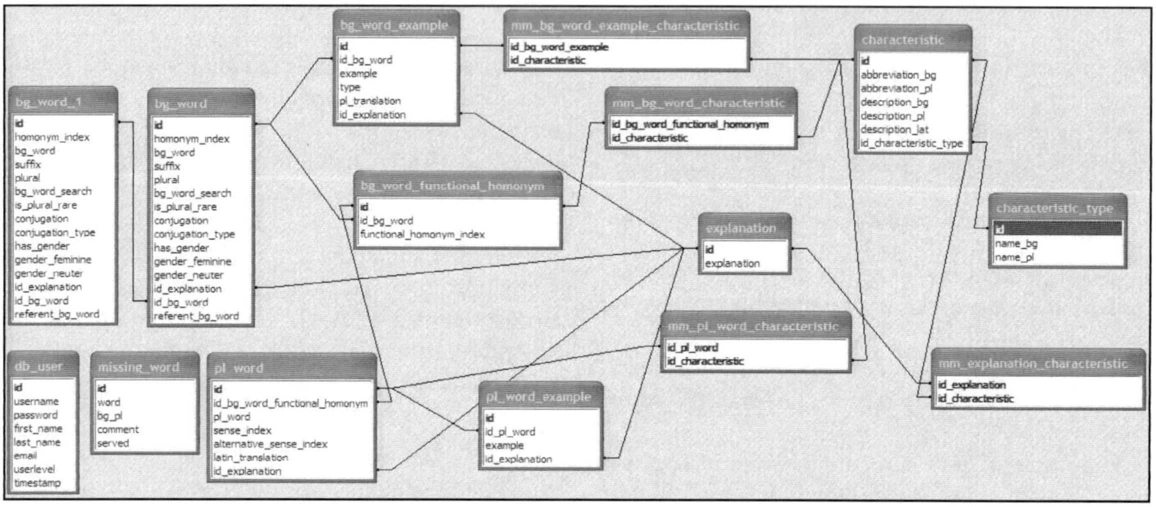

Figure 1. Relational database upon the LDB of the Bulgarian-Polish online dictionary

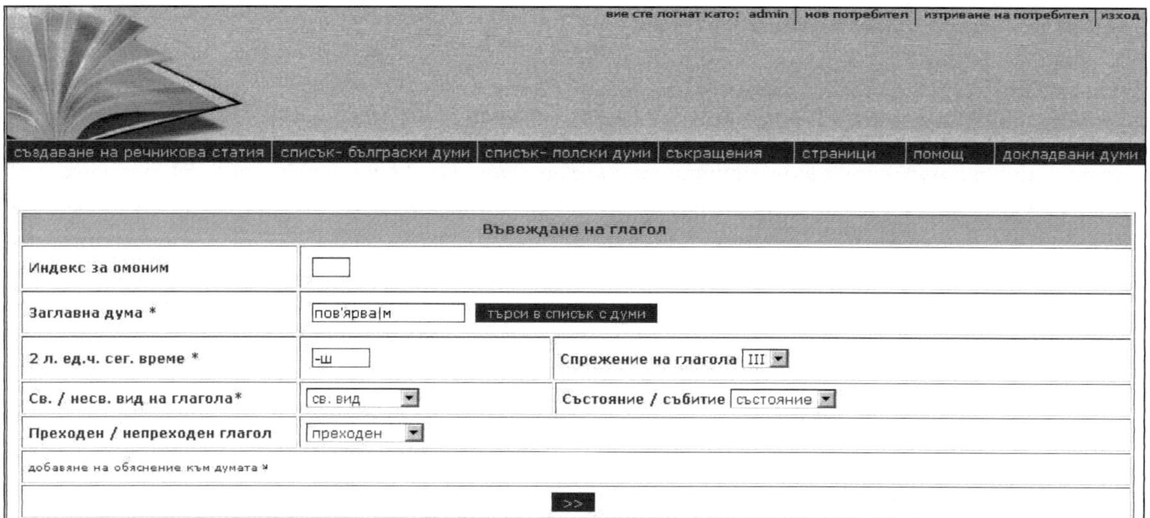

Figure 2. Administrative panel – 1st step of inserting of a Bulgarian verb

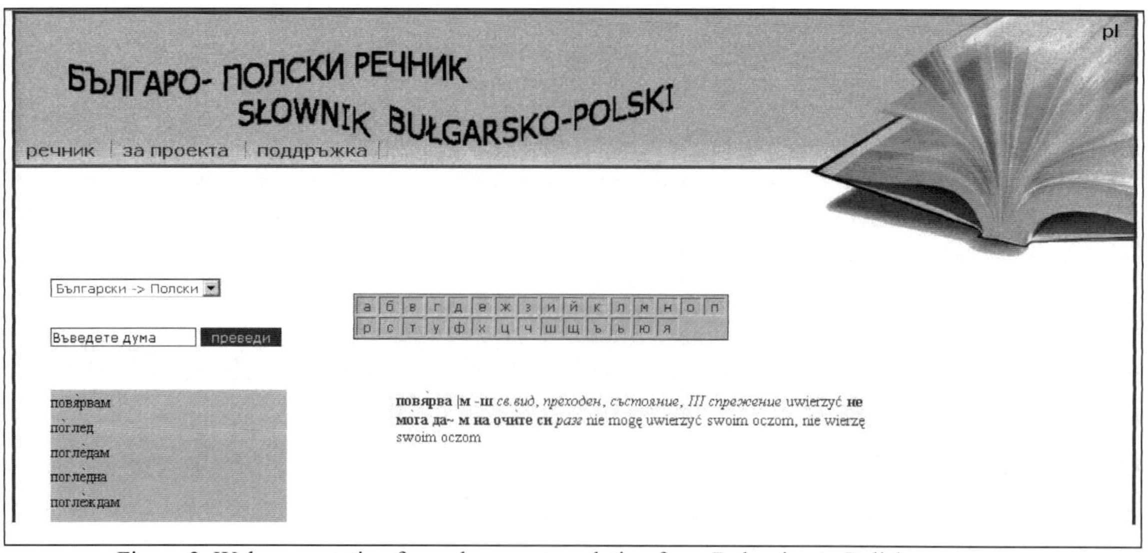

Figure 3. Web presentation for end users - translation from Bulgarian to Polish

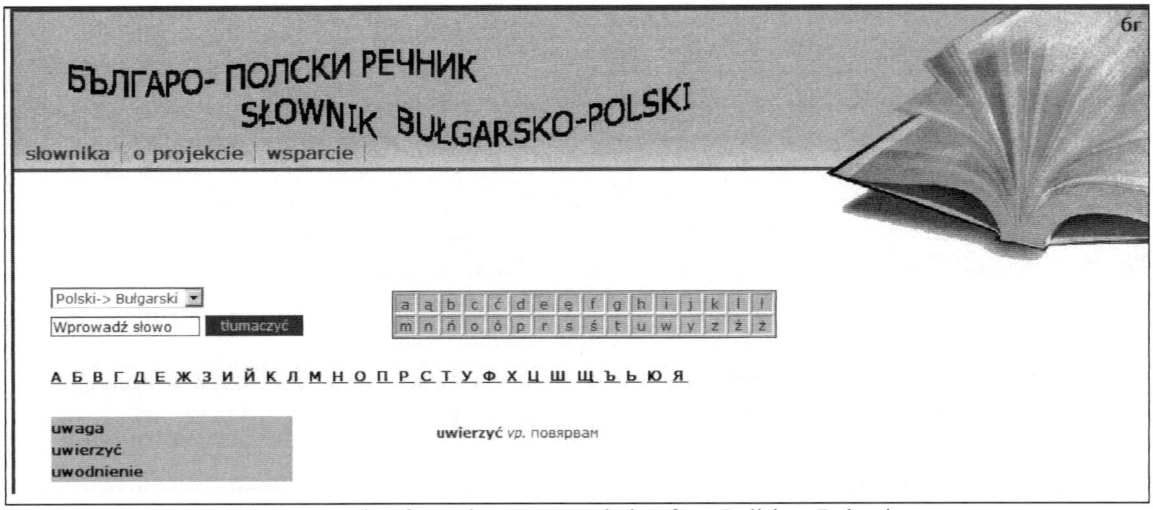

Figure 4. Web presentation for end users - translation from Polish to Bulgarian

Field	Comments
id	Id
homonym_index	Index of the homonym (if null, no homonym exists)
bg_word	Bulgarian headword
suffix	Suffix
plural	Plural form for a noun
is_plural_rare	Frequency of usage of the plural form for a noun (null – normal, 0 - often, 1 – rare)
conjugation	Conjugation form for a verb (2 p., present)
conjugation_type	Type of conjugation for a verb (1, 2 or 3)
has_gender	Whether a noun has feminine and neuter gender
gender_feminine	Feminine gender form for an adjective
gender_neuter	Neuter gender form for an adjective
id_explanation	Foreign key to "explanation"
id_bg_word	Id of the referent Bulgarian word
referent_bg_word	Referent Bulgarian word

Table 1. Presentation of the Bulgarian headwords

Field	Comments
id	Id
id_bg_word	Foreign key to "bg_word"
functional_homonym_index	Index of the functional homonym group

Table 2. Functional homonymy of the Bulgarian headwords

Field	Comments
id	Id
id_bg_word	Foreign key to "bg_word"
example	Example of the headword
type	Type of the usage (1 - Derivation; 2 - Phrase; 3 - Example)
pl_translation	Polish translation
id_explanation	Foreign key to "explanation"

Table 3. Derivations, phrases or examples of the Bulgarian headwords and their translation in Polish

Field	Comments
id	Id
id_bg_word_functional_homonym	Foreign key to "bg_word_functional_homonym"
pl_word	Polish headword
sense_index	Index of the sense
alternative_sense_index	Index of the alternative sense
latin_translation	Latin translation of the word
id_explanation	Foreign key to "explanation"

Table 4. Presentation of the Polish headwords

Field	Comments
id	Id
id_pl_word	Foreign key to "pl_word"
example	Example in Polish
id_explanation	Foreign key to "explanation"

Table 5. Examples of the Polish headwords

Field	Comments
id	Id
explanation	Explanation

Table 6. Explanations of the headwords, derivations, phrases and examples

Field	Comments
id	Id
username	Username
password	Password
first_name	Name
last_name	Family name

Table 7. Administrative users' authorization

Language Technology Support for Semantic Annotation of Iconographic Descriptions

Kamenka Staykova
IICT, BAS, Bulgaria
staykova@iinf.bas.bg

Gennady Agre
IICT, BAS, Bulgaria
agre@iinf.bas.bg

Kiril Simov
IICT, BAS, Bulgaria
kivs@bultreebank.org

Petya Osenova
IICT, BAS, Bulgaria
petya@bultreebank.org

Abstract

The paper describes an approach for semantic annotation of multimedia objects implemented for the purposes of SINUS Project[1]. Semantic annotations are supported by semantic annotation models based on ontological presentation of knowledge concerning Bulgarian Iconography. The process of semantic annotation includes automated data-lifting procedure and user-directed approach. The paper pays attention to a specific variant of the semantic annotation process directed by the user - application of Language Technologies for semi-automated creation of semantic text annotations (tags) based on analysis of descriptive texts. The 'ontology-to-text' approach has been adapted to the needs of the iconographic domain. Initial experiments are established to support the user during the process of manual semantic annotations in the context of SINUS environment.

1 Introduction

The main objective of the research project SINUS is to provide a semantic technology-based environment facilitating development of Technology-Enhanced Learning (TEL) applications, which are able to reuse existing heterogeneous software systems. The SINUS environment has a service oriented architecture allowing unified representation and use of heterogeneous systems as Web services. The environment is tested on a use case, which applies the basic TEL principles to the process of Learning-by-Authoring (Dochev and Agre, 2009). The domain of Bulgarian Iconography is chosen for constructing a SINUS Project scenario, since it provides an interesting example of TEL in humanities. The scenario requires an intensive use of multimedia objects stored in existing heterogeneous digital libraries.

In the SINUS environment a TEL-oriented application is created hierarchically, starting by converting an autonomous system for storing and retrieving a multimedia data (digital library) to a Web service, then transforming this service into a semantically-oriented digital library facilitated by Web services and ontologies, and finally, extending the library into a learning system based on service oriented architecture.

The current paper presents the processes of semantic annotation of multimedia objects (MO) implemented in the SINUS environment. Section 2 describes the basic decisions taken for organizing such annotations. Section 3 presents the first attempts to apply language technologies in order to develop a user-directed approach for semi-automatic creation of annotations. Section 4 discusses the future work.

2 Semantic Annotation of Multimedia Objects in SINUS Project

The domain of Bulgarian Iconography is a fruitful field to show how different multimedia documents (the digital photos of iconographic works, texts, video records, etc.) could be used in TEL applications. The multimedia resources for SINUS demo-examples come from the Multimedia Digital Library "Virtual Encyclopedia of East-Christian Art" described in (Pavlova-Draganova et al., 2007) and marked as "the Library" from here on. Its content is accessible via a special Web service developed in the SINUS environment.

[1] "Semantic Technologies for Web Services and Technology Enhanced Learning" (SINUS) sinus.iinf.bas.bg

2.1 Resources of Semantic Annotation

The Objects of semantic annotation in SINUS project are multimedia objects presenting information in digital form about icons, wall-paintings, miniatures and other iconographical works; also pictures and different texts concerning the iconographical works; information about authors, places, dating periods, religious characters and so on. The Library uses a fixed annotation schema for organizing all the resources and the available data. In order to allow more flexible and deep reasoning about the iconographical knowledge, the SINUS semantic space extends that schema to present the knowledge in a formalized, ontology-like manner.

The Ontologies. SINUSBasic Ontology is the main conceptual model of the SINUS semantic space. The fixed annotation schema of the Library is taken as a ground for creating this ontology, in order access to be provided to the Library from an upper, semantic level. However, the SINUSBasic Ontology itself (with minor exceptions) is created following the main principles of the standard SIDOC-CRM (Crofts et al., 2010). The SINUSBasic Ontology is implemented in OWL and comprises 58 classes, 38 object properties and 28 data-type properties. Main classes are: *Iconographical Object* with its sub-classes *Icon*, *Wall-Painting*, *Miniature*, *Mosaic*, *Vitrage* and so on, *Author*, *Iconographical Scene*, *Character*, *Iconographical Technique*, *Base Material* and so on.

The SINUS semantic space contains the so called "specialized ontologies", which encode experts' knowledge on particular aspect of the Bulgarian Iconography domain. It is assumed that specialized ontologies represent additional, more specialized domain knowledge that is not contained in the "basic" Library. For example, the specialized ontology on religious characters gives access to such notions as *Canonical Character*, *Apostle*, *Hierarch*, etc., the specialized ontology on iconographical technology gives access to notions as *Soft Material*, *Solid Material*, *Lacquering*, *Resin*, *Primer*, *Plaster*, etc. At the current stage of work the SINUSSpec Technology ontology is implemented in OWL and could be loaded into SINUS semantic space on demand. The ontology contains 16 classes, 14 object properties and 45 ontological individuals. Some concepts of the SINUSSpec Technology ontology represent extensions of concepts introduced in SINUSBasic ontology, and in this way basic domain ontology and specialized ontologies are linked. For example, the root ontological concept of SINUSBasic Ontology is *Iconographical Object*. Such concepts as *Author*, *Iconographical School*, *Collection* are used as root-concepts in SINUSSpec Technology ontology.

Basic Semantic Annotation Model (Basic SAM) is presented in the picture bellow.

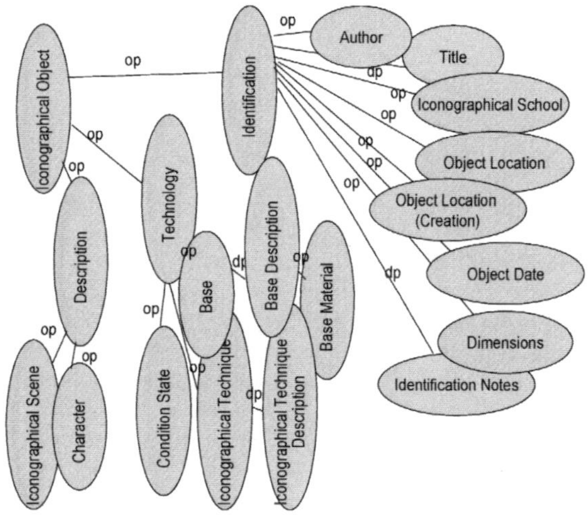

Some of the links between concepts represent object properties, others – datatype properties. Some of the object properties are realized as chains of 2 or 3 properties. Many of the datatype properties lead to textual data providing access to the descriptive texts collected in the Library.

Extended Semantic Annotation Model (Extended SAM) adds 14 new features to the Basic SAM of Iconographical Object individuals. All these additional features are supported by SINUSSpec Technology ontology as properties. For example, such features are: *base_has_component*, *gilding_has_type*, *laquering_has_evenness*, *primer_has_filler*, etc. In this way the instances of *Iconographical Object*, class defined in SINUSBasic ontology, is linked to concepts of *Primer*, *Gilding*, *Lacquering*, *Filler*, etc., defined in SINUSSpec Technology ontology.

Semantic Repository. SINUS environment employs SESAME RDF Semantic Repository that provides sufficient reasoning and standard functionalities of semantic repositories for realizing the SINUS scenario. All repository functionalities are accessible through the SINUS User Interface.

2.2 Search Process

The semantic annotation of MO in SINUS is organized as a two step process: at the first step a MO of interest should be found, and at the second step the desired new annotations should be added (manually or semi-automatically) to the object description. Semantic search of multimedia objects starts with preparing a "natural language"-like query, which is constructed on the base of described above SINUS ontologies and presented in user-friendly graphical way. The query is automatically transformed into SPARQL form, which is sent to the Extended Search Engine – a special component of the SINUS environment responsible for searching the information in the SINUS repositories. The component "lowers" the corresponding part of the query to the Library and then "lifts" the answer represented at the semantic level to the semantic repository, where the whole SPARQL query is executed. Practically, during this data lifting process some data from the Library is transformed to several SINUSBasic Ontology individuals that are added to ontologies stored in the semantic repository. The search result, which usually is a set of (identifiers to) multimedia objects, is presented to the user via the SINUS User Interface.

2.3 Semantic Annotation Process

Additional semantic annotations of MO made by the user are also supported. This user-directed semantic annotation process allows the user to add some new (specialized) annotation features to existing MO annotations or to create "basic" annotations for a new MO. The extension to the basic annotation model is supported by the SINUSSpec Technology ontology presented above. The process of user-directed semantic annotation has the following steps enabled by the SINUS User Interface:

1. All properties of a concrete object selected by the user are displayed. The number of properties depends on special ontologies the user is going to use for creating the annotations. Each property could be displayed with particular value (known annotation) or the value could be still unknown. In such case, a list of possible values of the property (stored in the corresponding ontology) is proposed as options to the user.

2. The user can either change a displayed value of a selected property (if this annotation has been created earlier by him or semi-automatically) or the user can create a new annotation by selecting a value from the corresponding list, if the current value of this property is empty.

3. After completing the annotation process and the user can save the new annotations in the SINUS semantic repository.

Opportunities for semi-automatic semantic annotation by use of descriptive texts analysis. The semantic annotation model of MO contains several links to descriptive texts concerning the MO. For example, each individual of the class Base of SINUSBasic Ontology is connected through the datatype property *has_Base_Description* to the particular text kept in the Library. An example of a short text describing the base of a particular Iconographical Object is given bellow.

```
BG: Основата е от иглолистна дървесина с
два кошака, добре запазена. Гипсов
грунд, нанесен тънко и равномерно.

EN: The base is of softwood with two
keys, well kept. Plaster ground coat,
applied thinly and evenly.
```

Most of the descriptive texts contain a lot of terminological notions of a particular domain and many of the terms are defined in the corresponding specialized ontologies. The main idea of semi-automatic semantic annotations is to help substantially the user in his/her attempt to annotate MO with notions presented in Extended Semantic Annotation Model. The support consists of access to preliminary created semantically annotated texts, which makes some (ontological) notions visible and sensitive, and also "technically" prepared to be used further in the process of used-directed semantic annotation.

The (preliminary) semantic annotations of texts are created off-line and stored in such a way that they can be seen as indexes to MO and used for on-line searching and retrieving the objects. The text annotation procedure is implemented as a special Web service accessible from the SINUS environment. The output of this process is a set of XML files, so in order to use them in the SINUS environment they have to be accessible during the on-line process of creating new annotations. The annotations (tags) in the texts are treated as parts of preliminary semantic annotations of particular MO. They could be acknowledged, extended or denied by the user during the semantic annotation process. The annotations suggested in texts are shown to the user as "default" values of the corresponding properties of the MO. SINUS platform has to be equipped with a special procedure that "translates" the annotated text into form of Extended Semantic Annotation Model.

The task of text annotation could be formulated in this way: given an ontology and text, return annotated text, which is sensitive to the ontological notions. This general task is known as *Ontology-to-Text* relation and is still a research challenge in the crossroad of Language Technologies and Semantic Technologies. Language Technologies operate with specific methods and tools to annotate text documents semantically.

3 Semantic Text Annotation for SINUS Project

Semantic text annotation presented here is based on a model of *Ontology-to-Text* relation developed within (Simov & Osenova, 2007; Simov & Osenova, 2008). *Ontology-to-Text* relation is defined with the help of two intermediate components: (terminological) lexicon and concept annotation grammar.

The lexicon plays twofold role. First, it interrelates the concepts in the ontology to the lexical knowledge used by the grammar in order to recognize the role of the concepts in the text. Second, the lexicon represents the main interface between the user and the ontology. This interface allows the ontology to be navigated or represented in a natural for the user way. For example, the concepts and relations might be named with terms used by the stakeholders in their everyday activities and in their own natural language. This could be considered as a first step to a contextualized usage of the ontology in a sense that the ontology could be viewed through different terms depending on the context. For example, the material names will vary from very specific terms within the domain of iconography to more common names used when a set of icons are exhibited to a wider audience. As the image depicts it, the lexical items contain the following information: a term, contextual information determining the context of the term usage, grammatical features determining the syntactic realization within the text. In the current implementation of the lexicons the contextual information is simplified to two values, *common term* and *others*.

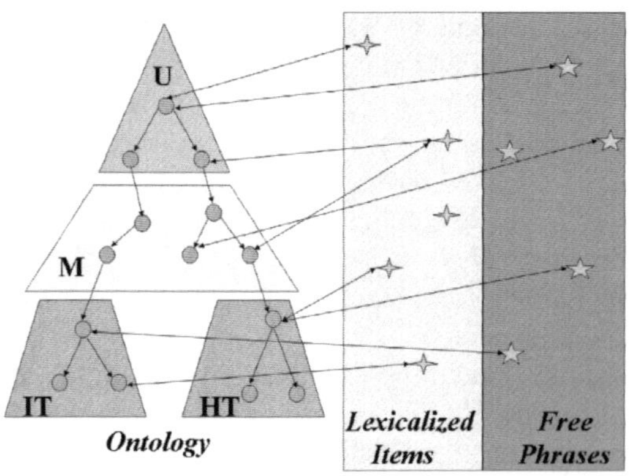

The second component of the *Ontology-to-Text* relation, the concept annotation grammar, is ideally considered as an extension of a general language deep grammar which is adapted to the concept annotation task. Minimally, the concept annotation grammar consists of a chunk grammar for concept annotation and (sense) disambiguation rules. The following picture demonstrates this part of the *Ontology-to-Text* relation.

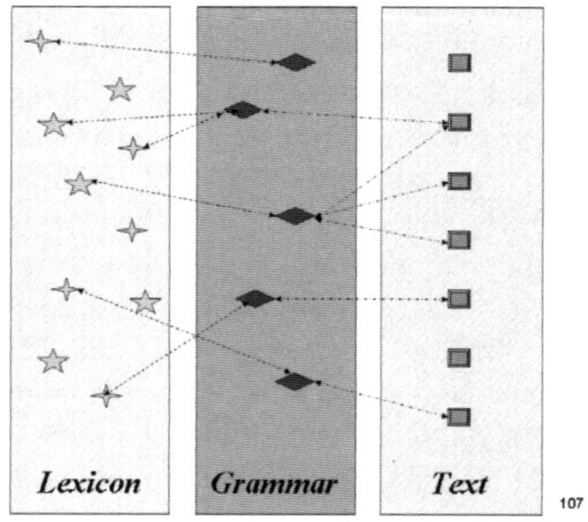

The chunk grammar for each term in the lexicon contains at least one grammar rule for recognition of the term. As a preprocessing step we consider annotation with grammatical features and lemmatization of the text. The disambiguation rules exploit the local context in terms of grammatical features, semantic annotation and syntactic structure, and also the global context, such as topic of the text, discourse segmentation, etc. Currently we have implemented chunk grammars for Bulgarian and English.

For the implementation of the annotation grammar we rely on the grammar facilities of the CLaRK System (Simov et al., 2001). The structure of each grammar rule in CLaRK is defined by the following DTD fragment:

```
<!ELEMENT line (LC?, RE, RC?, RM, Comment?) >

<!ELEMENT LC (#PCDATA)>

<!ELEMENT RC (#PCDATA)>

<!ELEMENT RE (#PCDATA)>

<!ELEMENT RM (#PCDATA)>

<!ELEMENT Comment (#PCDATA)>
```

Each rule is represented as a line element. The rule consists of regular expression (*RE*) and category (*RM* = return markup). The regular expression is evaluated over the content of a given XML element and could recognize tokens and/or annotated data. The return markup is represented as an XML fragment which is substituted for the recognized part of the content of the element. Additionally, the user could use regular expressions to restrict the context in which the regular expression is evaluated successfully. The *LC* element contains a regular expression for the left context and the *RC* for the right one. The element Comment is for human use. The application of the grammar is governed by *Xpath* expressions which provide additional mechanism for accurate annotation of a given XML document. Thus, the CLaRK grammar is a good choice for implementation of the initial annotation grammar.

The creation of the actual annotation grammars started with the terms in the lexicons for Bulgarian and English. Each term was lemmatized and the lemmatized form of the term was converted into regular expression of grammar rules. Each concept related to the term is stored in the return markup of the corresponding rule. Thus, if a term is ambiguous, then the corresponding rule in the grammar contains reference to all concepts related to the term.

The relation *Ontology-to-Text* implemented in this way provides facilities for solving different tasks, such as ontological search (including cross-lingual search), ontology browsing, ontology learning. In order to support multilingual access to semantic annotations we could implement the relation for several languages using the same ontology as starting point. In this way we implement a mapping between the lexicons in different languages and also comparable annotation of texts in them.

Within SINUS Project we have started the implementation of the *Ontology-to-Text* relation on the basis of the terms included in the ontology. In contrast to past applications where the concept grammars included only the concepts themselves, here also properties have been added. The relation from these terms to conceptual information is represented in two ways – direct terms for a given concept and terms for some property of a given concept. In order to keep this information within the annotation we keep it in the model. Thus, we annotated not only concrete concepts, but also fragments of conceptual information comprising a property and a concept (in the domain or the range of the property). In this way we provide annotation appropriate for future recognition of relations in the text.

The terms extracted from the ontology are lemmatized by the Bulgarian Morphological Lexicon. The lemmatized versions of the terms are converted automatically into CLaRK regular grammars which are used for the actual document annotation. In the following we present the example text from above annotated by the system. The actual annotation is done by the following format:

```
<OntoAnnotation>
… Term …
    <OntoFragment>
      … Ontology Fragment
    </OntoFragment>
</OntoAnnotation>
```

The Term is presented as a sequence of <tok> elements for each token of the term. Each token is annotated with the appropriate grammatical features. These features are used in the concept annotation grammars. The Ontology Fragment is represented by a set of <class> and <property> elements. Both kinds of elements have attribute @uri which represents the corresponding class or property identifier. This attribute is obligatory. Additionally the <property> element has @domain, @range and @value attribute. They determine the domain, range and the value of the attribute when recognized uniquely from the ontology and the annotation within the text. Bellow is given the resulting annotation for a part of our text example.

Two terms are recognized in the text extract: *Основа* (Base) and *Дървесина* (Wood). The first is annotated with one class and two properties, the second – with two classes and one property. The property in the second case received also a concrete value *дърво* (wood). At later stage the user can add a statement that the base, mentioned in the text, is made of *wood*. The user intervention is important in cases when the text contains ambiguity. The sublanguage of descriptive texts from the Library gives us the possibility to write rules for automatic addition of such statements in the future.

```
<OntoAnnotation>
  <tok ana="Ncfsd">Основата</tok>
  <OntoFragment>
   <class uri="sinus:OWLClass_Base"/>
   <property
      domain="sinus:OWLClass_Base"
      range="sinus:OWLClass_Primer"
      uri="sinus:OWLObjectProperty_base_
has_Component"/>
  <property domain="sinus:OWLClass_Base"
      range="owl:DataRange"
      uri="sinus:OWLDataProperty_base_ha
s_Cloth"/>
    </OntoFragment>
</OntoAnnotation>
    <tok ana="Vxitf-r3s">e</tok>
```

```
  <tok ana="R">от</tok>
  <tok ana="Afsi">иглолистна</tok>
<OntoAnnotation>
  <tok ana="Ncfsi">дървесина</tok>
  <OntoFragment>
    <class uri="sinus:OWLClass_BaseMa-
terial"/>
    <class uri="sinus:OWLClass_SolidMa-
terial"/>
    <property range="owl:DataRange"
      uri="sinus:OWLDataProperty_baseMa-
terial_has_Name"
      value="дърво"/>
  </OntoFragment>
</OntoAnnotation>
```

A Web service is implemented for the text annotation purposes. The input to it is a plain text. The output is an XML document according to the above format. The communication of Web service is made possible with the adoption of a RESTfull approach to the service communication with a simple but effective use of output XML files. In future the Web service will be integrated in the overall architecture of SINUS platform interacting directly with the Library and semantic repository.

4 Future Work

The experiment to support the user during the semantic annotation process with information extracted from texts is established to estimate the efforts against the benefits, and price of preliminary work on texts. The process of texts tagging (semantic text annotation) is applied for purposes of particular use-case suggested by SINUS platform for Bulgarian texts. The future work on SINUS project includes the usage of the pre-prepared annotations in texts and extensive tests on the semantic annotation process. The results will be analyzed in detail and compared to some related works as those reported in (Hare et al., 2006), (Ossenbruggen et al., 2007) and others. Another interesting topic arising here is the multilinguality and possible cross-references if the experiment is provided with texts in different languages (English, for example).

Acknowledgments

The research is supported by the National Science Fund of Bulgaria under the project No. D-002-189.

References

Crofts N., Doerr M., Gill T., Stead S., Stiff M. (editors). 2010. *Definition of the CIDOC Conceptual Reference Model*.

Dochev D., Agre G. 2009. *Towards Semantic Web Enhanced Learning*, In Proceedings. of Int. Conference on Knowledge Management and Information Sharing, Madeira, pp. 212-217.

Hare, J. S., Sinclair, P. A. S., Lewis, P. H., Martinez, K., Enser, P. G. B. and Sandom, C. J. 2006. *Bridging the Semantic Gap in Multimedia Information Retrieval: Top-down and Bottom-up approach*,. In: Mastering the Gap: From Information Extraction to Semantic Representation, 3rd European Semantic Web Conference, Budva, Montenegro.

Ossenbruggen J., Amin A., Hardman L., Hildebrand M., Assem M., Omelayenko B., Schreiber G., Tordai A., de Boer V., Wielinga B., Wielemaker J., de Niet M., Taekema J., van Orsouw M.-F., and Teesing A. 2007. *Searching and Annotating Virtual Heritage Collections with Semantic-Web Techniques*, In: Museums and the Web, pp.11-14.

Pavlova-Draganova L., Georgiev V., Draganov L. 2007. *Virtual Encyclopaedia of Bulgarian Iconography*, Information Technologies and Knowledge, vol.1, №3, pp. 267-271.

Simov K., Z. Peev, M. Kouylekov, A. Simov, M. Dimitrov, A. Kiryakov. 2001. *CLaRK - an XML-based System for Corpora Development*. In: Proc. of the Corpus Linguistics 2001 Conference, pp. 558-560.

Simov K. and P. Osenova. 2007. *Applying Ontology-Based Lexicons to the Semantic Annotation of Learning Objects*. In: Proceedings of the Workshop on NLP and Knowledge Represenattion for eLearning Environments, RANLP-2007, pp. 49-55.

Simov K. and P. Osenova. 2008. *Language Resources and Tools for Ontology-Based Semantic Annotation*, In: Proceedings of OntoLex 2008 Workshop at LREC 2008, eds. Al. Oltramari, L. Prévot, Chu-Ren Huang, P. Buitelaar, P. Vossen, pp. 9-13.

The Tenth-Century Cyrillic Manuscript *Codex Suprasliensis*: the creation of an electronic corpus UNESCO project (2010–2011)

Hanne Martine Eckhoff
University of Oslo
Kanonhallveien 10e
0585 Oslo
h.m.eckhoff@ifikk.uio.no

David J. Birnbaum
University of Pittsburgh
Department of Slavic Languages and Literatures
1417 Cathedral of Learning
djbpitt@pitt.edu

Anisava Miltenova
Bulgarian Academy of Sciences
Institute for Literature
52 Shipchenski prohod
amiltenova@gmail.com

Tsvetana Dimitrova
Bulgarian Academy of Sciences
Bulgarian Language Institute
52 Shipchenski prohod
cvetana@dcl.bas.bg

Abstract

This paper presents an overview of principles and problems connected with the preparation of an electronic edition of the largest Old Church Slavonic manuscript, the *Codex Suprasliensis*, in the context of a project funded by UNESCO. Specifications of the manuscript, its history, and previous paper-based and electronic editions are discussed, together with a strategy for the preparation of a complete digital edition, including newly acquired digital images, electronic text, analysis and commentaries, parallel Greek text, and updated bibliography. In particular, our paper sheds light on automating the morphosyntactic annotation of the text and the difficulties that had to be resolved in this part of the project.

1 Introduction

The UNESCO-funded project *The Tenth-Century Cyrillic Manuscript Codex Suprasliensis* aims at digitizing the largest Old Church Slavonic manuscript, the *Codex Suprasliensis* (http://csup.ilit.bas.bg/).

This early Cyrillic manuscript has been dated to the end of the tenth or the beginning of the eleventh century and has been published three times on paper (Miklošič, 1851; Severjanov, 1904; Zaimov and Capaldo, 1982–83). The most recent of these, the two-volume edition by Zaimov and Capaldo (1982, 1983), was published more than two decades ago and contains photographic images of the entire manuscript; a transcription reproduced from Severjanov, 1904 and corrected (not entirely without error) against the facsimile; and a Greek text (compiled from multiple Byzantine sources, which necessarily implies complications in its philological interpretation; see also Abicht and Schmidt, 1896).

In section 2, this paper presents information about the content, condition, and history of the manuscript. Section 3 reviews efforts in digitization of the manuscript, and section 4 discusses previous electronic editions of the deciphered text, reviewing problems with representation and availability and solutions adopted by the editors. Section 5 gives an overview of the principles of application of morphosyntactic annotation conditioned by the chosen annotation tool and strategy. The conclusion in section 6 explores distinctions among the publication of a text, digitization of a manuscript, development of language corpora, and a true electronic edition of the text, which is the goal of the UNESCO project.

2 The Manuscript

The *Codex Suprasliensis* is a Cyrillic manuscript, arguably copied at the end of the tenth or the beginning of the eleventh century (Krăstev and Bojadžiev, 1999). It is the largest extant Old Church Slavonic manuscript and it is associated with the Preslav literary school.

The *Codex* contains twenty-four vitae of Christian saints for the month of March and twenty-three homilies for the triodion cycle of the church year. In content it is a lectionary menaeum (or panaegyricon), combined with homilies from the movable Easter cycle, most of which written by or attributed to John Chrysostom (http://csup.ilit.bas.bg/node/7).

According to most researchers, the Miscellany was not translated as a stable compilation from any single Byzantine menological or hagiographical manuscript. Rather, it was compiled from texts translated at different times, long before the compilation of the *Codex Suprasliensis*. Presumably, at least one of the sources was the Glagolitic Epiphanius homily. Folio 104v of the manuscript has a marginal note that reads *g(ospod)i pomilui retьka amin* ('Lord have mercy on Retьk. Amen'), and some researchers have suggested that Retьk is the name of a scribe.

The language of the manuscript follows the Preslav literary norm of the tenth century. It is considered the most representative source of linguistic information about canonic Old Church Slavonic because of its size and because it contains texts otherwise unattested in the early mediaeval Slavic tradition. The codex is, thus, the main source for studying the language, writing, and culture of Bulgaria during the Preslav period.

The *Codex Suprasliensis* is written on parchment and shows careful writing and craftsmanship. It was discovered in 1823 in a Uniate Basilian monastery in Supraśl (then in Lithuania, now in Northeastern Poland in the Podlaskie Voivodeship) by Canon Michał Bobrowski. Bobrowski sent it for study to the Slovenian scholar Jernej Kopitar. After Kopitar's death, the first 118 folios were donated to the University Library in Ljubljana, where they are still kept. The following 16 leaves were purchased by A. F. Byčkov in 1856 and are now kept in the Russian National Library in St. Petersburg. The remaining 151 leaves were part of the collection of the Counts Zamoyski. The last, so-called Warsaw part had disappeared during World War II and were long considered lost until re-emerging in the US. In 1968, those folios were returned to Poland, where they are now part of the manuscript collection of the National Library in Warsaw.

The *Codex Supraslianis* has been listed in UNESCO's Memory of the World Register since 2007.

3 Digitization

In the present project, digital images of all three parts of the *Codex Suprasliensis*, currently located in repositories in three different countries (the National Library in Warsaw, Poland; the National Library of Russia in St. Petersburg; and the National University Library in Ljubljana, Slovenia), were reunited for publication in a single electronic edition. The digital images are already available at http://csup.ilit.bas.bg/galleries. The separate publication of the photographic facsimile is an interim stage in the project, and the photographs will eventually be republished together with a transcription that will be fully annotated, accompanied by commentary and updated bibliography.

Some previously unknown source materials, including some Byzantine originals identified only after the publication of the Zaimov and Capaldo edition in the early 1980s, have been used in the preparation of the Greek text of the new edition.

Eventually a diplomatic transcription of the text of the *Codex Suprasliensis* will be published together with critical apparatus, parallel Greek text, vocabulary, and grammatical analysis (in the form of corpora annotation). The annotation of the electronic corpus is at initial stage, with only one piece, namely the Life of St. Paul the Simple, completely annotated, and another (the Life of St. Paul and St. Juliana) under active preparation.

4 Electronic text

The principles of manuscript description follow a proposal developed in the context of *The Repertorium of Old Bulgarian Literature and Letters,* which includes descriptions, in both English and Bulgarian, of some 350 mediaeval Slavic manuscripts dated from the eleventh to the beginning of the eighteenth century. The *Repertorium* was designed in conformity with important standards and guidelines in humanities computing (Miltenova, Boyadzhiev, and Velev, 2000; Birnbaum, 1996). The description and analysis of the Cyrillic manuscripts contain comprehensive data drawn *de visu* from old texts (http://clover.slavic.pitt.edu/repertorium/).

The first electronic version of the *Codex Suprasliensis* was a 7-bit ASCII transliteration prepared under the direction of Jouko Lindstedt and distributed by the *Corpus Cyrillo-Methodianum Helsingiense: An Electronic Corpus of Old Church Slavonic Texts* (CCMH, http://www.helsinki.fi/slaavilaiset/ccmh/) and the TITUS project (http://titus.uni-frankfurt.de/texte/etcs/slav/aksl/suprasl/supra.htm). These transcriptions contain numerous errors and come completely without context and critical apparatus (no images, Greek text, commentary, grammatical annotation or analysis, etc.). The new edition under development takes the Helsinki transcriptions as a starting point, converts the text from ASCII to Unicode, corrects the errors, and includes the full range of supporting materials listed above.

A pilot model of an electronic edition of a small part of the *Codex Suprasliensis* with a search program was developed in 2008 (Birnbaum, 2008) at the University of Pittsburgh (http://paul.obdurodon.org). This electronic edition of the Life of St. Paul the Simple was developed in accord with the procedures and priorities described above: it is based on a corrected version of the text published by the CCMH, accompanied by parallel Greek (from the Zaimov/Capaldo edition), a new English translation, detailed linguistic commentary, and photographic facsimiles. Linguistic analysis in the commentary conforms to notation developed in Oscar Swan's *Old Church Slavic Inflectional Morphology* (2008).

There are many collections and editions of classical and mediaeval texts (such as the Perseus Project, http://www.perseus.tufts.edu/hopper/), but most of them are manually annotated. No rule-based morphological guesser is currently available for Old Church Slavonic, partially because of troublesome orthography, although there is preliminary finite-state morphology under development by Roland Meyer (http://rhssl1.uni-regensburg.de:8080/OCS/).

The research project *Pragmatic Resources in Old Indo-European Languages* (PROIEL), which aims at developing morphosyntactic means for the annotation of and research into the information structure in Ancient and Hellenistic Greek, Latin, Gothic, Classical Armenian, and Old Church Slavonic (Haug and Jøhndal, 2008), has developed a statistical morphological guesser and a semi-manual syntactic annotation tool supported by a set of morphology-based rules. The corpus to be built for the electronic edition of the *Codex Suprasliensis* will be annotated manually, but with the assistance of the morphological guesser already developed by the PROIEL project and trained for Old Church Slavonic morphology on the *Codex Marianus* (Haug et al., 2009). Thus, the *Codex Suprasliensis* will be annotated for morphology, syntax, and other features in the PROIEL annotation interface, and the information will be exported in XML for incorporation into the projected electronic edition.

5 Morphosyntactic Annotation

The morphosyntactic annotation tool to be used in the *Codex Suprasliensis* project is an integrated part of the PROIEL parallel treebank of ancient Indo-European languages. The core of the treebank is the New Testament in its Greek original and its earliest translations into each of the other project languages. PROIEL features an electronic version of the *Codex Marianus* fully annotated for morphology, syntax, and various other linguistic features. It has also been automatically aligned with the Greek Gospels at token level (Eckhoff and Haug, 2010).

Test annotation of the *Codex Suprasliensis* is currently in progress. Observations and solutions discussed in this section of the paper were drawn from the process of annotating of the Life of St Paul the Simple and the Life of St. Paul and St. Juliana (the annotated text is currently available at: http://foni.uio.no:3000/).

The PROIEL annotation tool (available at the same site) was developed with certain needs in mind:

When confronted with novel text styles and orthographical conventions (different from the already annotated *Codex Marianus*), annotation initially is primarily manual, but it becomes increasingly automatic as the tool learns from operator input. Because the annotation for some languages, including Old Church Slavonic, is being performed on a diplomatic transcription of a text with substantial orthographic variation (rather than on the normalized texts that are used more commonly in other disciplinary philological traditions), morphological analyzers and syntactic parsers are not available for all of the project languages.

Annotators had to be recruited internationally due to the specialized knowledge required. The application was, therefore, built to work with standards-compliant browsers, which did not require the annotators to perform any extra installation. For the annotators of Old Church Slavonic texts, the tool supports transliterated input, obviating the need for a specialized keyboard layout interface.

Texts are imported in a simple XML format, where they are split into tokens (words) based on spacing, and roughly into sentences based on punctuation. After the import and coarse automatic segmentation, the annotation proceeds as follows:

First, there is adjustment of sentence division. Since punctuation is not a reliable guide to sentence division in Old Church Slavonic, sentences must often be split or merged.

Second, the imported tokenization must be checked and corrected manually. A linguistic analysis of the text may need to normalize the word boundaries of the edition. In particular, contractions of prepositions and nouns may need to be dissolved.

Third, morphological annotation and lemmatization are implemented. The PROIEL annotation tool provides guesses for morphological features and lemmata based on previous reviewed annotations (Haug et al., 2009).

In the first stages of the annotation of the initial samples from the *Codex Suprasliensis*, the guesser recognized only 15% of the words on the basis of its prior annotation of the *Codex Marianus*. After annotating 2000 tokens of the *Codex Suprasliensis*, the accuracy of the guessing more than tripled, to approximately 50%. The low initial result and rapid improvement is mostly due to the use of diacritics in the *Codex Suprasliensis*, and we are developing an orthographic normalizer that will temporarily strip diacritics to facilitate recognition and automated linguistic tagging.

The lemmata were entered with support from a transliteration device, which also provides guesses based on extant lemmata. The lemmatization follows part-of-speech classification. A single form may, therefore, belong to several lemmata. For example, there are no fewer than four lemmata with the form *jako*: a subjunction, a relative adverb, and two regular adverbs that are deemed to have sufficiently different functions to be separated (one meaning 'as, like' and the other serving as an introductory 'for'). Morphological analysis disambiguates the morphological features as far as possible based on syntax and context, and the information is further stored in the database as a positional tag in the form of a string of symbols where each morphological feature represented by a given symbol has a fixed slot (for positional tags, see also Hajič, 2004).

Fourth, the annotators apply syntactic annotation in an enriched variety of dependency grammar (Haug, 2010). This level relies on overt elements and makes it possible to keep word order information and syntactic analysis in separate layers, which is essential in dealing with free-word-order languages such as Old Church Slavonic and Greek. The syntactic annotation is performed with a simple tool that provides good guesses from a set of morphologically based rules.

Fifth comes the review stage, where the morphological and syntactic analysis is reviewed by project members, and, when found correct, published on the PROIEL website.

In addition to the morphosyntactic annotation, there is an interface for annotating information status and anaphoric relations. There is also an option for customized tagging at the token, lemma, and sentence level. This option has been used to tag semantic features (such as animacy), derivational morphology (such as prefixation), and textual features (such as direct speech).

The annotations are all stored in a relational database, but may be exported in various XML formats. The rich linguistic information provided by the PROIEL-style annotation may, thus, be interwoven in XML format into an electronic text edition that also takes the many textological concerns implicit in the Suprasliensis project into account. The resulting edition will thus be one that can serve a very wide audience with different needs and interests.

6 Conclusion

The paper outlines the stages in creating an electronic edition of the *Codex Suprasliensis*: the digitization of the manuscript, preparation of the electronic text, and application of morphosyntactic annotation. All of these tasks can constitute objectives of separate projects (manuscript digitization; electronic text publication; language corpora compilation), but none of them alone would be sufficient to produce an electronic edition of the manuscript. Such an edition depends on all of these products, as well as the publication and annotation of the Byzantine sources, and the development of indices, a lexicon, glossary, bibliography, and others. The project therefore unites the efforts of an international working team with members with different but complimentary qualifications for the joint work on the edition. The electronic version of the *Codex Suprasliensis* will be freely available under a Creative Commons BY-NC-SA license.

Reference

Hajič, Jan. 2004. *Disambiguation of Rich Inflection (Computational Morphology of Czech)*. Karolinum Charles University Press, Prague.

Severjanov, S. 1904. *Suprasl'skaja rukopis' [Codex Suprasliensis, vol. 1-2]*. Pamjatniki staroslavjanskago jazyka, volume 1, 1-2. Sanktpeterburg.

Zaimov, Jordan and Mario Capaldo. 1982. *Suprasŭlski ili Retkov sbornik (Codex Supraslinesis or the Retkov Manuscript),* volume 1, Bulgarian Academy of Sciences Press, Sofia.

Zaimov, Jordan and Mario Capaldo. 1983. *Suprasŭlski ili Retkov sbornik (Codex Supraslinesis or the Retkov Manuscript),* volume 2, Bulgarian Academy of Sciences Press, Sofia.

Swan, Oscar. 2008. *Old Church Slavic. Inflectional Morphology*, volume 1, Berkeley Slavic Specialties, Berkeley.

Miltenova, Anissava, Andrei Boyadzhiev, and Stanimir Velev. 2000. Computerized Manuscript Corpus Data: Results and Further Development. *Bulgarian Studies at the Dawn of the 21st Century: a Bulgarian-American Perspective. Sixth Joint Meeting of Bulgarian and North American Scholars. Blagoevgrad, Bulgaria, May 30–June 2, 1999.* Gutenberg, Sofia, 237–243.

Birnbaum, David J. 1996. Standardizing Characters, Glyphs, and SGML Entities for Encoding Early Cyrillic Writing. *Computer Standards and Interfaces,* 18: 201–52.

Birnbaum, David J. 2008. Paul the Not-So-Simple. *Scripta & e-Scripta*, 6: 23–45

Krăstev, Georgi and Andrej Bojadžiev. 1999. Supras'lski sbornik: problemi na xronologijata i kompozicijata v iztočnoto-pravoslavie i v evropejskata kultura. *Materiali ot meždunarodnata naučna srešta, posvetena na 1100 godišninata ot načaloto na Zlatnija vek v bălgarskata kultura. Varna, 2–3 Juli 1993*. Guturanov, Sofia, 192–197.

Miklosich, Fr. 1851. *Monumenta linguae palaeoslovenicae e codice Suprasliensis*. Vindobonae, 456.

Abicht, R. and H. Schmidt. 1896. Quellennachweise zum Codex Suprasliensis. *Archiv für slavische Philologie*, 18: 138-155.

Haug, Dag. T. T. 2010. *PROIEL Guidelines for Annotation*: http://folk.uio.no/daghaug/syntactic_guidelines.pdf

Eckhoff, Hanne Martine and Dag Trygve Truslew Haug. 2010. Aligning Syntax in Early New Testament Texts: the PROIEL Corpus. *Wiener Slavistischer Almanach.*

Haug, Dag T. T., Marius Jøhndal, Hanne Martine Eckhoff, Eirik Welo, Mari J. B. Hertzenberg, and Angelika Muth. 2009. Computational and Linguistic Issues in Designing a Syntactically Annotated Parallel Corpus of Indo-European Languages. *Traitement Automatique des Langues*, volum 50.

Haug, Dag T. T., and Marius Jøhndal. 2008. *Creating a Parallel Treebank of the Old Indo-European Bible Translations.* http://www.hf.uio.no/ifikk/english/research/projects/proiel/Activities/proiel/publications/marrakech.pdf

SentiProfiler: Creating Comparable Visual Profiles of Sentimental Content in Texts

Tuomo Kakkonen
School of Computing
University of Eastern Finland
tuomo.kakkonen@uef.fi

Gordana Galić Kakkonen
Department of Croatian Language and Literature
University of Split, Croatia
ggalic@ffst.hr

Abstract

We introduce the concept of sentiment profiles, representations of emotional content in texts and the SentiProfiler system for creating and visualizing such profiles. We also demonstrate the practical applicability of the system in literary research by describing its use in analyzing novels in the Gothic fiction genre. Our results indicate that the system is able to support literary research by providing valuable insights into the emotional content of Gothic novels.

1 Introduction

In recent years, non-topical text analysis has become an active area of research. In contrast to "traditional" text analytics in which the aim is to extract and process the facts and concepts, non-topical text analysis aims at characterizing the attitudes, opinions and feelings present in a text.

Automatic detection and classification of sentiments has several potential areas of application. Hence, it has become an established field of *natural language processing* (NLP) research and a rising number of papers and articles dedicated to the analysis of the affective content of texts is being published each year. Feelings and sentiments are often represented within texts in complex and subtle ways, which makes their automatic detection an interesting research challenge.

Much of the work in *sentiment analysis* (SA) is concentrated on business applications, in particular the analysis of user-generated online content, such as customer reviews and tweets, in order to tap into what is sometimes referred to as the "Wisdom of the Crowds." This work departs from the general trends in SA research in more ways than one.

First, we apply SA to a field in which it has not, to the best of our knowledge, been applied before, namely the analysis of novels for literary research. Second, rather than concentrating on determining the polarity (negative vs. positive) of the analyzed document, we aim at providing more detailed classification affective content of the target texts. Third, although visualization of SA results has attracted some interest from the opinion mining and SA community, research contributions that particularly address the visual comparison of SA results are scarce.

We introduce a system called SentiProfiler that generates visual representations of affective content of texts and uses techniques to outline the differences and similarities between the pairs of texts under scrutiny. The design of the tool is centered on the idea of *sentiment profiles* (SPs), hierarchical representations of affective contents of the input documents. The SPs and the visual graphs representing them that the system generates are in effect summaries of the sentiment content of the input documents. The system makes use of various NLP and visualization resources and tools in tandem with Semantic Web technologies.

In addition calculating frequencies of sentiment-bearing words, a scoring measure is used to determine the prevalence of sentiments in the target texts. The hierarchical organization of the sentiment classes enables the system to aggregate these scores in order to gauge the prevalence of specific groups of sentiments. Our visualization technique uses vertex colors to denote the differences between the SPs that are being compared. This allows for quick browsing and detection of differences between the emotional content of the target documents.

We demonstrate the practical applicability of the SentiProfiler system by considering the ways in which it can support literary research by allowing visual comparisons of pairs of SPs created from works of a literary genre rich in dark and gloomy topics (and hence negative emotions), namely Gothic literature. The fact that Gothic novels are divided into two distinct subgenres of terror and horror allows us to experiment with the comparison functions of the system.

The paper is organized as follows. In Section 2, we outline the background of this research by shortly summarizing works on visualization of SA results and describing the tools and technologies on top of which SentiProfiler has been built. Section 3 introduces the architecture of the SentiProfiler system and explains the functioning of each of its main components. The practical applicability of the system is demonstrated and discussed in Section 4. Section 5 concludes by summarizing the paper and considering directions for future work.

2 Introduction

2.1 Related work

Most work on SA visualization has dealt with summarizing analysis results for collections of documents. Often, basic visualization methods, such as bar charts (Liu et al., 2005) and temporal graphs (Fukuhara et al., 2007) are utilized. The Pulse system by Gamon et al. (2005) generates treemap visualizations that display topic clusters and their associated sentiments. The size of the boxes indicates the number of sentences in the topic cluster, and the color denotes the average sentiment of the sentences belonging to that topic. Chen et al. (2006) generated multiple visualizations (such as decision trees and term variation networks) in order to enable the analysis of conflicting opinions.

One of the rare works that discusses visual comparison of SA results (Gregory et al., 2006) introduced a system that combines lexicon lookup-based SA with a visualization engine. The paper described an experiment with the well-known Hu and Liu (2004) customer review dataset.

The most relevant of the recent work on visualization of SA results is presented in Wu et al. (2010). They introduced OpinionSeer, a system that visualizes hotel customer feedbacks that is based on a visualization-centric analysis technique that considers uncertainty for modeling and analyzing customer opinions. They also suggested a type of visual representation that conveys customer opinions by augmenting scatterplots and radial visualization.

The only research work we are aware of that has applied SA to literary research is reported in (Taboda et el., 2006). In contrast to our work, rather than analyzing novels, Taboda et al. used SA techniques to extract information on the reputation of six early 20th century authors based on writings concerning them.

2.2 Tools and technologies applied

The SentiProfiler system uses WordNet-Affect (Strapparava and Valitutti, 2004) as the source for emotion-bearing words. WordNet-Affect is a linguistic resource for the lexical representation of affective knowledge. It was developed on the basis of WordNet (Miller, 1995) through the selection and labeling of the *synsets* (the WordNet technical term for semantically equivalent words) representing affective concepts. WordNet-Affect defines a hierarchy of emotions, in which the items are referred to as emotional categories. Each emotional category is linked with a set of WordNet synsets that contain the words that are connected with the emotional category. The WordNet-Affect hierarchy contains four main categories of emotions: negative, positive, ambiguous and neutral.

The WordNet-Affect hierarchy and the corresponding synsets from WordNet are represented in SentiProfiler as an ontology that is automatically generated from the WordNet-Affect hierarchy and WordNet synset definitions. The ontology is created and accessed by using the Jena framework (http://jena.sourceforge.net/). Jena is a well-known and stable Java framework for building Semantic Web applications that provides, among other things, an API for manipulating Semantic Web resources in the Resource Description Framework (RDF) format.

SentiProfiler makes use of several other well-known freely available Java tools and libraries. The MIT Java WordNet Interface (JWI) (http://projects.csail.mit.edu/jwi/) is an API for interfacing with WordNet. JWI is used by SentiProfiler for retrieving the relevant synsets from a local copy of the WordNet dictionaries.

GATE (Cunningham et al., 2002) is a widely used and flexible framework for developing text analysis systems. It is commonly applied in the NLP research community. SentiProfiler utilizes GATE in ontology-based tagging of sentiment-bearing words.

JUNG (the Java Universal Network/Graph Framework) (http://jung.sourceforge.net/) is a library for the modeling, analysis, and visualization of graphs. It provides an extensible set of graph operations, visualization methods and layouts. SentiProfiler usea JUNG for the visualization of sentiment profiles.

3 SentiProfiler

3.1 Introduction

The SentiProfiler system consists of three main components: ontology and ontology factory, sentiment analyzer and SP visualizer. Figure 1 outlines the system architecture.

As shown in Figure 1, the ontology that describes the hierarchy of the emotions to be detected is generated automatically from WN-Affect and WordNet data (see Section 3.2). The sentiment analyzer component (Section 3.3) consists of a GATE pipeline and a set of Java classes that analyze the tags assigned by GATE and creates the SPs of the input documents. The visualizer component (Section 3.3) is responsible for displaying SPs in a format that supports easy visual comparison.

3.2 Ontology of sentiments

The automatic ontology creation process from WordNet-Affect and WordNet data works as follows. First, the XML file containing the relevant part of the WordNet-Affect hierarchy is converted and stored in a graph data structure. Next, an ontology representing the sentiment hierarchy is created that contains the WordNet-Affect sentiment categories as classes. We refer to these as *sentiment classes*. The words from the relevant WordNet synsets are used as the individuals that instantiate each sentiment class. Finally, the ontology is written in an RDF/XML file that can be browsed and edited with any RDF-aware ontology editor. This allows automatically generated ontologies to be manually inspected and modified to the specific needs particular analysis tasks.

The JitterOnto ontology of negative sentiments that was generated for the experiments on Gothic literature described in Section 4 consisted of the 147 classes under the *negative-emotion* branch of the WordNet-Affect hierarchy. The maximum depth from the root class *negative-emotion* to a leaf sentiment class was five. This was the case, for example, with the sentiment class *negative-emotion/general-dislike/negative-fear/negative-unconcern/heartlessness/cruelty*. There are 823 individuals in the ontology, which means that the sentiment classes are described by a total of 823 nouns, verbs and adjectives. Hence, each class has on average of 5.6 instantiations. For instance, the *cruelty* class mentioned above is instantiated by the words "cruel," "cruelly," "cruelty," "mercilessness," "pitilessness," "ruthlessness" and "unkind."

Figure 2 shows an extract from the branch of the ontology that has to do with the set of emotions that are classified as *negative-fear*. The other seven classes that immediately follow the root class *negative-emotion* are as follows: *anxiety*, *daze*, *despair*, *general-dislike*, *humility*, *ingratitude* and *sadness*.

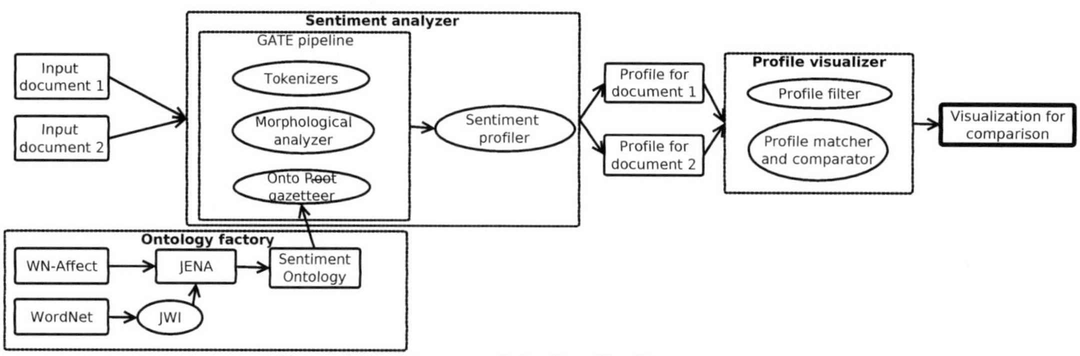

Figure 1. Architecture of the SentiProfiler system.

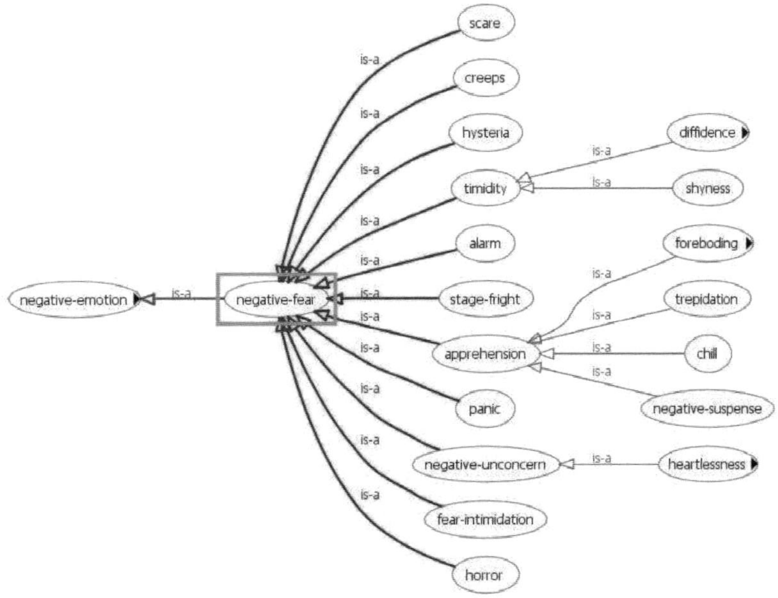

Figure 2. Extract from JitterOnto showing the two levels of more specific sentiment classes under the parent class negative-fear. The figure was created with the Protégé editor (Stanford Center for Biomedical Informatics Research, 2011).

3.3 Analysis of affective content

Sentiment analysis in SentiProfiler consists of creating a SP of an input document. A SP is a hierarchy of sentiment classes that contains all the classes of the source ontology that occurred in the document, and the classes that are part of a path from such a class to the root (*negative-emotion* in case of the ontology used for the experiments in this paper). That is, those sentiment classes that did not appear in the input document or have any children that appeared in the document are not included in the SP.

For instance, let us have a document in which the only negative sentiment classes that appear are *chill* and *timidity*. Following the paths from *negative-emotion* in Figure 2 to *chill* and *timidity* gives us the SP of the document.

The creation of SPs consist of three phases: detection of sentiment-bearing words, relating each such word with the relevant sentiment class and, finally, constructing the hierarchy that describes the SP of a document.

SA is performed in SentiProfiler with a GATE pipeline that consists of three basic ANNIE components (sentence splitter, word tokenizer and POS tagger), GATE morphological analyzer and an ontology-based tagging tool. Onto Root Gazetteer (Damljanovic et al., 2008) is a GATE processing resource that dynamically constructs a gazetteer from an ontology and creates, in combination with other GATE components, ontology-based annotations on the given content. In the SentiProfiler GATE pipeline Onto Root Gazetteer marks up in the input document the words that match with an individual found in the ontology. The relevant sentiment class names are used as the tags in the output.

Next, a graph presentation of the sentiment class hierarchy (i.e. the sentiment profile) is created for the input document in which each graph vertex is associated with the number of times a word relating to the relevant sentiment class appears in the document. In addition to the frequency counts we define a score that measures the prevalence of each sentiment class. The *sentiment class scores* (SCMs) measure the relative frequency with which a specific sentiment s_i appears in a document. SCM score is defined as follows:

$$SCM1_i = \frac{|s_i|}{|words|}$$

where $|S_i|$ is the number of times a word instantiating the sentiment class s_i appears in the document and $|S_i|$ is the total number of word tokens in the document. For instance, let us have a document with 1000 word tokens. Three of the sentiment-bearing words belong to the class s_1. The SCM score for the sentiment class s_1 is 0.15.

An *aggregate SCM score* (ASCM) is defined for all the non-leaf sentiment classes. It is calculated as the sum of the SCM scores of all the sentiment classes that succeed the current sentiment classes in the hierarchy plus the SCM score of the current sentiment class. This score provides a way of comparing whole branches of the SP rather than one single sentiment class at a time. Figure 3 illustrates the concept.

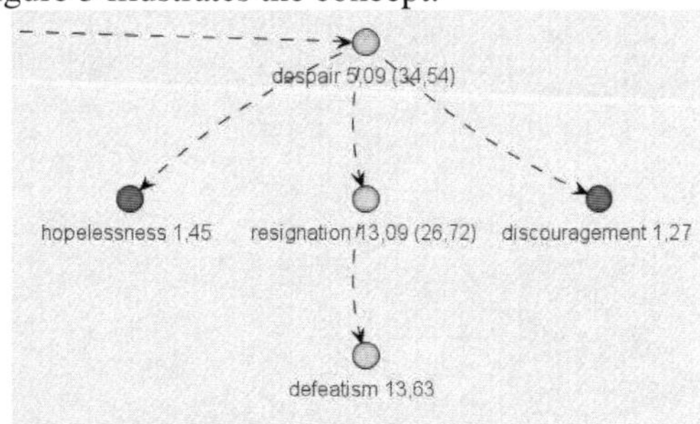

Figure 3. An example of SCM and ASCM scores. The scores that are not inside parentheses are SCMs (multiplied by 10 for easier interpretation). The figures inside the parentheses are aggregate SCM values.

3.4 Visualization

In the visualization of an SP, each sentiment class is represented as a vertex that indicates, in addition to the name of the sentiment class, any combination (depending on the system configuration) of frequency, SCM and ASCM values. User can also observe the occurrences of the sentiment-bearing words pertaining to specific sentiment category along with the context in which the word appeared.

The matching algorithm compares the profiles in order to find the sentiment classes that are present in only one of the profiles. We refer to these as *additional sentiment classes*. It also calculates the differences between the scores of those classes that occur in both of the profiles. The sentiment classes that receive a higher score are referred to as *higher score sentiment classes*. As a result of the matching process, the vertices representing additional and higher score sentiment classes are denoted by specific user-modifiable colors in the visualization.

4 Experiments with Gothic Novels

We evaluated the practical applicability of the SentiProfiler system by analyzing the SPs of Gothic novels. Such novels consist of stories of "terror and suspense, usually set in a gloomy old castle or monastery" (Baldick, 2004). The Gothic literary genre is further divided into works of terror and horror. Many explanations of the distinction between the two subgenres have been put forward in the literary research community (for example, Botting, 1996). In essence, the distinction between terror and horror can be summarized as the intensity and the type of emotions they depict and evoke in the fictional character as well as in the reader him/herself. Although the works of both subgenres of the Gothic novels contain emotions such as anxiety, fear and gloom, in terror these emotions are more connected to a threat, real or perceived, rather than actual events of cruelty and violence.

What makes this genre of novels so suitable for testing the profile comparison capabilities of SentiProfiler is, first, that they can be expected to contain a relatively high amount of (negative) emotional content. Second, the fact that there are two subgenres of Gothic novels provides a way of testing the practical use of our system in comparing SPs. If SentiProfiler is able, in addition to creating SP visualizations of Gothic novels, to distinguish differences in the types of emotions present in the SPs generated for samples of the two Gothic novel subgenres it provides evidence that the system can be used as a practical tool for supporting literature research.

Due to the nature of the target texts, we concentrated our analysis on negative emotions. What we were interested in observing, in particular, were differences in the SPs that support the distinction between the two subgenres of Gothic literature as it is understood in the theory of literature. What we were expecting to be able to recognize is that horror novels contain emotions that can be described as a sort of an "aftershock", a display of disgust that appears after a horrendous event has occurred. Terror, in contrast, raises anxiety and timidity caused by the fear of something terrible happening in the near future. In a sense, terror is of a more "psychological" nature than horror. Varma (1966) puts it succinctly: the difference between the two subgenres "is the difference between awful apprehension and sickening realization: between the smell of death and stumbling against a corpse."

Figure 4 illustrates an extract from the comparison of a horror and terror novel. The two novels used in the comparison were Matthew Lewis's (1796) "The Monk: A romance". It is considered as one of the prime examples of novels in Gothic horror. Ann Radcliffe's (1794) "The Mysteries of Udolpho" enjoys a similar status in the Gothic terror genre[1].

[1] All the novels for the research reported in this paper were obtained from the Project Gutenberg web site at http://www.gutenberg.org.

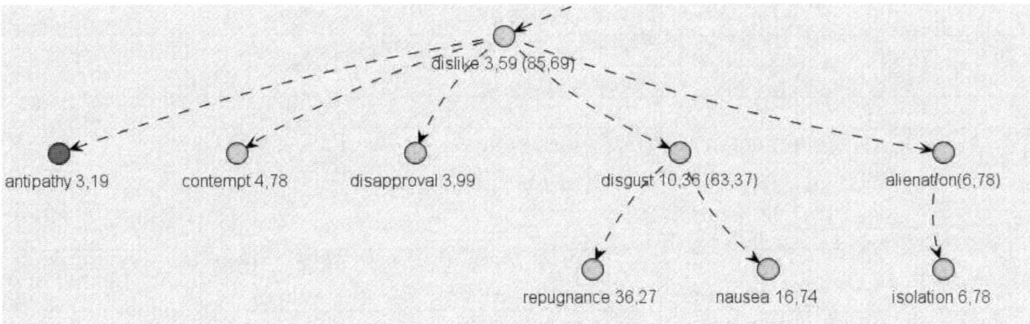

Figure 4. An extract from a sentiment profile comparison of the horror novel (The Monk) with the terror novel (Udolpho) from the perspective of the horror novel. Green vertices denote higher score sentiment classes. The red vertex (antipathy) indicates an additional sentiment class.

The SP extract in Figure 4 indicates, as expected under the definitions of the two subgenres, that the novel representative of the horror subgenre receives higher SCM scores for the sentiment classes pertaining to, for example, disgust and nausea. The same was observed, for example, for the sentiment class cruelty (not shown in the figure).

Figure 5 shows an extract from the same pair-wise comparison that was depicted in Figure 4, but in this case from the perspective of the terror novel.

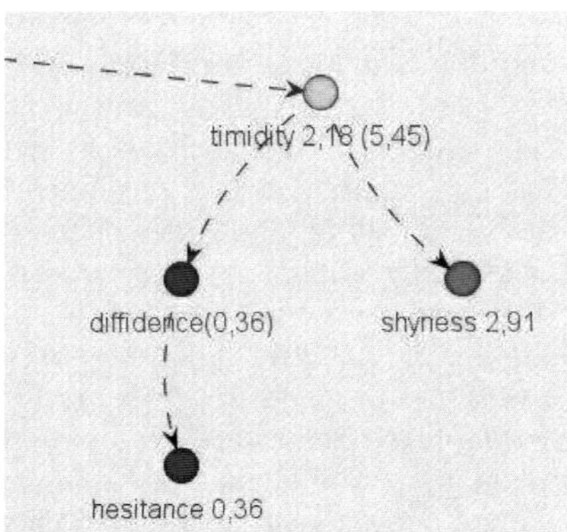

Figure 5. An extract from a comparison of the terror novel with the horror novel showing additional sentiment classes diffidence and hesitance and higher score class timidity.

As visualized in Figure 5, as expected, the terror novel more frequently contained sentiments that have to do with emotions that can be described as "less intense" and less connected with cruelty and the shock caused by acts of violence. In addition to the sentiment classes illustrated in Figure 5, this was the case, for instance, with the sentiment classes impatience and depression.

The color coding of vertices and the ability to zoom in and out (see Figure 6 for an example) enable the literary scholar to easily locate of the branches in the SP that show a significant number of differences between the novels explored. Moreover, the dialog that shows the contexts in which the words linked with a specific sentiment class occurred helps the comparative literature researcher to make more detailed analyses of, for instance, style and discourse.

Table 1 summarizes some of the observed differences between the SPs created based on the terror and horror novel discussed above, and the following two canonical works in the horror and terror subgenres: Frankenstein; or, The Modern Prometheus (Shelley, 1818) and the Castle of Otranto (Walpole, 1764).

The table does not give an exhaustive list of all the differences, but rather concentrates on those classes that support the notion of dividing the Gothic subgenres based on the "severity" of emotions.

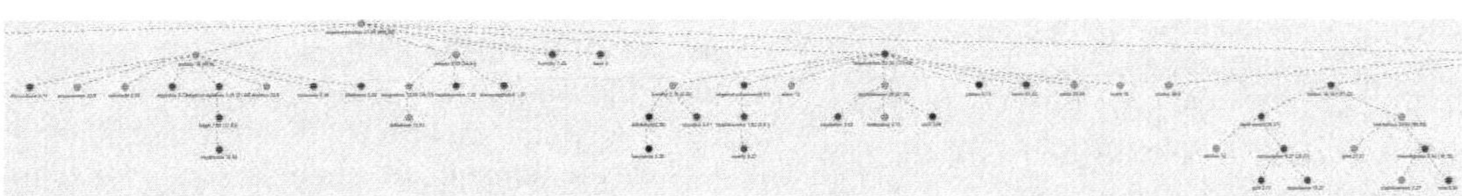

Figure 6. Zoomed-out view of a sentiment profile comparison that demonstrates how the system can be used for locating interesting branches in a sentiment profile. In this sample case, attention is drawn to the large branch in the middle, as it contains several blue vertices (denoting additional sentiment classes) and a mixture of red and green vertices. The user can zoom in to the interesting section of the visualization by turning the mouse wheel.

Novel pair		Sentiment classes			
		Higher score		Additional	
T	H	T	H	T	H
Udolpho	Franken-stein	timidity, shyness, anxiousness	horror, disgust, hate, lividity	hesitance, solicitude, insecurity	-
Otranto	Monk	sorrow, depression, anxiety	horror, disgust, repugnance	-	nausea, lividity
Udolpho	Monk	timidity, anxiety, impatience	horror, disgust, repugnance, cruelty	hesitance, diffidence	nausea, lividity
Otranto	Franken-stein	hopelessness, impatience	horror, disgust, repugnance	-	nausea, trepidation

Table 1: Pair-wise comparison of the two horror and terror novels. The two columns under the heading "higher score" lists examples of the sentiment classes that received higher score in the terror (T) and the horror (H) novel, respectively. The columns under the heading "additional" contain examples of sentiment classes that were present only either in the terror or the horror novel.

The results reported in Table 1 indicate that differences can indeed be observed in the relative frequency and presence of certain sentiment classes between representatives of the two subgenres of Gothic literature. Sentiment classes such as timidity, anxiety and shyness were more frequent in the terror novels than they were in the representatives of the horror subgenre. Horror and disgust were more frequent sentiment classes in horror novels in all the four pair-wise comparisons. Nausea was among sentiments that were present only in the horror novels included in the comparison.

It is also interesting to note that the terror novel Castle of Otranto had additional categories aggravation and wrath (not shown in Table1) that were not present in either of the horror novels. This observation did not seem to support the expected distinction between terror and horror novels. However, further analysis of relevant research literature (for instance, Hume (1969)) revealed that, while Otranto is often considered as a terror novel, it is somewhat of a borderline case between the two subgenres. Being able to capture such an ambiguity gives additional support to the practical applicability of SentiProfiler.

5 Conclusion

We introduced the concept of sentiment profiles (SPs) and the SentiProfiler system for creating easily comparable SPs created from pairs of documents. The system is built on the basis of various well-known NLP and Semantic Web technologies and tools. We demonstrated the use of the system by describing how it can support research in comparative literature. The visual comparisons allow the literary scholar to gain insights into the target texts that would be difficult, if not impossible, to obtain with the traditional "pen and paper" research methods that are typically used in the field.

The preliminary experiments we reported in Section 4 indicated that the tool can provide interesting insights for literary researchers. SentiProfiler was able to detect differences between the sentiments present in example novels of Gothic terror and horror subgenres. Moreover, many of the differences observed by the tool supported the literature theoretical distinction between these two subgenres.

Our planned future work includes applying the SentiProfiler tool to conduct a comprehensive study of a larger set of Gothic novels in order to verify whether the commonly accepted definition of the difference between the emotional content present in horror and terror subgenres holds true.

There are various ways in which SentiProfiler could be improved and extended. First, we plan to apply the system to a study of Gothic novels. Since we are dealing with books from the eighteenth and nineteenth centuries, extending the JitterOnto ontology of negative emotions with words that are not in use in modern English would presumably increase the accuracy of the system in that particular area of application.

The system has many potential uses beyond literary research. Negative emotions play a role in anti-social behavior. One of the future applications of SentiProfiler and the JittersOnto ontology used in the experiment reported in this paper includes automatic detection and prediction of potential acts of extreme anti-social behavior (such as school shootings) based on messages posted online. It is important to note that, despite the focus of this paper, SentiProfiler is designed and implemented in a way that allows any of the WordNet-Affect sentiment hierarchy branches, and in fact any ontologically represented class hierarchy, to be used. Hence, there is no reason why the tool and the method could not be applied in more general case of SA, rather than focusing on negative emotional content.

Acknowledgments

This work was supported by the project entitled "Detecting and Visualizing Changes in Emotions in Texts" funded by the Academy of Finland.

References

Chris Baldick. 2004. *The Concise Dictionary of Literary Terms (2nd edition).* Oxford University Press, Oxford, UK and New York, USA.

Fred Botting. 1996. *Gothic (The New Critical Idiom).* Routledge, New York, USA.

Chaomei Chen, Fidelia Ibekwe-SanJuan, Eric SanJuan and Chris Weaver. 2006. Visual Analysis of Conflicting Opinions. *Proceedings of the IEEE Symposium on Visual Analytics Science and Technology*, Baltimore, Maryland, USA.

Hamish Cunningham, Diana Maynard, Kalina Bontcheva and Valentin Tablan. 2002. GATE: A Framework and Graphical Development Environment for Robust NLP Tools and Applications. *Proceedings of the 40th Anniversary Meeting of the Association for Computational Linguistic*, Philadelphia, Pennsylvania, USA.

Danica Damljanovic, Valentin Tablan and Kalina Bontcheva. 2008 A Text-based Query Interface to OWL Ontologies. *Proceedings of the 6th Language Resources and Evaluation Conference*, Marrakech, Morocco.

Tomohiro Fukuhara, Hiroshi Nakagawa and Toyoaki Nishida. 2007. Understanding Sentiment of People from News Articles: Temporal Sentiment Analysis of Social Events. *Proceedings of the International Conference on Weblogs and Social Media*, Boulder, Colorado, USA.

Michael Gamon, Anthony Aue, Simon Corston-Oliver and Eric Ringger. 2005. Pulse: Mining Customer Opinions from Free Text. *Proceedings of the 6th International Symposium on Intelligent Data Analysis*, Madrid, Spain.

Michelle L. Gregory, Nancy A. Chinchor, Paul Whitney, Richard Carter, Elizabeth Hetzler and Alan Turner. 2006. User-Directed Sentiment Analysis: Visualizing the Affective Content of Documents. *Proceedings of the Workshop on Sentiment and Subjectivity in Text*, Sydney, Australia.

Minqing Hu and Bing Liu. 2004. Mining Opinion Features in Customer Reviews. *Proceedings of 19th National Conference on Artificial Intelligence*, San Jose, California, USA.

Robert D. Hume. 1969. Gothic Versus Romantic: A Revaluation of the Gothic Novel. *PMLA*, 84(2): 282-90.

Matthew G. Lewis. 1796. *The Monk: A Romance.* Printed for J. Saunders, Waterford, Ireland.

Bing Liu, Minqing Hu and Junsheng Cheng. 2005. Opinion Observer: Analyzing and Comparing Opinions on the Web. *Proc. of the 14th International Conference on World Wide Web*, Chiba, Japan.

George A. Miller. 1995. WordNet: A Lexical Database for English. *Communications of the ACM*, 38(11):39-41.

Ann Radcliffe. 1794. *The Mysteries of Udolpho.* Printed for G.G. and J. Robinson, London, UK.

Mary Shelley. 1818. *Frankenstein; or, The Modern Prometheus.* Lackington, Hughes, Harding, Mavor & Jones, London, UK.

Stanford Center for Biomedical Informatics Research. 2011. *Protégé.* http://protege.stanford.edu/ (Accessed March 23rd, 2011).

Carlo Strapparava and Alessandro Valitutti. 2004. WordNet-Affect: an Affective Extension of WordNet. *Proceedings of the 4th International Conference on Language Resources and Evaluation*, Lisbon, Portugal.

Maite Taboada, Mary Ann Gillies and Paul McFetridge 2006. Sentiment Classification Techniques for Tracking Literary Reputation. *Proceedings of LREC Workshop Towards Computational Models of Literary Analysis*, Genoa, Italy.

Horace Walpole. 1764. *The Castle of Otranto.* Thomas Lownds, London, UK.

Devendra P. Varma. 1966. *The Gothic Flame: Being a History of the Gothic Novel in England - Its Origins, Efflorescence, Disintegration, and Residuary Influences.* Scarecrow Press, New York, USA.

Yingcai Wu, Furu Wei, Shixia Liu, Norman Au, Weiwei Cui, Hong Zhou and Huamin Qu. 2010. OpinionSeer: Interactive Visualization of Hotel Customer Feedback. *IEEE Transactions on Visualization and Computer Graphics*, 16(6):1109-1118.

Character Profiling in 19th Century Fiction

Dimitrios Kokkinakis
Center for Language Technology &
Språkbanken, Department of Swedish
University of Gothenburg, Sweden
dimitrios.kokkinakis@svenska.gu.se

Mats Malm
Department of Literature, History of
Ideas and Religion
University of Gothenburg, Sweden
mats.malm@lit.gu.se

Abstract

This paper describes the way in which personal relationships between main characters in 19th century Swedish prose fiction can be identified using information guided by named entities, provided by a entity recognition system adapted to the 19th century Swedish language characteristics. Interpersonal relation extraction is based on the context between two relevant, identified person entities. The relationships extraction process also utilizes the content of on-line available lexical semantic resources (suitable vocabularies) and fairly standard context matching methods that provide a basic mechanism for identifying a wealth of interpersonal relations. Such relations can hopefully aid the reader of a 19th-century Swedish literary work to better understand its content and plot, and get a bird's eye view on the landscape of the core story.

1 Introduction

Digitized information and the task of storing, generating and mining an ever greater volume of (textual) data become simpler and more efficient with every passing day. Along with this opportunity, however, comes a further challenge: to create the means whereby one can tap this great potentiality and engage it for the advancement of (scientific) understanding and knowledge mining. The goal of this research is to generate a complete profile for all main characters in each arbitrary volume in a literature collection of 19th century fiction. We also aim at a methodology that should be easily transferable to any other piece of literary work. A complete profile implies an exhaustive list of any kind of interpersonal relationships, such as *Friend Of* and *Antagonist Of* that can be encountered between the main characters in a literary work.

Similarly to social network extraction, there are numerous imaginable semantically oriented relationships between named entity pairs, this paper however only examines interpersonal ones. It also provides a brief description of the lexical resources and extended named entities, used by a Swedish named entity recognition (NER) system applied for the annotation of the collection. The NER system is to a great extent rule-based and uses a large set of lexically-driven resources. The system originates from a generic NER system used for annotation of modern Swedish which has been enhanced and improved by respecting common orthographic norms of nineteenth-century Swedish spelling.

One of the purposes in mind for this work is to test the applicability of Natural Language Processing (NLP) technologies in data from a deviant domain and time period than the ones the technology is designed for (i.e., contemporary, modern Swedish) in order to get a clearer picture of the strengths and weaknesses of the resources and tools and thus identify ways to further improve the obtained outcomes. This way we can facilitate the extraction of content-related semantic metadata, an important element in the management, dissemination and sustenance of digital repositories.

Name extraction in combination with filtering scripts that model the vocabularies, as well as fairly standard context matching methods provide a mechanism for identifying interpersonal relations that can also aid the reader of a literary work to better understand its content and plot, and get a bird's eye view on the landscape of the core story. Despite the risks of *spoiling* the enjoyment that some readers of the narrative would otherwise have experienced without revealing of any plot elements, we still believe that such supporting aid can be used for an in-depth story understanding (for the human reader). Moreover, creating biographical sketches (e.g., birthplace) and extracting facts for entities (e.g., individuals) can be easily exploited in various possible ways by NLP technologies such as summarization and question answering (e.g., Jing *et al.*, 2007).

2 Related Work

Natural-language processing is an attractive approach to processing large text collections for relation extraction (usually defined as a relation predicate ranging over two arguments, e.g., concepts or people) and there exist a number of techniques that have applicability to any type of text; for a general review see Hachey (2009). Such techniques can facilitate more advanced research on literature and provide the appropriate mechanisms for generating multiple views on corpora and insights on people, places, and events in a large scale, through various types of relations.

Relation extraction was introduced in the mid 1990s by the *Template Element* and *Template Relation* tasks in MUC-6 (Message Understanding Conferences) and followed by the ACE (Automatic Content Extraction) *Relation Detection/Recognition* tasks (*cf.* Doddington *et al.*, 2004). Since then it has been an active and fruitful area of research, partly driven by the explosion of the available information via the Web and partly by the evidence that embedded relations are useful for various NLP tasks such as Q&A and Information Retrieval.

Relation extraction approaches (particularly binary ones) can be classified in various ways. Knowledge engineering approaches (e.g., rule-based, linguistic based), learning approaches (e.g., statistical, machine learning, bootstrapping) and hybrid ones; for an overview of techniques see Jinxiu (2007). Learning approaches become more and more common in the open domain i.e. large corpora of web scale, *cf.* Agichtein & Gravano, (2000); Christensen *et al.* (2010); relations are also of particular interest and prominent in the (bio)medical domain; e.g. Rosario & Hearst (2004); Giles & Wren (2008); Roberts *et al.* (2008). Elson *et al.* (2010) describe a method to extract social networks from literature (nineteenth-century British novels and serials) depending on the ability to determine when two characters are in conversation. The authors use a named-entity tagger to automatically locate all the names in a novel and then a classifier that automatically assigns a speaker to every instance of direct speech in the novel using features of the surrounding text. A "conversation" occurs if two characters speak within 300 words each other, and finally, a social network is constructed from the conversations. Nodes are named speakers and edges appear if there was a conversation between two characters, a heavier edge means more conversations. Our approach is mainly influenced by the work by Hasegawa *et al.* (2004) who proposed an unsupervised, domain-neutral approach to relation extraction by clustering named entity pairs according to the similarity of context words intervening between two entities and selecting the most frequent words from the context to label the relation.

3 Material: *a Prose Fiction Corpus*

Prose fiction is a just one type of textual material that has been brought into the electronic "life" using large scale digitized efforts. Prose fiction is an essential source within many disciplines of humanities (history, religion, sociology, linguistics etc) and social studies and an invaluable source for understanding the movements of society by its ability to demonstrate what forces and ideas are at work in the society of its time. Prose fiction is complex and difficult to use not only because of interpretational complexity but also because of its limited availability. The "19th Century Sweden in the Mirror of Prose Fiction" (*Det svenska 1800-talet speglat i prosafiktionen*) project (2009-12) aims at developing a representative corpus which mirrors society at given points in time, chronologically selected in such a way that historical comparisons can be made. The material is all fiction, written in the original and published separately for the first time, that appeared in Swedish during the years 1800, 1820, 1840, 1860, 1880 and 1900 (300 publications, ca 60,000 pages). The material provides a whole century of evolution and social, aesthetic, scientific, technical, cultural, religious and philosophical change.

3.1 Lexical Resources

The main focus of this research is the extraction of main character profiles[1], in literary archives and as a starting point we only look into interpersonal relationships. There is a number of suitable, freely available resources that we have started to exploit in order to aid the relation identification process, particularly the *RELATION-*

[1] Currently, this work is similar to the extraction of social networks but in the long run it is also desirable to extract more than merely interdependency relations of individuals (e.g., birth place, workplace etc.).

SHIP[2] vocabulary and two Swedish lexical semantic resources, namely the *FrameNet++*[3] and the *Swesaurus*[4]. These resources are useful and provide the appropriate machinery for our goals, namely to both identify appropriate relationship oriented lexical units and also appropriate relationship labels.

The RELATIONSHIP vocabulary defined by Davis & Vitiello (2010) is a good starting point for the labeling of the interpersonal relations. In their work Davis & Vitiello provide a description of 35 possible relationships that can occur between individuals. The description is not unproblematic since some of these relationships may be partially overlapping or even tautological such as *ChildOf* vs. *AncestorOf* / *DescedentOf* and *friendOf* vz. close*FriendOf*, The two other resources, namely the Swedish Swesaurus (Borin & Forsberg, 2010), that is fuzzy synsets in a WordNet-like resource under active development, and the Swedish FrameNet++ (Borin *et al.*, 2009) provides a large, and constantly growing number of synonyms and related words that are important for the relation extraction task.

In the Swedish FrameNet++ such words are called *lexical units* and are described by a number of *frames*. A frame is a script-like structure of concepts, which are linked to the meanings of linguistic units and associated with a specific event or state. A number of frames and particularly the lexical units encoded therein are relevant for interpersonal relationship extraction, such frames are for instance the *Personal_Relationship* (with lexical units: *flickvän* 'girl friend' and *make* 'husband', etc.), the *Kinship* (with lexical units: *barnbarn* 'grandchild', *bror* 'brother', *brorsdotter* 'niece', *dotter* 'daughter', etc.) and the *Forming_Relationship* (with lexical units: *förlova_sig* 'become engaged with', *gifta_sig* 'marry with', etc.). These frames are semi-automatically mapped to the RELATIONSHIP vocabulary and their containing lexical units become the actual lexical manifestation of the relationship in question. Similarly, we have experimented with the Swedish Swesaurus in order to identify synonyms for some of these lexical units. This way we can increase the amount of the words that can be part of various relations types. Thus, for the word *kollega* 'colleague' we can get a set of acceptable near synonyms such as *arbetskamrat* 'co-worker' but unfortunately also a number of not so suitable near synonyms such as *kompis* 'buddy', therefore we had to manually go through such near synonym lists and discard erroneous entries.

3.2 Named Entities and Animacy

There has been some work in the past on defining and applying rich name hierarchies, both specific (Fleischman & Hovy, 2002) and generic (Sekine, 2004) to various corpora. However, in other approaches (Kokkinakis, 2004) the wealth of name types is captured by implementing a fine-grained named entity taxonomy by keeping a small generic set of named entity types as *main* types and modeling the rest using a *subtype* mechanism. In this latter work a *Person entity* (a reference to a real word entity) is defined as proper nouns – personal names (forenames, surnames), animal/pet names, mythological names, names of Gods etc. – and common nouns and noun phrases denoting groups/sets of people. In this work the rule-based component for Person entity identification utilizes a large set of designator words (e.g., various types of nominal mentions) and phrases (e.g., typically verbal constructions) that require animate subjects, a relevant piece of knowledge which is explored for the annotation of animate instances in literary texts and other related tasks (*cf.* Orasan & Evans, 2001). These designators are divided into four groups according to their semantic denotation:

- nationality or the ethnic/racial group of a person (e.g. *tysken* 'the German [person]')
- profession (e.g. *läkaren* 'the doctor')
- family ties and relationships (e.g. *svärson* 'son in law'; *moster* 'aunt [from the mother's side]')
- individual that cannot be unambiguously categorized into any of the other three groups (e.g. *patienten* 'the patient')

Animacy markers are further marked for gender (male, female or unknown/unresolved such as *barn* 'child'). An example of animacy annotation is given below. In this example the animacy attribute, *ANI*, has a value *FAF* which stands for *FA*mily and *F*emale, while the attributes *TYPE* and *SuBT*ype refer to *PeRS*on and *HUM*an respectively: <ENAMEX TYPE="PRS" SBT="HUM" ANI="FAF">*Didriks mor*</ENAMEX> i.e. 'Didriks mother'. An important use of the animacy attribute is that it can be helpful for ruling out some erroneous non-allowable, gender-bearing

[2] http://vocab.org/relationship/.html
[3] http://spraakbanken.gu.se/eng/swefn
[4] http://spraakbanken.gu.se/swe/forskning/swefn/swesaurus

relations such as the one given in example 5. In this example there in an obvious *anomaly* involved considering the otherwise erroenous final relation, *SiblingOf*. *Stina* is recognized as female (through the attribute *UNF*) while in the preceding context the word *broder* 'brother' implies a following mention of a male gender, such features could be perhaps rule out spurious relationhips.

4 Method

NLP techniques, such as Information Extraction, provide methods for identifying domain specific relations and event information. From a initial perspective such methods seem to be doomed to fail since each literary work is in itself a kind of *closed world* or domain where one may deal with death and resurrection and another on travelogues. However, each piece of work has certain general characteristics that can be captured by applying fairly standard NLP components such as named entity recognizers and indexers using various generic lexical resources, such as lexical units extracted from the Swesaurus. Also, inspired by similar methodologies that have shown high recall and precision figures, such as Hasegawa *et al.* (2004) we also try to capture interpersonal relationships by investigating ways in which the context between two entities can be modeled using unsupervised methods. Our basic approach is outlined below:

1. *Entity detection*: annotate corpora with named entities and animacy markers
2. *Context extraction*: extract sentences with co-occurring pairs of person named entities
3. *Relation detection and labeling:* label the extracted pairs of person entities
   a. automatically; for window size of 1-3 tokens using pattern matching templates with lexical units from the resources
   b. for window size of 4-10 tokens measure the context similarity between the extracted pairs of person entities
      i. make clusters of pairs and their context
      ii. semi-automatically label the clusters
4. *Merging:* filter, join and plot the results of (3a and 3b)

We automatically annotated each available volume in the collection with a slightly tuned to 19th century Swedish system; for details *cf.* Borin *et al.* (2007) and Borin & Kokkinakis (2010). We started by first clustering *all* possible context lengths and also applied template pattern matching once again on *all* possible contexts. After some experiments we split the process into two separate ones guided by the number of tokens between the entities. Very short contexts can be quickly and reliably captured in a pattern matching fashion. Therefore, we decided to *first* apply template pattern matching involving two recognized person entities and matched the intervened context with the lexical information extracted and modeled from the various lexical sources. Example of manually designed, pattern matching templates are provided below:

GrandparentOf: morfar|mormor|farfar|farmor|morfader|...

<PRSentity-1> *any?* {GrandparentOf} <PRSentity-2>
<PRSentity-1> {GrandparentOf} *any?* <PRSentity-2>
<PRSentity-1> *any?* <PRSentity-*s*-2> {GrandparentOf}

These template-examples attempt to capture the *GrandparentOf* relation by testing whether any of the lexical units, extracted from the resources as previously described, are between two person entities or immediately to the right of the second if this is in genitive form, i.e., ends in '-s'; *any* refers here to any optional non-empty sequence of characters while *GrandparentOf* is simply a convenient shorthand notation that gives a single name to a set of related lexical units. The results with this method were reliable when the intervening context is only a couple of tokens. The examples below illustrate the process; examples 1-3 contain the metadata obtained by the NER, and 1′-3′ the obtained relations after pattern matching and filtering.

(1) <ENAMEX TYPE="PRS" SBT="HUM" ANI="UNM"> *Muhammeds*</ENAMEX> *dotter* <ENAMEX TYPE= "PRS" SBT="HUM" ANI="FAF">*Fatima*</ENAMEX>; i.e., "Muhammeds daughter Fatima"

(2) <ENAMEX TYPE="PRS" SBT="HUM" ANI="UNU"> *Strindberg*</ENAMEX> *hade träffat* <ENAMEX TYPE ="PRS" SBT="HUM" ANI="UNF">*Nennie*</ENAMEX>; i.e., "Strindberg had met Nennie"

(3) <ENAMEX TYPE="PRS" SBT="HUM" ANI="UNF"> *Taube*</ENAMEX> *anställde nu* <ENAMEX TYPE= "PRS" SBT="HUM" ANI="UNF">*Marie Susanne Cederlöf*</ENAMEX>; i.e., "Taube employed now Marie Susanne Cederlöf"

(1′) *Muhammeds=>dotter/*ParentOf*=>Fatima*
ParentOf (Fatima, Muhammed)
(2′) *Strindberg=>träffat/*HasMet*=>Nennie*
HasMet (Strindberg, Nennie)
(3′) *Taube=>anställde/*EmployerOf*=>Marie Susanne Cederlöf*
EmployerOf (Taube, Marie Susanne Cederlöf)

For contexts between 4 and 10 tokens we produce context vectors (bag of words) from all intervening tokens of all contexts, with the exclusion of punctuation and numerical tokens. We chose not to include the very short contexts since pattern matching is reliable for short window sizes. After some test we limited the maximum window to be 10 tokens;, larger size of intervening tokens introduce in many cases noisy results. Examples 4-6 illustrate cases with a context between the person entities of >2 tokens. Note that the extracted relations in example 5′ is actually erroneous probably caused by one of the context words, namely *brodern* 'the brother'. This could be actually eliminated if the animacy attribute *ANI=UN**F** (**Female**)* could be considered, a case left for future developments of this work. Example (6) illustrates another issue namely that of a potential relations that cannot be captured by the existing vocabulary; i.e. a tautology. For such relations there seems to be a *default* one, labeled, *Relationship* which is defined as "A class whose members are a particular type of connection existing between people related to or having dealings with each other", which we also use[5].

(4) <ENAMEX TYPE="PRS" SBT="HUM" ANI="UNF"> *Mafalda*</ENAMEX> *var van att se upp till syster* <ENAMEX TYPE ="PRS" SBT="HUM" ANI="FAF"> *Linda*</ENAMEX>; i.e., “Mafalda was used to seeing up to sister Linda”

(5) <ENAMEX TYPE="PRS" SBT="HUM" ANI="UNM"> *Ivar*</ENAMEX> *eggade med minspel och ögonkast brodern att trotsa, medan* <ENAMEX TYPE="PRS" SBT= "HUM" ANI="UNF">*Stina* </ENAMEX>; i.e., “Ivar edged with facial expressions and looks brother to defy, while Stina”

(6) <ENAMEX TYPE="PRS" SBT="HUM" ANI="UNU"> *Modén*</ENAMEX> *som av kamraterna också kallades* <ENAMEX TYPE="PRS" SBT="HUM" ANI="UNU"> *Moderat*</ENAMEX>; i.e., “Modén who of the colleagues also called Moderat”

[5] Here we could imagine an "Identical" relation since both names refer to the same individual. As a matter of fact we have recently initiated work in order to extend the list with missing relation types.

(4′) *Mafalda=>syster/*SiblingOf *=> Linda*
SiblingOf (Mafalda, Linda)
(5′) **Ivar=>brodern/*SiblingOf *=> Stina*
?SiblingOf (Ivar, Stina)
(6′) *Modén => kallades/Relationship => Moderat*
Relationship(Modén, Moderat))

5 Results

The context similarity between extracted pairs of entities can be measured in various ways. We applied hierarchical clustering (Seo & Shneiderman, 2002) with complete linkage and with cosine similarity as a similarity measure. We then manually evaluated obtained clusters and picked-up the top-5 most frequent words in these clusters as a means to characterize the cluster and tried to map these to the RELATIONSHIP vocabulary. Unfortunately, this activity revealed limitations since it was challenging to point to an appropriate label possibly because the data was *too* limited in size and also because most clusters had very few members (see more discussion below). For the evaluation (Precision, Recall and F-score) we chose to examine in more detail three randomly distinct volumes (see the References' section). *Precision (Pr)* is the fraction of relation instances that is correct, and for clustering Pr_{hc} the correct contexts that could be mapped among the contexts clustered automatically. *Recall (R)* is the fraction of relation instances that has been correctly extracted among all possible that involve two person named entities.

Table 1 summarizes these results, here *All* is the number of all window sizes with two person entities for a book and *<4* the number of contexts matched with the pattern matching approach. The abbreviated B1-B3 stand for the three volumes examined; B1 (Almqvist, 1847); B2 (Lo-Johansson, 1935) and B3 (Bergman, 1910).

	All	*<4*	$Pr_{<4}$	$R_{<4}$	$F_{<4}$	Pr_{hc}
B1	428	219	91.7% *24 rels*	70,6%	79,7%	47,1%
B2	227	115	93,7% *16 rels*	84,2%	88,7%	39,8%
B3	130	80	100% *9 rels*	75%	85,7%	41,8%

Table 1: Evaluation of relations in three books
$F_{<4}=2\times Pr\times R/Pr+R$

We manually inspected the <4 contexts and we found that only a small fraction of those (9) were wrong due to errors produced by the named entity tagger, e.g., <ENAMEX TYPE="PRS" SBT="HUM" ANI="UNM">*Kring*</ENAMEX> *sig hade* <ENAMEX

TYPE="PRS" SBT="HUM" ANI="UNU">*Kurt*</ENAMEX> *några...*; i.e., "Around him had Kurt some...", here *Kring* is simply an adverb..

6 Discussion

Our preliminary results showed that we need different strategies for modeling context between entities of interest and accordingly we have separated this modeling into two different relation detection methods, for short and longer context depending on the number of tokens intervening between named entities (within a single sentence). As one might expect, the use of patterns over very short contexts is much more successful than the clustering approach taken for long contexts. It seems that the unsupervised relation discovery approach is inappropriate to the application of extracting relationships from individual works of fiction. A problem with clustering such contexts is that one often gets a lot of small clusters and labeling is hard. Possibly because other work in the field or relation extraction generally assumes a very large corpus of (mainly) news texts, where relationships can be expected to be expressed multiple times in different documents and precision is improved through aggregation of mentions. However, in an individual work of fiction relationship are not expressed multiple times but rather once or twice. Therefore, this requires approaches with very high accuracy on individual relation mentions.

There is still another method that it would be lies in the gray zone between pattern matching and clustering. For instance Riloff (1996) applied more *generalised patterns* using regular expressions, e.g., *X* * *daughter* * *Y* where *X* and *Y* are person entities and * is any string of tokens, and she showed good results with this approach back in the 1990s.

The combined relations extracted can be viewed as a social network, i.e. a graph of relationships that indicate the important entities in a literary work and can be used to study or summarise interactions. The networks could also provide an alternative to standard presentation of information retrieval results when interacting with a litterary collection, e.g. by providing browsable representation of entities and their relationships that link to text passages where they are described.

Our first attempt to character profiling resulted in moderate precision and recall scores, at least for the clustering approach. But we believe that there is also plenty of scope for improvements and even of new research directions. For example, negations and speculative language might be a tricky issue since it can completely change the scope of a relation, e.g., *Han visste, att* <ENAMEX TYPE="PRS" SBT="HUM" ANI="UNF">*Mafalda* </ENAMEX> *icke tyckte om* <ENAMEX TYPE="PRS" SBT="HUM" ANI="UNM">*Zini*</ENAMEX> i.e., "He knew that Mafalda didn't like Zini". There are other issues that so far we have not confronted with, such as nameless characters, infrequently-appearing named characters, questions and opinions that once again can change the quality of a social network one experiences in a novel, e.g., *do you think X likes Y?*.

7 Conclusions

This paper has reported on initial experiments to automate character profiling in 19th century Swedish prose fiction. Profile implies intra-sentential relationship discovery between person entities. The aim is to support the users of digitized literature collections with tools that enable semantic search and browsing. In this sense, we can offer new ways for exploring the volumes of literary texts being made available through cultural heritage digitization projects.

In the future we also intend to even elaborate with relationships between main characters and other categories driven by named entities, such as between persons and locations and improve both the quantity and quality of the results. This way we can also extract significant properties of the characters and not only interpersonal relationships. It should be fairly straightforward since named entities can be reliably identified and a similar methodology as the one outlined in this paper can be applied. Applying other types of named entity types will eventually detect more relations about the characters and this will make the profiling more comprehensive than at the moment, which will reveal a clearer picture of the main characters' activities and associations. Another issue that needs attention is contexts with conjunctive mentions of entities, e.g. *X and Y*, since tokens in the near context might be good indicators of a relations as in the example: *Bröderne* <ENAMEX TYPE="PRS" SBT="HUM" ANI= "UNM">*Tage*</ENAMEX> *och* <ENAMEX TYPE="PRS" SBT="HUM" ANI="UNM">*Robert*</ENAMEX>, i.e. "The brothers Tage and Robert".

At the moment we are looking at *explicit* relationships supported by textual evidence and did not include relations that dependent on the reader's understanding of the document's meaning and/or her world knowledge, also a number of implicit relations could be inferred (e.g. *X ChildOf Y* implies *Y ParentOf X*). Moreover we would like to explore co-reference (pronominal references) since it plays an important role for profiling (biographical) extraction and for recognizing a larger set of relations between characters. Also *learning* of relationships in a complementary fashion in the future is envisaged and we plan to annotate data for this purpose.

Acknowledgments

This work is partially supported by the Centre for Language Technology (CLT) <http://clt.gu.se/> and the project *19th Century Sweden in the Mirror of Prose Fiction* financed by the "Research infrastructures" programme by the Swedish Research Council.

References

Carl Jonas Love Almqvist. 1847. *Herrarne på Ekolsund, del 1&2*. Samlade Verk 31. Almqvist & Wiksell International

Eugene Agichtein and Luis Gravano L. 2000. Snowball: Extracting Relations from large Plain-Text Collections. Proceedings of the 5th ACM International Conf. on Digital Libraries. New York.

Hjalmar Bergman. 1910. *Amourer*. Albert Bonniers Förlag, Stockholm.

Lars Borin, Dimitrios Kokkinakis and Leif-Jöran Olsson. 2007. Naming the Past: Named Entity and Animacy Recognition in 19th Century Swedish Literature. Workshop on Language Technology for Cultural Heritage Data (LaTeCH 2007), pages 1–8. Prague.

Lars Borin, Dana Dannélls, Markus Forsberg, Maria Toporowska Gronostaj and Dimitrios Kokkinakis. 2009. Thinking Green: Toward Swedish FrameNet++. Proceedings of the FrameNet Masterclass and Workshop. Milan, Italy.

Lars Borin and Markus Forsberg. 2010. Beyond the synset: Swesaurus – a fuzzy Swedish wordnet. Proceedings of the symposium: Re-thinking synonymy: semantic sameness and similarity in languages and their description. Helsinki, Finland.

Lars Borin and Dimitrios Kokkinakis. 2010. Literary Onomastics and Language Technology. In *Literary Education and Digital Learning. Methods and Technologies for Humanities Studies*. van Peer W., Zyngier S., Viana V. (eds). Pp. 53-78. IGI Global.

Janara Christensen, Mausam, Stephen Soderland and Oren Etzioni. 2010. Semantic Role Labeling for Open Information Extraction. Proceedings of the NAACL HLT First International Workshop on Formalisms and Methodology for Learning by Reading. Pp 52–60, Los Angeles, California.

Ian Davis and Eric Vitiello Jr E. 2010. RELATIONSHIP: A vocabulary for describing relationships between people. <http://vocab.org/relationship/ .html>.

David K. Elson, Nicholas Dames, Kathleen R. McKeown. 2010. Extracting Social Networks from Literary Fiction. Proceedings of the 48th Annual Meeting of the Association for Computational Linguistics (ACL 2010), Uppsala, Sweden.

George Doddington, Alexis Mitchell, Mark Przybocki, Lance Ramshaw, Stephanie Strassel and Ralph Weischedel. 2004. The automatic content extraction (ACE) program tasks, data, and evaluation. Proc of the 4th Int Conf on Language Resources and Evaluation (LREC), pp 837–840, Lisbon.

Michael Fleischman and Eduard Hovy. 2002. Fine Grained Classification of Named Entities. Proceedings of the 19th International Conference on Computational Linguistics. Taipei, Taiwan. 1–7.

Cory B. Giles and Jonathan D. Wren. 2008. Large-scale directional relationship extraction and resolution. BMC Bioinformatics 2008, 9 (Suppl 9): S11doi:10.1186/1471-2105-9-S9-S11.

Benjamin Hachey 2009, *Towards Generic Relation Extraction*. PhD Thesis. Institute for Communicating and Collaborative Systems School of Informatics, University of Edinburgh.

Takaaki Hasegawa, Satoshi Sekine and Ralph Grishman. 2004. Discovering relations among named entities from large corpora. The 42nd Annual Meeting on Association for Computational Linguistics. Barcelona, Spain.

Hongyan Jing, Nanda Kambhatla, and Salim Roukos. (2007). Extracting social networks and biographical facts from conversational speech transcripts. Proceedings of the 45th Meeting of the Assoc. of Computational Linguistics, Prague, Czech Rep.

Chen Jinxiu. 2007. *Automatic relation extraction among named entities from text contents*. PhD thesis, University of Singapore.

Ivar Lo-Johansson. 1935. *Kungsgatan*. Albert Bonniers Förlag, Stockholm.

Dimitrios Kokkinakis. 2004 Reducing the Effect of Name Explosion. LREC Workshop: Beyond Named Entity Recognition, Semantic Labelling for NLP tasks. 4th LREC. Lissabon, Portugal.

Constantin Orasan and Richard Evans. 2001. Learning to Identify Animate References. Proceedings of the Workshop on Computational Natural Language Learning (CoNLL-2001). Toulouse, France.

Ellen Riloff. 1996. Automatically Generating Extraction Patterns form Untagged Text. Proceedings of the Thirteenth National Conference on Artificial Intelligence (AAAI-96), pp. 1044-1049.

Angus Roberts, Robert Gaizauskas and Mark Hepple. 2008. Extracting Clinical Relationships from Patient Narratives. BioNLP 2008. Pp 10–18, Ohio, USA.

Barbara Rosario and Marti A. Hearst. 2004. Classifying Semantic relations in Bioscience Texts. Proceedings of the 42nd Annual Meeting on ACL. Barcelona, Spain.

Satoshi Sekine. 2004. Definition, Dictionaries and Tagger for Extended Named Entity Hierarchy. Proceedings of the Language Resources and Evaluation Conf (LREC). Lisbon, Portugal.

Jinwook Seo and Ben Shneiderman, 2002. Interactively Exploring Hierarchical Clustering Results. IEEE Computer, Vol. 35:7, pp. 80-86. <http://www.cs.umd.edu/ hcil/hce/>

Diachronic Stylistic Changes in British and American Varieties of 20th Century Written English Language

Sanja Štajner and **Ruslan Mitkov**
Research Group in Computational Linguistics
University of Wolverhampton
Stafford Street, Wolverhampton, WV1 1SB, UK
{S.Stajner, R.Mitkov}@wlv.ac.uk

Abstract

In this paper we present the results of a study investigating the diachronic changes of four stylistic features: average sentence length, Automated Readability Index, lexical density and lexical richness in 20th century written English language. All experiments were conducted on the largest existing diachronic corpora of British and American English – the Brown 'family' corpora, employing NLP techniques for automatic extraction of the features. Additionally, we compare the trends of changes between the two English varieties and make suggestions for future studies of diachronic language change.

1 Introduction

As time elapses, language changes and those changes are present at various levels of the language structure: vocabulary, phonology, morphology and syntax (Kroch, 2001). Most of the previous studies of language change in English tended to focus on the phonetic and lexical rather than the stylistic or syntactic changes. Furthermore, the vast majority of the early sociolinguistic and historical linguistic studies of language change did not provide textual evidence for their claims, i.e. they were not corpus-based or the used corpora were not large and representative enough. Bauer (1994) set higher methodological standards for diachronic studies as he was among the first who sought to support his statements with textual evidence (Mair and Leech, 2006).

In his study of authorship attribution, Holmes (1994) defines style of the text "as a set of measurable patterns which may be unique to an author". In the context of language change, this definition could be slightly amended and the style defined as a set of measurable patterns which may be unique to a particular period of time. In an extensive overview of applications in stylochronometric approaches in the last sixty years (Stamou, 2008) it is hypothesised that changes in certain aspects of an author's writing style ought to be detectable by using appropriate methods and stylistic markers. Inspired by this hypothesis, one of the main goals of our study is to investigate whether diachronic changes in certain aspects of the writing style used in a specific text genre can be detected by using the appropriate methods and stylistic markers (features).

Different authors, even from the same period of time, will exhibit various styles. Consequently, this will be epitomised by very heterogeneous results in each observed year and genre, making general changes in style not readily detectable. Therefore, our first goal is to establish a methodology which would be appropriate for the investigation of these types of diachronic changes. This would lead to more precise and statistically justified conclusions in the corpus-based studies of diachronic linguistics.

Our second goal is to explore diachronic changes of several well-known stylistic markers: average sentence length, Automated Readability Index, lexical density and lexical richness in two major English language varieties – British and American and to detect whether those changes were present in both of those varieties. As we are using the mutually comparable corpora of British and American English, we are able to compare the changes of these two language varieties and to examine whether they followed the same trends of stylistic changes.

We base our methodology on the largest publicly available diachronic corpora of the 20th century written English language – Brown 'family' corpora (Leech and Smith, 2005) and NLP tools provided by the state-of-the-art Connexor Machinese Syntax parser[1].

[1] www.connexor.eu

2 Related Work

Various studies in the field of stylistic variation and change use both the historical and sociolinguistic approach. Typical examples of this can be seen in the early studies of author's and period styles (Gordon, 1966; Adolph, 1968; Bennett, 1971). A preponderance of subsequent studies allude to the textual dimensions and relations used in Biber (1988) and follow the works of Biber and Finegan (1986, 1988, 1989). Westin (2002) and Westin and Geisler (2002) explore stylistic changes in the 20th century in the Corpus of English Newspaper Editorials (CENE) across the five linguistic dimensions described in (Biber and Finegan, 1988). They employ the methodology based on a multi-dimensional framework presented in (Biber, 1985; 1988).

The emergence of the FLOB and Frown corpora in the 1990s, compared with the previous LOB and Brown corpora, offered new possibilities for diachronic studies of written English language in the 20th century across two major English varieties – American and British English. Mair and Hundt (1995), Mair (1997, 2002), Mair, Hundt, Leech and Smith (2002), Smith (2002, 2003a, 2003b), Leech (2003, 2004), Leech and Smith (2006) and Mair and Leech (2006) exploited the possibilities of the Brown 'family' corpora by investigating the trends of changes in various lexical, grammatical and syntactic features. All of these studies were conducted on manually corrected POS tagged corpora and used the log likelihood test as a measure of the statistical significance of the results.

To our best knowledge, there is no mention of any investigation of diachronic changes of the four stylistic features we used in our study nor studies which describe automatic extraction of the features from the raw text corpora by using NLP techniques. All methodologies used in the previous studies of language changes required a great amount of human annotation or manual corrections which are time-consuming and labour-intensive or they relied on the use of very specific language tools.

3 Corpora

The Brown 'family' corpora (Leech and Smith, 2005) consist of four mutually comparable corpora publicly available as part of the ICAME Corpus Collection[2]. Two of these contain texts written in British English, published in 1961 and 1991, respectively:

- The Lancaster-Oslo/Bergen Corpus of British English (**LOB**)
- The Freiburg-LOB Corpus of British English (**FLOB**)

The other two contain texts written in American English, published in 1961 and 1992, respectively:

- The Brown University corpus of written American English (**Brown**)
- The Freiburg-Brown Corpus of American English (**Frown**)

All four corpora share the same sampling frame, as the LOB[3], FLOB[4] and Frown[5] corpora were designed to closely match the structure of the Brown corpus[6] with the aim to provide an opportunity to compare diachronic changes within two major varieties of the written English language (Leech and Smith, 2005).

Each corpus is a one-million-word corpus, consisting of 500 texts of about 2000 running words each, selected at a random point in the original source. The sampling range covers 15 text genres, which can be grouped into four more generalised categories:

- **Press** (Press: Reportage; Press: Editorial; Press: Review)
- **General Prose** (Religion; Skills, Trades and Hobbies; Popular Lore; Belles Lettres, Biographies, Essays)
- **Learned** (Miscellaneous; Science)
- **Fiction** (General Fiction; Mystery and Detective Fiction; Science Fiction; Adventure and Western; Romance and Love Story; Humour)

In this study we separately investigate diachronic stylistic changes in each of the four main text categories.

[2] http://www.hit.uib.no/icame
[3] http://khnt.aksis.uib.no/icame/manuals/lob/
[4] http://khnt.aksis.uib.no/icame/manuals/flob/
[5] http://khnt.aksis.uib.no/icame/manuals/frown/
[6] http://khnt.aksis.uib.no/icame/manuals/brown/

4 Methodology

Although all four corpora are available in their tagged versions with the annotated sentence boundaries, those boundaries are not consistent throughout them. The LOB and FLOB tagged versions were manually corrected and therefore 100% accurate, while the Brown and Frown corpora are not manually corrected. Furthermore, some inconsistencies regarding the sentence boundaries in the cases of direct speech and itemised sentences are present among different corpora. Therefore, we decided to use the raw text versions of the LOB, FLOB, Brown and Frown corpora (divided into original portions of 500 texts of approximately 2,000 words each) and parse them with the Connexor Machinese Syntax parser in order to achieve more consistent sentence splitting, tokenisation and lemmatisation. The sentence boundaries identified by the parser offered a fairer comparison of the results among the corpora which was of primary importance for this study.

Connexor Machinese Syntax parser is based on linguistic methods and its lexicon contains hundreds of thousands of base forms. For compilation of the lexicon various large corpora were used, among which the most common were news texts, bureaucratic documents and literature (Connexor Oy, 2006b). In cases when the word cannot be found in the lexicon, word class and base form are determined by using the heuristic methods (Connexor Oy, 2006b). POS accuracy of the Machinese Syntax parser measured on Standard Written English (benchmark from the Maastricht Treaty) was 99.3% with no ambiguity (Connexor Oy, 2006b). The earlier research of Samuelsson and Voutilainen (1997) reported excellent accuracy of the software used as the base for the current version of the parser. The fact that the lexicon of the Machinese parser was built by using similar text genres as those represented in the Brown 'family' corpora ensures a high accuracy of the analysis completed in this study.

In the following two sub-sections we list some of the specificities of the tokenisation and lemmatisation procedures used by the Machinese parser. This is important for better understanding and interpreting the results provided in this study.

4.1 Tokenisation

The Connexor Machinese parser has a specific treatment of the contracted negative form and *'s*.

Contracted negative form and its antecedent verb are treated as separate tokens. E.g. in the case of *isn't*, the verb and negation are treated as two separate tokens *is* and *not* and correspondingly as two separate base forms *be* and *not*.

Treatment of *'s* depends on its role in the sentence (Connexor Oy, 2006a). In the cases where *'s* represents a genitive form, e.g. " ... *Roy's United Federal Party* ..." (LOB:A01), *Roy's* is treated as one token *Roy's* and corresponding base form is *roy*. In other cases where *'s* represents the contraction of the verb *to be (is)* or *to have (has)*, e.g. " ... *he's nice* ... " (LOB:P05), the personal pronoun and verb contraction are treated as two separate tokens – *he* and *is*. Accordingly, they are treated as two separate base forms – *he* and *be*.

4.2 Lemmatisation

In this sub-section, we describe the results of the lemmatisation process for the three word types – possessive pronouns, derived adverbs and EN and ING forms, as they differ between the current and the previous versions of the parser.

4.2.1 Base forms of possessive pronouns and derived adverbs

The current version of the Machinese parser assigns to possessive pronouns their own base forms (lemmas), e.g. the base form of the word *yours* in the current version of the parser is *yours*, while in the previous versions possessive pronouns were assigned the base forms of their corresponding personal pronouns, e.g. the base form of the word *yours* in the previous versions of the parser was *you* (Connexor Oy, 2006b).

Base forms of derived adverbs, e.g. *immediately, fundamentally, absolutely, directly* (LOB:A01) are assigned *immediately, fundamentally, absolutely, directly* as their base forms in the current version of the parser while in the previous versions they were assigned the following base forms: *immediate, fundamental, absolute, direct.*

4.2.2 EN and ING forms

The current version of the parser assigns different base forms for EN and ING forms which represent the present or past participle of a verb than for those representing corresponding nouns or adjectives. Previous versions of the parser were assigning the same base forms for all four possible cases of EN and ING forms. For example, in the sentence:

"The Government decided to adjust the financing ..." (LOB:A01)

the assigned base form for the noun *financing* is *financing* while the older versions of the parser would assign *finance* as the base form for the same word *financing* in the given context.

Similarly, in the sentence:

"Sir Roy is violently opposed to Africans getting an elected majority in Northern Rhodesia ..." (LOB:A01)

the assigned base form for the adjective *elected* is *elected* while the older versions of the parser would assign *elect* as the base form for the same word *elected* in the given context.

In the above sentence, the words *opposed* and *getting* are assigned *oppose* and *get* as the base forms in all versions of the Machinese parser, as they represent the past and present participle of the verbs *oppose* and *get*, respectively.

5 Experimental settings

We conducted two sets of experiments:

- Stylistic diachronic changes in British English in the period 1961–1991
- Stylistic diachronic changes in American English in the period 1961–1992

The first experiment was conducted on LOB (1961) and FLOB (1991) corpora and the second experiment on Brown (1961) and Frown (1992) corpora.

In both experiments we investigated the diachronic changes over the four main text categories: Press, General Prose, Learned and Fiction separately, as the preliminary results had shown different trends of changes among these four text categories.

As stylistic markers we used the following four features:

- Average sentence length (ASL)
- Automated Readability Index (ARI)
- Lexical density (LD)
- Lexical richness (LR)

Average sentence length was measured as the total number of words divided by the total number of sentences for each text (eq.1), using the sentence and word boundaries returned by the parser. Words containing only punctuation marks were not counted.

$$ASL = \frac{total\_number\_of\_words}{total\_number\_of\_sentences} \quad (1)$$

Automated Readability Index (Senter and Smith, 1967; Smith and Kincaid, 1970) belongs to the formative era of readability studies and was listed among eleven most commonly used readability formulas (McCallum and Peterson, 1982) of that time. It is calculated using the following formula:

$$ARI = 4.71\frac{c}{w} + 0.5\frac{w}{s} - 21.43 \quad (2)$$

where *c*, *w* and *s* represent, respectively, total number of characters, words and sentences in the text. The result of the Automated Readability Index gives the US grade level necessary to understand the given text.

Lexical density is computed as the number of unique word types (tokens) divided by the total number of tokens in the text (eq.3).

$$LD = \frac{number\_of\_unique\_tokens}{total\_number\_of\_tokens} \quad (3)$$

Low lexical density indicates many repetitions of the same words throughout the text, while high lexical density suggests a use of a wider range of vocabulary. This feature has been used as a stylistic marker in (Ule, 1982) and for dating works in (Smith and Kelly, 2002).

Lexical richness is computed as the number of unique lemmas divided by the total number of tokens in the text (eq.4).

$$LR = \frac{number\_of\_unique\_lemmas}{total\_number\_of\_tokens} \quad (4)$$

The use of lexical richness separately from lexical density was proposed by Corpas Pastor et al. (2008) who argued that "lexical density is not indicative of the vocabulary variety of an author as it counts morphological variants of the same word as different word types". Following this argument, we make a distinction between lexical density and lexical richness and investigate both features separately.

6 Results and Discussion

The results of the first and second experiment are given separately (sub-sections 6.1 and 6.2, respectively). The results of each experiment are divided into two tables, where the first table contains the results of the investigation of diachronic changes of ASL and ARI, and the second table contains results of the investigation of diachronic changes of LD and LR. Each feature contains two columns – 'change' and 'p'.

Column 'change' represents the relative change of the feature over the period 1961–1991/2, measured as a percentage of the starting value in 1961. The sign before the value signifies the direction of the change; '+' corresponds to an increase and '−' to a decrease. Both the starting and ending values in years 1961 and 1991/2, respectively, were previously calculated as an arithmetic mean of the feature values in all texts of the relevant text category (Press, Prose, Learned or Fiction) and corpus (LOB or FLOB in the sub-section 6.1 or Brown and Frown in the sub-section 6.2).

Column 'p' represents the p-value of the two-tailed t-test applied on the results obtained for each text separately (in the corresponding text category and corpus) and used as a measure of statistical significance. For the results with a p-value lower than the chosen critical value 0.05, we are more than 95% sure that they represent real diachronic changes rather than being a consequence of faulty sampling. Those results were considered as statistically significant and reliable enough to be used for making further hypotheses.

Given that the corpora used in the two experiments are mutually comparable, we are able to make a comparison of the trends of changes between British and American English in sub-section 6.3.

6.1 Diachronic changes in British English

Results of the first experiment – diachronic stylistic changes in British English over the period 1961–1991 are presented in Table 1 and Table 2.

Genre	ASL		ARI	
	change	**p**	**change**	**p**
Press	+4.39%	0.114	**+6.43%**	**0.046**
Prose	+1.64%	0.490	**+9.07%**	**0.002**
Learned	−5.05%	0.060	+3.07%	0.254
Fiction	−4.85%	0.184	−1.97%	0.726

Table 1: British English: ASL and ARI.

Automated Readability Index shows a statistically significant increase over the observed period 1961–1991 in the Press and Prose text categories (Table 1) which can be interpreted as a tendency to render texts in these categories in a difficult-to-read manner.

The results of the first experiment (Table 1) indicate that ASL did not change significantly in the period 1961–1991 in any of the four investigated text categories of British English.

Genre	LD		LR	
	change	**p**	**change**	**p**
Press	**+7.43%**	**0.000**	**+7.17%**	**0.000**
Prose	**+3.90%**	**0.000**	**+4.40%**	**0.000**
Learned	+2.35%	0.248	+1.76%	0.416
Fiction	**+3.92%**	**0.008**	**+4.28%**	**0.012**

Table 2: British English: LD and LR.

On the basis of the data analysed (Table 2), we can draw the conclusion that the vocabulary was enriched in three text categories of British English – Press, Prose and Fiction, over the observed period 1961–1991. The strongest intensity of these changes can be noticed in the Press category.

6.2 Diachronic changes in American English

Results of the second experiment – diachronic stylistic changes in American English over the period 1961–1992 are presented in Table 3 and Table 4.

Genre	ASL		ARI	
	change	**p**	**change**	**p**
Press	**−4.90%**	**0.034**	−1.43%	0.598
Prose	−3.35%	0.164	+3.32%	0.242
Learned	**−10.49%**	**0.000**	−3.29%	0.278
Fiction	−7.37%	0.058	−9.92%	0.082

Table 3: American English: ASL and ARI.

The Press and Learned text categories manifested a decrease of ASL in the observed period 1961–1992 (Table 3). This could be interpreted as an example of colloquialisation – "a tendency for the written language gradually to acquire norms and characteristics associated with the spoken conversational language" (Leech, 2004), as it is known that shorter sentences are a characteristic of the spoken language.

The results in Table 3 indicate that ARI did not change significantly in the period 1961–1991 in any of the four investigated text categories of American English.

Lexical density and lexical richness demonstrated a statistically significant increase only in the Prose text category (Table 4).

Genre	LD		LR	
	change	p	change	p
Press	+2.03%	0.084	+0.71%	0.588
Prose	**+4.06%**	**0.000**	**+3.85%**	**0.004**
Learned	+3.89%	0.082	+3.90%	0.092
Fiction	−2.51%	0.106	−3.04%	0.088

Table 4: American English: LD and LR.

These results lead to the conclusion that the vocabulary used in the Prose category of American English was enriched over the observed period 1961–1992.

6.3 British vs. American diachronic changes

From the results presented in the above four tables we are able to make a comparison of the trends of diachronic changes between British and American English for the four investigated stylistic features and provide some general observations.

The central conclusion is that British and American English do not follow the same trends of stylistic diachronic changes in all genres and for all features. The most striking differences are in the cases of ASL and ARI. They demonstrated statistically significant changes in only one of the two investigated varieties of the English language. ASL had a statistically significant decrease in the Press and Learned categories of American English over the period 1961–1991 (Table 3), while at the same time did not manifest any statistically significant changes in any of the four text categories of British English (Table 1). ARI demonstrated a statistically significant increase in the Press and Prose categories of British English (Table 1) and no statistically significant changes in any of the four text categories of American English (Table 3).

LD and LR manifested a statistically significant increase in three text categories of British English – Press, Prose and Fiction (Table 2). In American English, this trend was followed only in the Press category, while the other two text categories – Prose and Fiction, did not exhibit any statistically significant changes of LD or LR (Table 4).

In order to better understand noticed diachronic changes and investigate possible influence between the two English language varieties, we conducted an additional experiment of synchronic comparison between British and American English in both starting and ending years – 1961 and 1991/2, for each genre and each feature separately. These results were consistent with the results of the previous two experiments – diachronic changes in British and diachronic changes in American English, thus supporting the hypotheses made in the previous two subsections.

Of most interest were the results obtained from the Press category (Table 5), as they suggested the presence of Americanisation – "the influence of north American habits of expression and behaviour on the UK (and other nations)" (Leech, 2004) in the observed period 1961-1991/2. They indicated that the influence between the British and American English written styles was more pronounced in the Press category than in the other three – Prose, Learned and Fiction.

Feature	1961		1991/2	
	Br.	Am.	Br.	Am.
ASL	20.63	21.50	**21.53***	**20.45**
ARI	**11.34**	**12.08***	12.07	11.91
LD	**36.37**	**37.65***	39.08	38.41
LR	**32.61**	**33.83***	34.95	34.07

Table 5: Synchronic comparison: Press category.

In Table 5, the value of the LD and LR calculated using equations 3 and 4 (Section 5) is multiplied by 100. Statistical significance of the differences between the feature values in British and American English is measured by the two-tailed t-test. The results significant at the 0.05 level are shown in bold. In those cases, the higher of the two values (Br. or Am.) is marked with an '*'.

Statistically significant increases of the ARI, LD and LR in the Press category of British English during the period 1961–1991 (Table 1 and Table 2) together with the significantly higher values of these features in the same text category of American English in 1961 (Table 5) could be explained using the aforementioned Americanisation hypothesis.

7 Conclusions

On the basis of the data analysed in the previous section, we can draw the following conclusions about the trends of stylistic changes in the British and American varieties of English language over the period 1961–1991/2:

1) The Prose text category followed the same trend of enriching the vocabulary in both varieties of the English language.

2) Average sentence length had a statistically significant decrease in the Press and Learned text categories in American English and no statistically significant changes in any of the four text categories in British English.

3) Automated Readability Index had a statistically significant increase in the Press and Prose text categories in British English and no statistically significant changes in any of the four text categories in American English.

Additionally, the presented study allowed us to make several more general conclusions:

1) NLP tools can be successfully used in the studies of language change and make use of the raw text corpora customising it for the specific purposes thus saving a great amount of human effort for annotation or manual corrections.

2) Stylistic changes are present and are noticeable even after the 30 year time gap in various categories of the written language.

3) Different genres show different trends of stylistic changes over the same period of time. Therefore, it is of great importance to investigate them separately in order to obtain a better picture of the process of language change and the possible influences between different genres.

4) As different language varieties show different trends of stylistic changes inside the same text categories, no general conclusions about the trends of stylistic changes should be made before a detailed investigation in each of the language varieties. Furthermore, results of the separate investigations of stylistic changes among different language varieties enable a better understanding of the noticed trends and their possible mutual influence. However, it is important to ensure that the corpora of different language varieties are mutually comparable and thus any similarities or differences among their trends of change are not due to different sampling methods and text selection.

Finally, we demonstrated the possibility of using the Brown 'family' corpora and NLP techniques for the investigation of diachronic stylistic changes. It has created a path for many other stylistic features to be investigated using the same corpora and utilising the full potential of the current state-of-the-art NLP tools and techniques.

Acknowledgements

This project was supported by the European Commission, Education & Training, Erasmus Mundus: EMMC 2008-0083, Erasmus Mundus Masters in NLP & HLT.

References

Adolph Robert. 1966. *The Rise of Modern Prose Style*. Cambridge, Mass.: M.I.T. Press.

Bauer Laurie. 1994. *Watching English change: and introduction to the study of linguistic change in standard English in the twentieth century*. London: Longman.

Bennett R. James. 1971. *Prose Style: A Historical Approach through Studies*. San Francisco: Chandler.

Biber Douglas. 1985. Investigating Macroscopic Textual Variation through Multifeature / Multidimensional Analyses. *Linguistics*, 23: 337–360.

Biber Douglas and Finegan Edward. 1986. An Initial Typology of English Text Types. In: J. Aarts and W. Meijs, eds. *Corpus Linguistics H: New Studies in the Analysis and Exploitation of Computer Corpora*. Amsterdam, Rodopi, 19–46.

Biber Douglas. 1988. *Variation across speech and writing*. Cambridge: Cambridge University Press.

Biber Douglas and Finegan Edward. 1988. Drift in three English genres from the 18th to the 20th century: A multi-dimensional approach. In: M. Kyt, O. Ihalainen, and M. Rissanen, eds. *Corpus linguistics, hard and soft. Proceedings of the Eighth International Conference on English Language Research on Computerized Corpora*: 83–101. Amsterdam: Rodopi.

Biber Douglas and Finegan Edward. 1989. Drift and the evolution of English style: A history of three genres. *Language*, 65: 487–517.

Connexor Oy. 2006a. *Machinese Language Model*.

Connexor Oy. 2006b. *Machinese Language Analysers*.

Corpas Pastor Gloria, Mitkov Ruslan, Afzal Navid and Pekar Viktor. 2008. Translation Universals: Do they exist? A corpus-based NLP study of convergence and simplification. *In Proceedings of the AMTA*. Waikiki, Hawaii.

Gordon A. Ian. 1966. *The Movement of English Prose*. Bloomington: Indiana University Press.

Holmes I. David. 1994. Authorship Attribution. *Computers and the Humanities*, 28(2): 87–106. Springer Netherlands.

Kroch Anthony. 2001. Syntactic change. In: M. Baltin and C. Collins, eds. *The Handbook of Contemporary Syntactic Theory*. Malden, MA: Blackwells, 699–730.

Leech Geoffrey. 2003. Modality on the move: the English modal auxiliaries 1961-1992. In: R. Facchinetti, M. Krug and F. Palmer, eds. *Modality in contemporary English*. Berlin/New York: Mouton de Gruyter, 223–240.

Leech Geoffrey. 2004. Recent grammatical change in English: data, description, theory. In: K. Aijmer and B. Altenberg, eds. *Advances in Corpus Linguistics: Papers from the 23rd International Conference on English Language Research on Computerized Corpora (ICAME 23) Gteborg 22-26 May 2002*. Amsterdam: Rodopi, 61–81.

Leech Geoffrey and Smith Nicholas. 2005. Extending the possibilities of corpus-based research on English in the twentieth century: a prequel to LOB and FLOB. *ICAME Journal*, 29: 83–98.

Leech Geoffrey and Smith Nicholas. 2006. Recent grammatical change in written English 1961–1992: some preliminary findings of a comparison of American with British English. In: A. Renouf and A. Kehoe, eds. *The Changing Face of Corpus Linguistics*. Amsterdam: Rodopi, 186–204.

Mair Christian and Hundt Marianne. 1995. Why is the progressive becoming more frequent in English? A corpus-based investigation of language change in progress. *Zeitschrift fr Anglistik und Amerikanistik*, 43: 111–122.

Mair Christian. 1997. The spread of the going-to-future in written English: a corpus-based investigation into language change in progress. In: R. Hickey and St. Puppel, eds. *Language history and linguistic modelling: a festschrift for Jacek Fisiak on his 60th birthday*. Berlin: Mouton de Gruyter, 1536–1543.

Mair Christian. 2002. Three changing patterns of verb complementation in Late Modern English: a real-time study based on matching text corpora. *English Language and Linguistics*, 6: 105–131.

Mair Christian, Hundt Marianne, Leech Geoffrey and Smith Nicholas. 2002. Short term diachronic shifts in part-of-speech frequencies: a comparison of the tagged LOB and F-LOB corpora. *International Journal of Corpus Linguistics*, 7: 245–264.

Mair Christian and Leech Geoffrey. 2006. Current change in English syntax. In: B. Aarts and A. MacMahon, eds. *The Handbook of English Linguistics*, Ch.14. Oxford: Blackwell.

McCallum R. Douglas and Peterson L. James. 1982. Computer-based readability indexes. *In Proceedings of the ACM '82 Conference*: 44–48. New York, NY.

Samuelsson Christer and Voutilainen Atro. 1997. Comparing a linguistic and a stochastic tagger. *Proceedings of the 35th Annual Meeting of the Association for Computational Linguistics and Eighth Conference of the European Chapter of the Association for Computational Linguistics*, (ACL '98): 246–253. Association for Computational Linguistics, Stroudsburg, PA, USA.

Senter, R. J. and Smith E. A. 1967. *Automated readability index*. Technical Report (AMRLTR-66-220). University of Cincinnati, Cincinnati: Ohio.

Smith A. Edgar and Kincaid J. Peter. 1970. Derivation and Validation of the Automated Readability Index for Use with Technical Materials. *Human Factors: The Journal of the Human Factors and Ergonomics Society*, 12(5): 457–464.

Smith A. Joseph and Kelly Colleen. 2002. Stylistic Constancy and Change Across Literary Corpora: Using Measures of Lexical Richness to Date Works. *Computers & the Humanities*, 36(4): 411–431.

Smith Nicholas. 2002. Ever moving on? The progressive in recent British English. In: P. Peters, P. Collins and A. Smith, eds. *New frontiers of corpus research: papers from the twenty first International Conference on English Language Research on Computerized Corpora, Sydney 2000*. Amsterdam: Rodopi, 317–330.

Smith Nicholas. 2003a. A quirky progressive? A corpus-based exploration of the will + be + -ing construction in recent and present day British English. In: D. Archer, P. Rayson, A. Wilson and T. McEnery, eds. *Proceedings of the Corpus Linguistics 2003 Conference*: 714–723. Lancaster University: UCREL Technical Papers.

Smith Nicholas. 2003b. Changes in the modals and semi-modals of strong obligation and epistemic necessity in recent British English. In: R. Facchinetti, M. Krug and F. Palmer, eds. *Modality in contemporary English*. Berlin/New York: Mouton de Gruyter, 241–266.

Stamou Constantina. 2008. Stylochronometry: Stylistic Development, Sequence of Composition, and Relative Dating. *Literary & Linguistic Computing*, 23(2): 181–199.

Ule Louis. 1982. Recent progress in computer methods of authorship determination. *Association of Literary and Linguistic Computing Bulletin*, 10(3): 73–89.

Westin Ingrid and Geisler Christer. 2002. A multi-dimensional study of diachronic variation in British newspaper editorials. *ICAME Journal*, 26: 133–152.

Westin Ingrid. 2002. *Language Change in English Newspaper Editorials*. Amsterdam: Rodopi.

AVATecH: Audio/Video Technology for Humanities Research

Sebastian Tschöpel
Daniel Schneider
Rolf Bardeli
Fraunhofer IAIS
http://www.iais.fraunhofer.de

Oliver Schreer
Stefano Masneri
Fraunhofer HHI
http://www.hhi.fraunhofer.de

Peter Wittenburg
Han Sloetjes
MPI for Psycholinguistics
http://www.mpi.nl/

Przemek Lenkiewicz
Eric Auer
MPI for Psycholinguistics
http://www.mpi.nl/

Abstract

In the AVATecH project the Max-Planck Institute for Psycholinguistics (MPI) and the Fraunhofer institutes HHI and IAIS aim to significantly speed up the process of creating annotations of audio-visual data for humanities research. For this we integrate state-of-the-art audio and video pattern recognition algorithms into the widely used ELAN annotation tool. To address the problem of heterogeneous annotation tasks and recordings we provide modular components extended by adaptation and feedback mechanisms to achieve competitive annotation quality within significantly less annotation time. Currently we are designing a large-scale end-user evaluation of the project.

1 Introduction

The AVATecH project[1] is a collaborative research project between the Max-Planck Institute for Psycholinguistics (MPI) on the one hand and the Fraunhofer Institutes HHI and IAIS on the other hand. The aim of the project is to enable researchers in the field of humanities to significantly speed up their annotation process. This process is inevitable, for example, for carrying out deep linguistic studies (Wittenburg et al., 2010; Masneri et al., 2010).

To reach this goal the Fraunhofer institutes provide audio and video pattern recognition technology for (semi-) automatic extraction of content related annotations. By integrating them into the common annotation process for linguistic research we expect a significant reduction of the overall annotation time. High potential of such technologies and tools for increasing annotation speed has been shown in (Roy and Roy, 2009).

The main challenge in the project is to tackle audio and video pattern recognition where the standard methods based on stochastic engines trained on large training sets cannot be applied to noisy field and complex lab recordings because: (1) there are only small training corpora available; (2) there are in general no models for the languages or visual setups in focus; (3) the recordings are usually of limited quality, e.g., affected by noise in the background or disadvantageous lighting conditions; (4) there are no or only few annotations that can be used to train a model. The central ideas in the AVATecH project are to adapt models to the given annotation scenario and exploit iterative feedback from the human annotator.

2 System Landscape

The system landscape of AVATecH is detailed in Figure 1. The Fraunhofer institutes are technology providers delivering recognizers in form of executables. These recognizers are integrated into existing annotation tools using a common recognizer interface that is based on a derivate of the CMDI (Component Metadata Infrastructure) specification, developed within the CLARIN research infrastructure project (Váradi et al., 2008; Broeder et al., 2010). The annotation tools are developed and maintained by the MPI. The interactive ELAN[2] tool is a widely used, open source annotation tool with a graphical frontend to annotate audiovisual content for linguistic research (Auer et al., 2010; Wittenburg et al., 2006). ELAN is not only used by many of the MPI researchers but also by a lot of other researchers worldwide. The main areas of application include language documentation,

[1] http://www.mpi.nl/avatech/

[2] http://www.lat-mpi.eu/tools/elan/

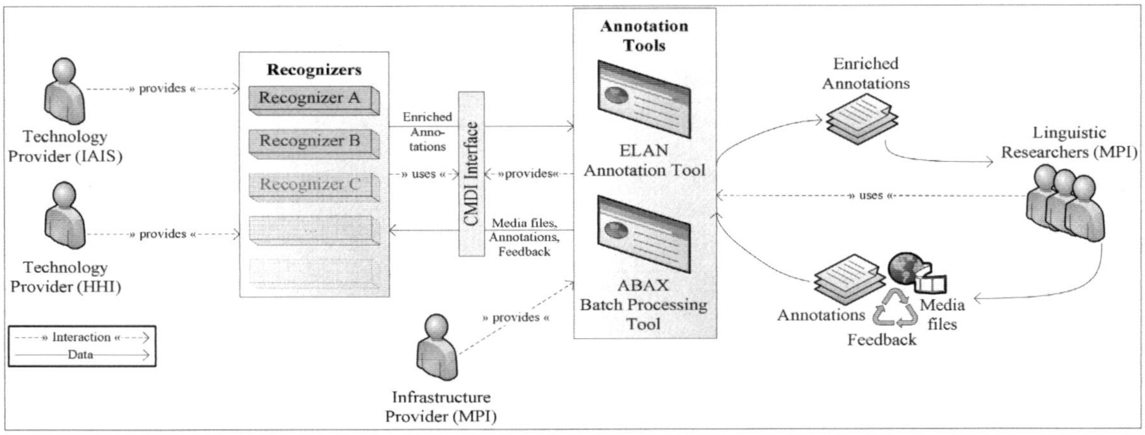

Figure 1. AVATecH System landscape

sign language research and gesture research. An additional tool, ABAX, has been created in the AVATecH project. In contrast to ELAN it is used to perform a series of annotation tasks on multiple files. ABAX provides a CMDI-interface as well. Researchers can use either ELAN or ABAX to create enriched annotations using the recognizers provided by the Fraunhofer institutes. Researchers provide media files to be annotated and, depending on the recognizer, existing annotations or additional feedback information, e.g., parameter settings, to optimize the performance of the recognizers.

3 State of work

During the beginning of the AVATecH project, we carried out intensive corpora studies to identify typical annotation scenarios and their costs in terms of hours spend by the humanities researchers. The sample corpora provided by MPI consist of 38 sub-corpora with a total file size of 730 GB and about 43,000 individual media documents. We concluded that the material is highly varying in audio and video quality (from office or lab experiments with good recording quality to field recordings in noisy environments), in language, genre (from monologues to interviews and other discourse situations), and in the amount of information that can be derived directly from the audio or video stream. This led to the conclusion that IAIS and HHI have to assemble flexible solutions in order to cope with the large variety of annotation problems.

In the first half of the project we mainly addressed three types of annotation scenarios and the utilization of user feedback.

3.1 Annotation of field recordings

Within the first scenario, researchers come back from an extensive field trip with tens of hours of unstructured media data. We aim at supporting annotation of arbitrary field recordings with only little manual interaction. The researchers provide their recordings to the analysis components via ELAN or ABAX in their usual working environment. If required, they can provide prior knowledge about the recordings, e.g., they can adjust analysis parameters or label a few segments for providing examples to a detection algorithm. After the analysis, they will obtain a pre-annotated set of field recordings, where they can quickly navigate to the portions of interest that requires more detailed manual annotation. We already integrated a number of recognizers to address this task:

Audio Recognizers

- *Audio Activity Detection*
- *Acoustic Segmentation*
- *Detection of Speech*
- *Speaker Diarization*
- *Vowel and Pitch contour detection*

Video Recognizers

- *Detection of Shot Cuts*
- *Extraction of Key frames*
- *Camera Motion / Motion Inside-the-Scene Detection*
- *Hands and Head Tracking*

3.2 Annotation of interview recordings

For a second scenario we exploit the resulting annotations of the first workflow described above. In this scenario, the researchers have a large set of interview recordings where they are just interested in the responses of the interviewee. We add further prior knowledge in the form of speech examples of the interviewer, and create separate tiers for the interviewer and the subjects of an interview situation. To address this task we incorporate widely used state-of-the-art audio analysis technology for the automatic detection of specific speakers. To use this component the researcher must provide a few minutes of samples of the desired speaker.

3.3 Annotation of sign language studio recordings

In the third scenario, the researchers want to create gesture annotations based on a corpus without any pre-annotations. The MPI-corpora contain sign language studio recordings that can be partitioned in two groups. The first group consists of single person videos, where the subject can be filmed from several positions, e.g., from above or facing the camera and at different camera distances. The other group consists of interviews with two to four people in the scene, none of them facing the camera. Resolution and quality of the recordings vary heavily depending on the sub-corpus.

Typical gesture annotations require the user to manually select the start and end point of each gesture as well as the appropriate descriptions. For each gesture, glosses for each hand can be included, as well as mouth position and information about eye aperture, gaze direction, head movements, etc. Accurate gesture analysis can be an extremely time consuming task. In the project, the videos are automatically prioritized, allowing the researchers to decide which ones are worth annotating without the necessity to view them in advance. The aim is to provide the automatic extraction of low level features (like position of the hands during a movement, average speed of the hands, duration of a gesture), allowing the researchers to focus on higher level gesture analysis. We integrated a recognizer to automatically estimate skin colour parameters and, building up on this, a recognizer for automatic hands and head detection and tracking. The latter also detects interaction between different body parts, for example, when two hands join or an arm is overlapping the face.

3.4 Using user-feedback for optimization

On the heterogeneous data in this project, some of the baseline recognizers perform poorly without additional adaptation. Moreover, in order to really speed up the annotation process, the researchers need to be able to rely on those automatic annotations that exclude data from the manual process. Hence, we investigate the potential of each analysis component to support either an adaptation mechanism or a feedback-loop mechanism or both. Furthermore, the graphical user interface will support fast correction of typical annotation errors produced by the recognizers.

By an adaptation mechanism we mean that the researchers provide examples of aspects they would like to detect, e.g., samples of a speaker for automatic speaker detection. Alternatively, they can choose from presets for typical acoustic environments, e.g., different presets for the acoustic segmentation of studio or field recordings.

By a feedback-loop mechanism we mean strategies where the user first runs a recognition process, gives feedback about the quality of the result and then runs the process with the updated information again. For example, for speaker identification the user adapts the recognizer by selecting some examples of the speaker, then runs the recognizer, and then verifies a number of segments. The recognizer uses this response to adapt the algorithm before running the process again.

To support this, the user interface must support various techniques to interact with the recognizers, e.g., to quickly jump from segment to segment, to allow a decision whether a segment is correctly labeled or not (feedback-loop), or to select segments that will be used for the adaptation mechanism.

User interaction is an essential part of our annotation workflows and it directly addresses the goal of reducing the overall annotation time since some of the originally unsupervised algorithms will not be able to provide the necessary high-quality annotation.

4 Evaluation Phase

For the evaluation, we are interested in two sets of information: qualitative statements from the human annotators that assess the annotation experience when using the AVATecH system and a quantitative evaluation of the actual annotation speed-up compared to manual annotation.

During the qualitative evaluation we are interested how the work of annotators is supported by automatic analysis, and whether annotators think that the system is beneficial. In the evaluation, subjects annotate their own material with ELAN supported by recognizers. We record their experience with a questionnaire. Within the qualitative evaluation we aim to cover all three annotation tasks mentioned above. The questionnaire consists of 20 questions addressing the quality of the ELAN interface, the productivity using recognizers during annotating, the quality of the delivered results and the overall experience. We aim to incorporate at least thirty MPI researchers or students who want to annotate their data with recognizer support.

Within quantitative evaluation, we want to measure the speed-up for annotation by using automatic tools. We ask a limited number of people to perform a specific annotation task for a subset of field recordings or studio recordings from our corpus, both with and without support from automatic analysis. The annotation will consist of labeling the speech of the interviewee, such that the researcher can quickly browse from answer to answer (for interview recordings) and labeling the gesture of the person in the video, so that the researcher can quickly see when a gesture begins, ends and what kind of motion is associated to it (for studio recordings).

To measure the annotation speed we have defined a metric that can be used not only for our evaluation, but can give a good insight about the general annotation speed of a researcher. This is not straightforward to assess, because researchers work with recordings of varying complexity (e.g. having few or many relevant events per time unit) and they are looking for different information in them, hence creating very different annotations (from very basic to multi-level, complex annotations with long descriptions).

Our general metric is based on two measures: 1) the number of created annotation blocks per unit of time; 2) the length of the media file. These values considered together will allow assessing the average annotation speed and complexity of annotation created for a given media file. Calculating these measures will be done by extending ELAN to record the overall annotation time from opening to closing the project file and to log certain annotation events, e.g., "created a new label" or "created a new segment", with corresponding timestamps. However, if the same data is annotated twice by the same subject, the second annotation will be biased as the subject already knows the structure of the file. Therefore we penalize the automatic annotation and do it first. Moreover, we split the runs over two days (1^{st}day: annotation with automatic tools, 2^{nd}day manual annotation). Also we measure active vs. passive annotation time, i.e., waiting for recognizers to finish processing. This can be achieved with proper logging of the times when recognizers start and finish their execution. As population we will incorporate five to ten advanced ELAN users.

5 Future work

After carrying out the study presented above we plan to do iterations of recognizer advancements and subsequent user-reviews to further reduce the overall annotation time and to increase the user satisfaction. Also we will add more recognizers for more specialized tasks such as language-independent and -dependent forced alignment (already in an advanced stage of development), acoustic and visual query-by-example. Furthermore we expect advancements by carefully evaluating and implementing more ways of adaption and user-feedback to overcome the difficulties of heterogeneous and low-quality field recordings.

Acknowledgments

AVATecH is a joint project of Max Planck and Fraunhofer, started in 2009 and funded by both Max Planck Society and Fraunhofer Society.

References

Stefano Masneri, Oliver Schreer, Daniel Schneider, et al. 2010. *Towards semi-automatic annotations for video and audio corpora*. Proc. CSLT Workshop, LREC 2010.

Peter Wittenburg, Eric Auer, Han Sloetjes, et al. 2010. *Automatic Annotation of Media Field Recordings*. Proc. LaTECH, Workshop, ECAI 2010.

Eric Auer, Albert Russel, Han Sloetjes, et al. 2010. *ELAN as Flexible Annotation Framework for Sound and Image Processing Detectors*. Proc. LREC 2010.

Brandon C. Roy and Deb Roy. 2009. *Fast Transcription of Unstructured Audio Recordings*. Proc. Interspeech 2009.

Peter Wittenburg, Hennie Brugman, Albert Russel, et al. 2006. *ELAN: a Professional Framework for Multimodality Research*. Proc. LREC 2006

Tamás Váradi, Steven Krauwer, Peter Wittenburg, et al. 2008. *CLARIN: Common Language Resources and Technology Infrastructure*. Proc. LREC 2008

Daan Broeder, Marc Kemps-Snijders, Dieter Van Uytvanck, et al. 2010. *A Data Category Registry- and Component-based Metadata Framework*. Proc. LREC 2010

Handwritten Text Recognition for Historical Documents

Verónica Romero, Nicolás Serrano, Alejandro H. Toselli,
Joan Andreu Sánchez and **Enrique Vidal**
ITI, Universitat Politècnica de València, Spain
{vromero,nserrano,jandreu,atoselli,evidal}@iti.upv.es

Abstract

The amount of digitized legacy documents has been rising dramatically over the last years due mainly to the increasing number of on-line digital libraries publishing this kind of documents. The vast majority of them remain waiting to be transcribed into a textual electronic format (such as ASCII or PDF) that would provide historians and other researchers new ways of indexing, consulting and querying them. In this work, the state-of-the-art Handwritten Text Recognition techniques are applied for the automatic transcription of these historical documents. We report results for several ancient documents.

1 Introduction

In the last years, huge amount of handwritten historical documents residing in libraries, museums and archives have been digitalized and have been made available to the general public through specialized web portals. The vast majority of these documents, hundreds of terabytes worth of digital image data, remain waiting to be transcribed into a textual electronic format that would provide historians and other researchers new ways of indexing, consulting and querying them.

The automatic transcription of these ancient handwritten documents is still an incipient research field that has been started to be explored in recent years. For some time in the past decades, the interest in Off-line Handwritten Text Recognition (HTR) was diminishing, under the assumption that modern computer technologies will soon make paper-based documents useless. However, the increasing number of on-line digital libraries publishing large quantities of digitized legacy documents has turned HTR up in an important research topic.

HTR should not be confused with Optical Character Recognition (OCR). Nowadays, OCR systems are capable to recognizing text with a very good accuracy (Breuel, 2008; Ratzlaff, 2003). However, OCR products are very far from offering useful solutions to the HTR problem. They are simply not usable, since in the vast majority of the handwritten documents, characters can by no means be isolated automatically. HTR, specially for historical documents, is a very difficult task. To some extent HTR is comparable with the task of recognizing continuous speech in a significantly degraded audio file. And, in fact, the nowadays prevalent technology for HTR borrows concepts and methods from the field of Automatic Speech Recognition (ASR) (Rabiner, 1989) as Hidden Markov Models (HMMs) (Bazzi et al., 1999) and n-Gram (Jelinek, 1998). The most important difference is that the input feature vector sequence of the HTR system represents a handwritten text line image, rather than an acoustic speech signal.

In this sense, the required technology should be able to recognize all the text elements (sentences, words and characters) as a whole, without any prior segmentation of the image into these elements. This technology is generally referred to as segmentation-free *off-line Handwritten Text Recognition* (HTR) (Marti and Bunke, 2001; Toselli and others, 2004; España-Boquera et al., 2011).

Given that historical documents suffered from the typical degradation problems of this kind of documents and, in order to obtain accurately transcription of them, different methods and techniques of the document analysis and recognition field are needed. Among them are the layout analysis and text line extraction methods, image preprocessing techniques, lexical and language modeling and HMMs. In this paper we study the adaptation/application of the above mentioned techniques on historical documents, testing the system on four sort of different ancient documents characterized, among other things, by different handwritten styles from diverse places and time periods.

This paper is divided as follows. First, the HTR framework is introduced in section 2. Then, the different corpora used in the experiments are described in subsection 3.1. The experiments and results are commented in subsection 3.2. Finally, some conclusions are drawn in the section 4.

2 Handwritten Text Recognition

The handwritten text recognition (HTR) problem can be formulated in a similar way to ASR, as the problem of finding the most likely word sequence, $\mathbf{w} = (w_1\ w_2\ \ldots\ w_n)$, for a given handwritten sentence image represented by an observation sequence, $\mathbf{x} = (x_1\ x_1\ \ldots\ x_m)$, i.e., $\mathbf{w} = \text{argmax}_{\mathbf{w}} P(\mathbf{w} \mid \mathbf{x})$. Using the Bayes' rule we can decompose this probability into two probabilities, $P(\mathbf{x} \mid \mathbf{w})$ and $P(\mathbf{w})$:

$$\hat{\mathbf{w}} = \underset{\mathbf{w}}{\text{argmax}}\, P(\mathbf{w} \mid \mathbf{x}) \approx \underset{\mathbf{w}}{\text{argmax}}\, P(\mathbf{x} \mid \mathbf{w}) P(\mathbf{w}) \tag{1}$$

$P(\mathbf{x} \mid \mathbf{w})$ can be seen as a morphological-lexical knowledge. It is the probability of the observation sequence $\mathbf{x}$ given the word sequence $\mathbf{w}$ and is typically approximated by concatenated character HMMs (Jelinek, 1998). On the other hand, $P(\mathbf{w})$ represents a syntactic knowledge. It is the prior probability of the word sequence $\mathbf{w}$ and is approximated by a word language model, usually n-grams (Jelinek, 1998).

In practice, the simple multiplication of $P(\mathbf{x} \mid \mathbf{w})$ and $P(\mathbf{w})$ needs to be modified in order to balance the absolute values of both probabilities. To this end a language model weight α (Grammar Scale Factor, GSF), which weights the influence of the language model on the recognition result, and an insertion penalty β (Word Insertion Penalty, WIP), which helps to control the word insertion rate of the recognizer (Ogawa et al., 1998) are used. In addition, log-probabilities are usually used to avoid the numeric underflow problems that can appear using probabilities. So, Equation (1) can be rewritten as:

$$\hat{\mathbf{w}} = \underset{\mathbf{w}}{\text{argmax}}\ \log\ P(\mathbf{x} \mid \mathbf{w}) + \alpha\ \log\ P(\mathbf{w}) + l\beta \tag{2}$$

where l is the word length of the sequence $\mathbf{w}$ and α and β are optimized for all the training sentences of the corpus.

The HTR system used here follows the classical architecture composed of three main modules: a document image preprocessing module, in charge to filter out noise, recover handwritten strokes from degraded images and reduce variability of text styles; a line image feature extraction module, where a feature vector sequence is obtained as the representation of a handwritten text line image; and finally a HMM training/decoding module, which obtains the most likely word sequence for the sequence of feature vectors (Bazzi et al., 1999; Toselli and others, 2004).

2.1 Preprocessing

It is quite common for ancient documents to suffer from degradation problems (Drida, 2006). Among these are the presence of smear, background of big variations and uneven illumination, spots due to the humidity or marks resulting from the ink that goes through the paper (generally called bleed-through). In addition, there are other kinds of difficulties appearing in these pages as different font types and sizes in the words, underlined and/or crossed-out words, etc. The combination of all these problems contributes to make the recognition process difficult, and hence, the preprocessing module quite essential.

The following steps take place in the preprocessing module: first, the skew of each page is corrected. We understand as "skew" the angle between the horizontal direction and the direction of the lines on which the writer aligned the words. Then, a conventional noise reduction method is applied on the whole document image (Kavallieratou and Stamatatos, 2006), whose output is then fed to the text line extraction process which divides it into separate text lines images. The method used for the latter case is based on the horizontal projection profile of the input image. Local minimums in this projection are considered as potential cut-points located between consecutive text lines. When the minimum values are greater than zero, no clear separation is possible. This problem has been solved using a method based in connected components (Marti and Bunke, 2001). Finally, slant correction and size normalization are applied on each separate line. More detailed description can be found in (Toselli and others, 2004; Romero et al., 2006).

2.2 Feature Extraction

The feature extraction process approach used to obtain the feature vectors sequence follows similar ideas described in (Bazzi et al., 1999). First, a grid is applied to divide the text line image into $M \times N$ squared cells. M is chosen empirically and N is such that N/M equals the original line image aspect ratio. Each cell is characterized by the following features: *average gray level*, *horizontal gray level derivative* and *vertical gray level derivative*. To obtain smoothed values of these features, an $s \times s$ cell analysis window, centered at the current cell, is used in the computations (Toselli and others, 2004). The smoothed cell-averaged gray level is computed through convolution with two 1-d Gaussian filters. The smoothed horizontal derivative is calculated as the slope of the line which best fits the horizontal function of column-average gray level in the analysis window. The fitting criterion is the sum of squared errors weighted by a 1-d Gaussian filter which enhances the role of central pixels of the window under analysis. The vertical derivative is computed in a similar way.

Columns of cells (also called *frames*) are processed from left to right and a feature vector is constructed for each *frame* by stacking the three features computed in their constituent cells. Hence, at the end of this process, a sequence of M $3 \cdot N$-dimensional feature vectors (N normalized gray-level components and N horizontal and vertical derivatives components) is obtained. Figure 1 shows a representative visual example of the feature vectors sequence for the Spanish word "cuarenta" ("forty") and how a continuous density HMM models two feature vector subsequences corresponding to the character "a".

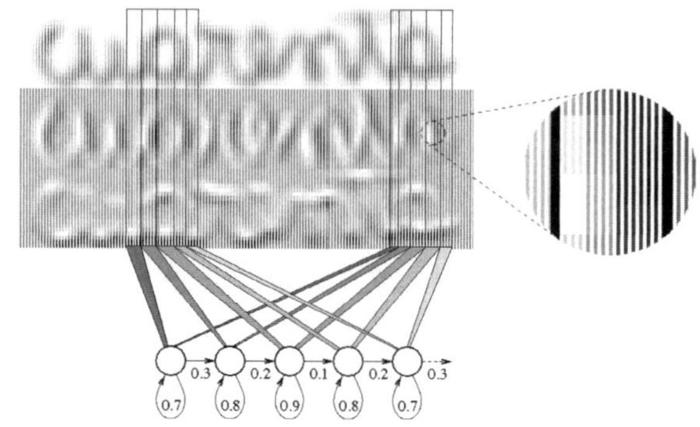

Figure 1: Example of feature-vector sequence and HMM modeling of instances of the character "a" within the Spanish word "cuarenta" ("forty"). The model is shared among all instances of characters of the same class. The zones modeled by each state show graphically subsequences of feature vectors (see details in the magnifying-glass view) compounded by stacking the normalized grey level and its both derivatives features.

2.3 Recognition

Characters (or graphemes) are considered here as the basic recognition units in the same way as phonemes in ASR, and therefore, they are modeled by left-to-right HMMs. Each HMM state generates feature vectors following and adequate parametric probabilistic law; typically, a Gaussian Mixture. Thereby, the total amount of parameters to be estimated depends on the number of states and their associated emission probability distributions, which need to be empirically tuned to optimize the overall performance on a given amount of available training samples. As in ASR, character HMMs are trained from images of continuously handwritten text (without any kind of segmentation and represented by their respective observation sequences) accompanied by the transcription of these images into the corresponding sequence of characters. This training process is carried out using a well known instance of the EM algorithm called forward-backward or Baum-Welch re-estimation (Jelinek, 1998).

Each *lexical entry (word)* is modeled by a stochastic finite-state automaton which represents all possible concatenations of individual characters that may compose the word. By embedding the character HMMs into the edges of this automaton, a *lexical HMM* is obtained.

Finally, the concatenation of words into text lines or sentences is usually modeled by a bi-gram *language model*, with Kneser-Ney back-off smoothing (Katz, 1987; Kneser and Ney, 1995), which uses the previous $n-1$ words to predict the next one:

$$P(\mathbf{w}) \approx \prod_{i=1}^{N} P(w_i|\mathbf{w}_{i-n+1}^{i-1}) \qquad (3)$$

This n-grams are estimated from the given transcriptions of the trained set.

However, there are tasks in which the relation of running words and vocabulary size is too low causing that bi-gram language models hardly contributes to restrict the search space. This is the case of one of the documents used in the experiments reported in section 3.2 called "Index". In the following subsection we describe the language model used for recognition in this specific task.

Once all the *character*, *word* and *language* models are available, the recognition of new test sentences can be performed. Thanks to the homogeneous finite-state (FS) nature of all these models, they can be easily *integrated* into a single *global* (huge) FS model. Given an input sequence of feature vectors, the output word sequence hypothesis corresponds to a path in the integrated network that produces the input sequence with highest probability. This optimal path search is very efficiently carried out by the well known Viterbi algorithm (Jelinek, 1998). This technique allows for the integration to be performed "on the fly" during the decoding process.

2.3.1 "Index" Language Model

The Index task (see section 3.2) is related to the transcription of a marriage register book and corresponds to the transcription of the index at the beginning of one of these books. This index registers the page in which each marriage record is located. These marriage register books were usually used for centuries to register marriages in ecclesiastical institutions and have been used recently for migratory studies. Their transcription is considered an interesting problem (Esteve et al., 2009). These index pages have some regularities and a very easy syntactic structure. The lines of the index pages used in this study have first a man surname, then the word "ab" (that in old Catalan means "with"), then a woman surname and finally the page number in which that marriage record was registered.

In this work, in order to improve the accuracy and speed up the transcription process of this document, we have defined a very simple language model that strictly accounts for the easy syntactic structure of the lines. Figure 2 shows a graphical representation of this language model. First a surname must be recognized, then the word "ab", and then another surname that can be preceded by the word "V.". This letter means that the woman was widow and she was using her previous husband surname. Finally a page number or the quotation marks symbol must be recognized.

3 Experimental Results

In order to assess the effectiveness of the above-presented off-line HTR system on legacy documents, different experiments were carried out. The

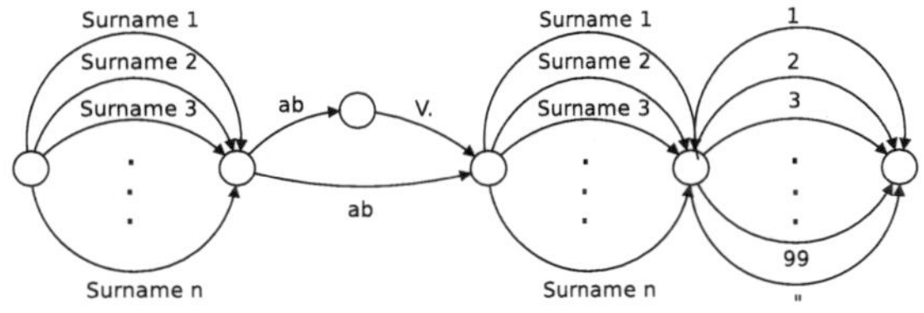

Figure 2: Language model for the Index task.

corpora used in the experiments, as well as the different measures and the obtained experimental results are summarized in the following subsections.

3.1 Corpora and Transcription Tasks

Four corpora with more or less similar HTR difficulty were employed in the experiments. The first three corpora, CS (Romero et al., 2007), Germana (Pérez et al., 2009) and Rodrigo (Serrano and Juan, 2010), consist of cursive handwritten page images in old Spanish from 16th and 19th century. The last corpus: Index (Romero et al., 2011), was compiled from the index at the beginning of a legacy handwritten marriage register book. Figure 3 shows examples of each of them.

Cristo-Salvador This corpus was compiled from the legacy handwriting document identified as *"Cristo-Salvador"*, which was kindly provided by the *Biblioteca Valenciana* (BIVAL)[1].

It is composed of 53 text page images, written by only one writer and scanned at 300dpi. As has been explained in section 2, the page images have been preprocessed and divided into lines, resulting in a data-set of 1,172 text line images. The transcriptions corresponding to each line image are also available, containing 10,911 running words with a vocabulary of 3,408 different words.

Two different partitions were defined for this data-set. In this work we are going to use the partition called *hard* (Romero et al., 2007), where the test set is composed by 497 line samples belonging to the last 20 document pages, whereas the remaining 675 were assigned to the training set.

Germana The GERMANA corpus is the result of digitizing and annotating the Spanish manuscript *"Noticias y documentos relativos a Doña Germana de Foix, última Reina de Aragón"* written in 1891. It is a single-author book and a limited-domain topic, and the original manuscript

[1] http://bv2.gva.es

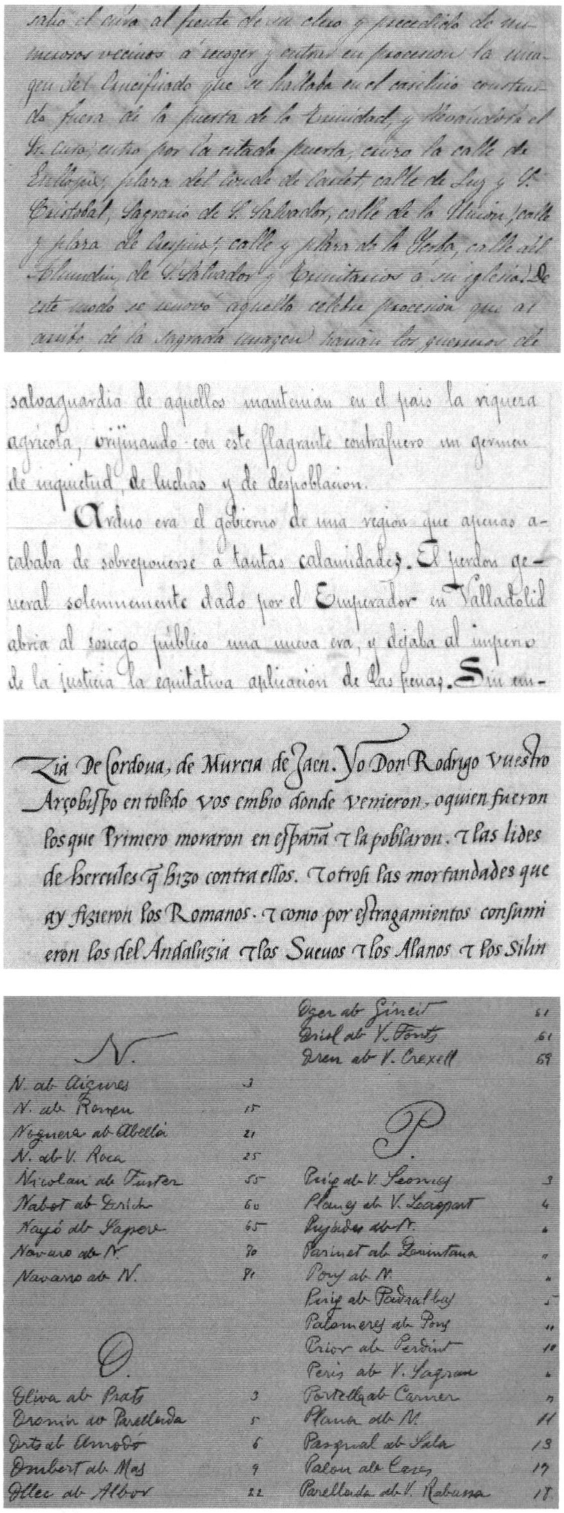

Figure 3: From top to bottom: Single-Writer Manuscripts from the XIX Century (CS and Germana), Single-Writer Spanish manuscript from XVI century (Rodrigo) and index page of a marriage register book (Index).

was well-preserved (Pérez et al., 2009). It is composed of 764 pages, with approximately $21k$ lines.

The page images were preprocessed and divided into lines 2. These lines have been transcribed by paleography experts, resulting in a data-set of $217k$ running words with a vocabulary of $30k$ words. To carry out the experiments, we have used the same partition described in (Pérez et al., 2009), that only uses the first 180 pages of the corpus.

Rodrigo The Rodrigo database corresponds to a manuscript from 1545 entitled *"Historia de España del arçobispo Don Rodrigo"*, and written in old Spanish by a single author. It is 853-page bound volume divided into 307 chapters.

The manuscript was carefully digitized by experts at 300 dpi and annotated in a procedure very similar to the one used for the Germana database. The complete annotation of Rodrigo comprises about $20K$ text lines and $231K$ running words form a lexicon of $17K$ words. In this work, the experiments have been carried out using the same partition described in (Serrano and Juan, 2010)

Index This corpus was compiled from the index at the beginning of a legacy handwritten marriage register book. This book was kindly provided by the *Centre d'Estudis Demogràfics* (CED) of the *Universitat Autònoma de Barcelona*. As previously said, the lines in these pages have some syntactic regularities that could be used to reduce the human effort needed to carry out the transcription (Romero et al., 2011).

The Index corpus was written by only one writer and scanned at 300 dpi. It was composed by 29 text pages. For each page, the GIDOC (Serrano et al.,) prototype was used to perform text block layout, line segmentation, and transcription. The results were visually inspected and the few line-separation errors were manually corrected, resulting in a data-set of $1,563$ text line images, containing $6,534$ running words from a lexicon of $1,725$ different words. Four different partitions were defined for cross-validation.

3.2 Results

The quality of the transcriptions obtained with the off-line HTR system is given by the well-known Word Error Rate (WER). It is widely used in HTR (Toselli and others, 2004; Toselli et al., 2010; España-Boquera et al., 2011) and in ASR (Jelinek, 1998). It is defined as the minimum number of words that need to be substituted, deleted or inserted to convert a sentence recognized by the system into the corresponding reference transcription, divided by the total number of words in the reference transcription.

The corresponding morphological (HMMs) and language models (the different *bi*-grams and the special language model for the Index task) associated with each corpus were trained from their respective training images and transcriptions. Besides, all results reported in Table 1 have been obtained after optimizing the parameters values corresponding to the preprocessing, feature extraction and modeling processes for each corpus.

Concerning to the CS corpus, the obtained WER (%) results was 33.5 using in this case a closed-vocabulary. For the Germana corpus, the best WER achieved were around 8.9% and 26.9% using closed-vocabulary and open-vocabulary respectively. Regarding the out-of-vocabulary (OOV) words, it becomes clear that a considerable fraction of transcription errors is due to the occurrence of unseen words in the test partition. More precisely, unseen words account here for approximately 50% of transcription errors. Although comparable in size to GERMANA, RODRIGO comes from a much older manuscript (from 1545), where the typical difficult characteristics of historical documents are more evident. The best WER figure achieved in this corpus until the moment is around 36.5%, where most of the errors are also caused by the occurrence of OOV words. Respect to the Index corpus, in which the transcription process used a specific language model, WER of 28.6% and 40.3% were obtained for closed-vocabulary and open-vocabulary respectively.

From the results we can see that current state-of-the-art segmentation-free "off-line HTR" approach produces word error rates as high as 9-40% with handwritten old documents, depending whether open or closed vocabulary is used. These results are still far from offering perfect solutions to the transcription problem. However, this accuracy could be enough for indexing and searching tasks or even to derive adequate metadata to roughly describe the ancient document contents.

4 Conclusions

In this paper the nowadays technology of HTR, which borrows concepts and methods from the field of Automatic Speech Recognition technology, has been tested for historical documents. This HTR technology is based on Hidden Markov Models using Gaussians as state emission probability function. The HMM-based HTR has a hierarchical structure with character HMMs modelling the basic recognition units. These models are concatenated forming word models, and these in turn concatenated forming sentence models. The HMM used in this work was furthermore enhanced by a language model incorporating linguistic information beyond the word level.

Several tasks have been considered to assess this HTR approach. Considering all the difficulties involving the old handwritten documents used in the experiments, although the results achieved are not perfect they are really encouraging. In addition, as previously commented, this accuracy could be enough for tasks such as document indexing and searching or even could be used to derive adequate metadata that describes roughly the content of documents. Moreover, other applications such as word-spotting can be easily implemented using this segmentation-free HTR technology. In this sense, results are expected to be much more precise than using the popular approaches which do not take advantage of the context of spotted words.

Finally, to obtain perfect transcriptions, instead of the heavy human-expert "post-editing" work, that generally results inefficient and uncomfortable to the user and also it is hardly accepted by expert transcribers, computer assisted interactive predictive solutions (Toselli et al., 2010) can be used. These solutions offer promising significant improvements in practice and user acceptance. In these approaches, the user and the system work interactively in tight mutual cooperation to obtain the final perfect transcription of the given text images.

Acknowledgments

Work supported by the Spanish Government (MICINN and "Plan E") under the MITTRAL (TIN2009-14633-C03-01) research project and under the research programme Consolider Ingenio 2010: MIPRCV (CSD2007-00018), the Generalitat Valenciana under grant Prometeo/2009/014 and FPU AP2007-02867.

Table 1: Basic statistics information from each corpus along with the WER(%) obtained using the segmentation-free off-line HTR system.

Corpus		CS	GERMANA		RODRIGO	INDEX	
Language		19th C Sp.	19th C Sp.		16th C Sp.	Old Catalan	
Lan. Model	Lexicon	2 277	7 477		17 300	1 725	
	Train. Ratio	2.8	4.5		12.5	3.8	
HMMs	Characters	78	82		115	68	
	Train. Ratio	460	2 309		7 930	453	
Open Vocabulary		N	N	**Y**	**Y**	N	**Y**
WER (%)		**33.5**	**8.9**	**26.9**	**36.5**	**28.6**	**40.3**

References

I. Bazzi, R. Schwartz, and J. Makhoul. 1999. An Omnifont Open-Vocabulary OCR System for English and Arabic. *IEEE Transactions on PAMI*, 21(6):495–504.

Thomas M. Breuel. 2008. The ocropus open source ocr system. In *DRR*, page 68150.

F. Drida. 2006. Towards restoring historic documents degraded over time. In *Proceedings of the DIAL'06*, IEEE Computer Society, pages 350–357. Washington, DC, USA.

S. España-Boquera, M.J. Castro-Bleda, J. Gorbe-Moya, and F. Zamora-Martínez. 2011. Improving offline handwriting text recognition with hybrid hmm/ann models. *IEEE Transactions on PAMI*, 33(4):767–779.

A. Esteve, C. Cortina, and A. Cabré. 2009. Long term trends in marital age homogamy patterns: Spain, 1992-2006. *Population*, 64(1):173–202.

F. Jelinek. 1998. *Statistical Methods for Speech Recognition*. MIT Press.

S. M. Katz. 1987. Estimation of Probabilities from Sparse Data for the Language Model Component of a Speech Recognizer. *IEEE Transactions on Acoustics, Speech and Signal Processing*, ASSP-35:400–401, March.

E. Kavallieratou and E. Stamatatos. 2006. Improving the quality of degraded document images. In *Proceedings of the DIAL '06*, pages 340–349, Washington, DC, USA. IEEE Computer Society.

R. Kneser and H. Ney. 1995. Improved backing-off for m-gram language modeling. volume 1, pages 181–184, Los Alamitos, CA, USA. IEEE Computer Society.

U.-V. Marti and H. Bunke. 2001. Using a Statistical Language Model to improve the preformance of an HMM-Based Cursive Handwriting Recognition System. *IJPRAI*, 15(1):65–90.

A. Ogawa, K. Takeda, and F. Itakura. 1998. Balancing acoustic and linguistic probabilites. In *Proceeding IEEE CASSP*, volume 1, pages 181–184, Seattle, WA, USAR, May.

Daniel Pérez, Lionel Tarazón, Nicolás Serrano, Francisco-Manuel Castro, Oriol Ramos-Terrades, and Alfons Juan. 2009. The germana database. In *Proceedings of the ICDAR'09*, pages 301–305, Barcelona (Spain), July. IEEE Computer Society.

L. Rabiner. 1989. A Tutorial of Hidden Markov Models and Selected Application in Speech Recognition. *Proceedings IEEE*, 77:257–286.

E. H. Ratzlaff. 2003. Methods, Report and Survey for the Comparison of Diverse Isolated Character Recognition Results on the UNIPEN Database. In *Proceedings of ICDAR '03*, volume 1, pages 623–628, Edinburgh, Scotland, August.

V. Romero, M. Pastor, A. H. Toselli, and E. Vidal. 2006. Criteria for handwritten off-line text size normalization. In *Proceedings of the VIIP 06*, Palma de Mallorca, Spain, August.

V. Romero, A. H. Toselli, L. Rodríguez, and E. Vidal. 2007. Computer Assisted Transcription for Ancient Text Images. In *Proocedings of the ICIAR 2007*, volume 4633 of *LNCS*, pages 1182–1193. Springer-Verlag, Montreal (Canada), August.

V. Romero, Joan Andreu Sánchez, Nicolás Serrano, and E. Vidal. 2011. Handwritten text recognition for marriage register books. In *Proceedings of the 11th ICDAR*, IEEE Computer Society. To be published, September.

Nicolás Serrano and Alfons Juan. 2010. The rodrigo database. In *Proceedings of the LREC 2010*, Malta, May 19-21.

N. Serrano, L. Tarazón, D. Pérez, O. Ramos-Terrades, and A. Juan. The GIDOC prototype. In *Proceedings of the 10th PRIS 2010*, pages 82–89, Funchal (Portugal).

A. H. Toselli et al. 2004. Integrated Handwriting Recognition and Interpretation using Finite-State Models. *IJPRAI*, 18(4):519–539.

A.H. Toselli, V. Romero, M. Pastor, and E. Vidal. 2010. Multimodal interactive transcription of text images. *Pattern Recognition*, 43(5):1824–1825.

Reducing OCR Errors in Gothic-Script Documents

Lenz Furrer
University of Zurich
`Lenz.Furrer@uzh.ch`

Martin Volk
University of Zurich
`volk@cl.uzh.ch`

Abstract

In order to improve OCR quality in texts originally typeset in Gothic script, we have built an automated correction system which is highly specialized for the given text. Our approach includes external dictionary resources as well as information derived from the text itself. The focus lies on testing and improving different methods for classifying words as correct or erroneous. Also, different techniques are applied to find and rate correction candidates. In addition, we are working on a web application that enables users to read and edit the digitized text online.

1 Introduction

The State Archive of Zurich currently runs a digitization project, aiming to make publicly available online governmental texts in German of almost 200 years. A part of this project comprises the resolutions by the Zurich Cantonal Government from 1887 to 1902, which are archived as printed volumes in the State Archive. These documents are typeset in Gothic script, also known as *blackletter* or *Fraktur*, in opposition to the *antiqua* fonts of modern typesetting. In a cooperation project of the State Archive and the Institute of Computational Linguistics at the University of Zurich, we digitize these texts and prepare them for public online access.

The tasks of the project are automatic image-to-text conversion (OCR) of the approximately 11,000 pages, the segmentation of the bulk of text into separate resolutions, the annotation of metadata (such as the date or the archival signature) as well as improving the text quality by automatically correcting OCR errors.

As for OCR, the data are most challenging, since the texts contain not only Gothic type letters – which already lead to a lower accuracy compared to antiqua texts – but also particular words, phrases and even whole paragraphs are printed in antiqua font (cf. figure 1). Although we are lucky to have an OCR engine capable of processing mixed Gothic and antiqua texts, the alternation of the two fonts still has an impairing effect on the text quality. Since the interspersed antiqua tokens can be very short (e. g. the abbreviation *Dr.*), their diverting script is sometimes not recognized by the engine. This leads to heavily misrecognized words due to the different shapes of the typefaces; for example antiqua *Landrecht* (Engl.: "citizenship") is rendered as completely illegible *I>aii<lreclitt*, which is clearly the result of using the inappropriate recognition algorithm for Gothic script.

Aktum Dienstags den 3. März 1891.

Vor versammeltem Regierungsrathe.

456. Gewerkschaftskammern. Der von der Justiz- und Polizeidirektion vorgelegte Gesetzesentwurf betreffend die fakultative Einführung von Gewerkschaftskammern und die Kompetenzen derselben wird in Berathung gezogen und bis und mit § 8 in erster Lesung erledigt.

457. Statistik. Nach Einsicht:

a) Eines Gesuchschreibens der Zentralkommission der schweiz. statistischen Gesellschaft vom 12. November 1890 um Ertheilung eines Staatsbeitrages an ihre Ausgaben für das Jahr 1891;

b) eines Antrages der Direktion des Innern,

beschließt der Regierungsrath:

1. Der schweiz. statistischen Gesellschaft (Sekretär und Kassier: Herr C. Mühlemann in Bern) ist wie bisher ein Staatsbeitrag von 300 Fr. aus dem Kredite des Regierungsrathes (Büdget Tit. B. XII. a.) zu verabreichen.

2. Mittheilung an die Petentin, sowie an die Direktion der Finanzen zur Vollziehung.

Figure 1: Detail of a session header, followed by two resolutions, in German. The numbered titles as well as Roman numerals are typeset in antiqua letters.

In section 2 we present the OCR system used in the project. The focus of our work lies on section 3, which discusses our efforts in post-correcting OCR

```
- <par align="Center">
  - <line baseline="5974" l="3786" t="5870" r="5568" b="6002">
    - <formatting lang="OldGerman" ff="Arial" fs="15." spacing="-12">
        <charParams l="3786" t="5870" r="3868" b="5986" wordStart="1" wordFromDictionary="0"
          wordNormal="1" wordNumeric="0" wordIdentifier="0" charConfidence="98" serifProbability="255"
          wordPenalty="15" meanStrokeWidth="161">A</charParams>
        <charParams l="3874" t="5872" r="3926" b="5974" wordStart="0" wordFromDictionary="0"
          wordNormal="1" wordNumeric="0" wordIdentifier="0" charConfidence="92" serifProbability="255"
          wordPenalty="15" meanStrokeWidth="161">k</charParams>
        <charParams l="3932" t="5874" r="3966" b="5976" wordStart="0" wordFromDictionary="0"
          wordNormal="1" wordNumeric="0" wordIdentifier="0" charConfidence="96" serifProbability="255"
          wordPenalty="15" meanStrokeWidth="161">t</charParams>
        <charParams l="3970" t="5902" r="4022" b="5974" suspicious="1" wordStart="0"
          wordFromDictionary="0" wordNormal="1" wordNumeric="0" wordIdentifier="0" charConfidence="92"
          serifProbability="255" wordPenalty="15" meanStrokeWidth="161">u</charParams>
        <charParams l="4028" t="5900" r="4106" b="5974" wordStart="0" wordFromDictionary="0"
          wordNormal="1" wordNumeric="0" wordIdentifier="0" charConfidence="98" serifProbability="255"
          wordPenalty="15" meanStrokeWidth="161">m</charParams>
```

Figure 2: Output XML of Abbyy Recognition Server 3.0, representing the word "Aktum".

errors. Section 4 is concerned with a web application.

2 OCR system

We use Abbyy's Recognition Server 3.0 for OCR. Our main reason to decide in favour of this product was its capability of converting text with both antiqua and Gothic script. Another great advantage in comparison to Abbyy's FineReader and other commercial OCR software is its detailed XML output file, which contains a lot of information about the recognized text.

Figure 2 shows an excerpt of the XML output. The fragment contains information about the five letters of the word *Aktum* (here meaning "governmental session"), which corresponds to the first word in figure 1. The first two XML tags, `par` and `line`, hold the contents and further information of a paragraph and a line respectively, e. g. we can see that this paragraph's alignment is centered. Each character is embraced by a `charParams` tag that has a series of attributes. The graphical location and dimensions of a letter are described by the four pixel positions `l`, `t`, `r` and `b` indicating the left, top, right and bottom borders. The following boolean-value attributes specifie if a character is at a left word boundaries (`wordStart`), if the word was found in the internal dictionary (`wordFromDictionary`) and if it is a regular word or rather a number or a punctuation token (`wordNormal`, `wordNumeric`, `wordIdentifier`). `charConfidence` has a value between 0 and 100 indicating the recognition confidence for this character, while `serifProbability` rates its probability of having serifs on a scale from 0 to 255. The fourth character *u* shows an additional attribute `suspicious`, which only appears if it is set to true. It marks characters that are likely to be misrecognized (which is not the case here).

We are pleased with the rich output of the OCR system. Still, we can think of features that could make a happy user even happier. For example, post-correction systems could gain precision if the alternative recognition hypotheses made during OCR were accessible.[1] Some of the information provided is not very reliable, such as the attribute "wordFromDictionary" that indicates if a word was found in the internal dictionary: on the one hand, a lot of vocabulary is not covered, whereas on the other, there are misrecognized words that are found in the dictionary (e. g. *Bandirektion*, which is an OCR error for German *Baudirektion*, Engl.: "building ministry"). While the XML attribute "suspicious" (designating spots with low recognition confidence) can be useful, the "charConfidence" value does not help a lot with locating erroneous word tokens.

An irritating aspect is, that we found the dehyphenation to be done worse than in the previous engine for Gothic OCR (namely FineReader XIX). Words hyphenated at a line break (e. g. *fakul- tative* on the fourth line in figure 1) are often split into two halves that are no proper words, thus looking up the word parts in its dictionary does not help the OCR engine with deciding for the cor-

[1] Abbyy's Fine Reader Software Developer Kit (SDK) is capable of this.

rect conversion of the characters. Since Abbyy's systems mark hyphenation with a special character when it is recognised, one can easily determine the recall by looking at the output. We encountered the Recognition Server's recall to be significantly lower than that of FineReader XIX, which is regrettable since it goes along with a higher error rate in hyphenated words.

The Recognition Server provides dictionaries for various languages, including so-called "Old German".[2] In a series of tests the "Old German" dictionary has shown slightly better results than the Standard German dictionary for our texts. Some, but not all of the regular spelling variations compared to modern orthography are covered by this historical dictionary, e. g. old German *Urtheil* (in contrast to modern German *Urteil*, Engl.: "jugdement") is found in Abbyy's internal dictionary, whereas *reduzirt* (modern German *reduziert*, Engl.: "reduced") is not. It is also possible to include a user-defined list of words to improve the recognition accuracy. However, when we added a list of geographical terms to the system and compared the output of before and after, there was hardly any improvement. Although the words from our list were recognized more accurately, the overall number of misrecognized words was almost completely compensated by new OCR errors unrelated to the words added.

All in all, Abbyy's Recognition Server 3.0 serves our purposes of digitizing well, especially in respect of handling large amounts of data and for pipeline processing.

3 Automated Post-Correction

The main emphasis of our project is on the post-correction of recognition errors. Our evaluation of a limited number of text samples yielded a word accuracy of 96.7 %, which means that one word out of 30 contains an error (as e. g. *Regieruug* instead of correct *Regierung*, Engl.: "government"). We aim to significantly reduce the number of misrecognized word tokens by identifying them in the OCR output and determining the originally intended word with its correct spelling.

In order to correct a maximum of errors in the corpus with the given resources, we decided for an automated approach to the post-correction. The great homogeneity of the texts concerning the layout as well as the limited variation in orthography are a good premise to achieve remarkable improvements. Having in mind the genre of our texts, we followed the idea of generating useful documents ready for reading and resigned from manually correcting or even re-keying the complete texts, as did e. g. the project *Deutsches Textarchiv*[3], which has a very literary, almost artistic standard in digitizing first-edition books from 1780 to 1900.

The task resembles that of a spell-checker as found in modern text processing applications, with two major differences. First, the scale of our text data – with approximately 11 million words we expect more than 300,000 erroneous word forms – does not allow for an interactive approach, asking a human user for feedback on every occurrence of a suspicious word form. Therefore we need an automatic system that can account for corrections with high reliability. Second, dating from the late 19th century, the texts show historic orthography, which differs in many ways from the spelling encountered in modern dictionaries (e. g. historic *Mittheilung* vs. modern *Mitteilung*, Engl.: "message"). This means that using modern dictionary resources directly cannot lead to satisfactory results.

Additionally, the governmental resolutions contain, typically, many toponymical references, i. e. geographical terms such as *Steinach* (a stream or place name) or *Schwarzenburg* (a place name). Many of these are not covered by general-vocabulary dictionaries. We also find regional peculiarities, such as pronunciation variants or words that are not common elsewhere in the German spoken area, e. g. *Hülfstrupp* vs. standard German *Hilfstruppe*, Engl.: "rescue team". Of course there is also a great amount of genre-specific vocabulary, i. e. administrative and legal jargon. We are hence challenged to build a fully-automated correction system with high precision that is aware of historic spelling and regional variants and contains geographical and governmental language.

3.1 Classification

The core task of our correction system with respect to its precision is the classification routine, that determines the correctness of every word. This part is evidently the basis for all correcting steps.

[2]The term has not to be confused with the linguistic epoch *Old High German*, which refers to texts from the first millenium A. D. Abbyy's "Old German" seems to cover some orthographical variation from the 19th, maybe the 18^{th}century.

[3]see www.deutschestextarchiv.de

Misclassifications are detrimental, as they can lead to false corrections. At the same time it is also the hardest task, as there are no formal criteria that universally describe orthography. Reynaert (2008) suggests building a corpus-derived lexicon that is mainly based on word frequencies and the distribution of similarly spelled words. However, this is sometimes misleading. For example, *saumselig* (Engl.: "dilatory") is a rare but correct word, which is found only once in the whole corpus, whereas *Liegenschast* is not correct (in fact, it is misrecognized for *Liegenschaft*, Engl.: "real estate"), but it is found sixteen times in this erroneous form. This shows that the frequency of word forms alone is not a satisfactory indicator to distinguish correct words from OCR errors; other information has to be used as well.

An interesting technique for reducing OCR errors is comparing the output of two or more different OCR systems. The fact that different systems make different errors is used to localize and correct OCR errors. For example, Volk et al. (2010) achieved improvements in OCR accuracy by combining the output of Abbyy FineReader 7 and Omnipage 17. However, this approach is not applicable to our project for the simple reason that there is to our knowledge, for the time being, only one state-of-the-art OCR system that recognizes mixed antiqua / Gothic script text.

The complex problem of correcting historical documents with erroneous tokens is addressed by Reffle (2011) with a two-channel model, which integrates spelling variation and error correction into one algorithm. To cover the unpredictable number of spelling variants of texts with historical orthography (or rather, depending on their age, texts without orthography), the use of static dictionaries is not reasonable as they would require an enormous size. Luckily, the orthography of our corpus is comparatively modern and homogenous, which means that there is a manageable number of deviations in comparison to modern spelling and between different parts of the corpus.

In our approach, we use a combination of various resources for this task, such as a large dictionary system for German that covers morphological variation and compounding (such as *ging*, a past form of *gehen*, Engl.: "to go", or German *Niederdruckdampfsystem*, a compound of four segments meaning "low-pressure steam system"), a list of local toponyms (since our texts deal mostly with events in the administered area) and the recognition confidence values of the OCR engine. Every word is either judged as correct or erroneous according to the information we gather from the various resources.

The historic and regional spelling deviations are modelled with a set of handwritten rules describing the regular differences. For example, with a rule stating that the sequence *th* corresponds to *t* in modern spelling, the old form *Mittheilung* can be turned into the standard form *Mitteilung*. While the former word is not found in the dictionary, the derived one is, which allows for the assumption that *Mittheilung* is a correctly spelled word.

The classification method is applied to single words, which are thus considered as a correct or erroneous form separately and without their original context. This reduces the number of correction candidates significantly, as not every word is to be handled, but only the set of the *distinct* word forms. However, this limits the correction to non-word errors, i. e. misrecognized tokens that cannot be interpreted as a proper word. For example, *Fcuer* is clearly a non-sense word, which should be spelled *Feuer* (Engl.: "fire"). In contrast, the two word forms *Absatze* and *Absätze* (Engl.: "paragraph") are two correct morphological variants of the same word, which are often confused during OCR. To decide which one of the two variants is correct in a particular occurrence, the word has to be judged in its original context, which is outside the scope of our project.

The decision for the correctness of a word is primarily based on the output of the German morphology system Gertwol by Lingsoft, in that we check every word for its analyzability. Although the analyses of Gertwol are reliable in most cases, there are two kinds of exceptions that can lead to false classifications. First, there are correct German words that are unknown to Gertwol, such as Latin words like *recte* (Engl.: "right") or proper names. Second, sometimes Gertwol finds analyses for misrecognized words, e. g. correct *Regierungsrat* (Engl.: "member of the government") is often rendered *Negierungsrat*, which is then analysed as a compound of *Negierung* (Engl.: "negation") and *Rat* (Engl.: "councillor"). To avoid these misclassifications we apply heuristics which include word lists for known frequent issues, the frequency of the word form or the feedback values of the OCR system concerning the recognition confidence.

3.2 Correction

The set of all words recognized as correct words plus their frequency can now serve as a lexicon for correcting erroneous word tokens. This corpus-derived lexicon is by nature highly genre-specific, which is desirable. On the other hand, rare words might remain uncorrected if all of their few occurrences happen to be misspelled, in which case there will be no correction candidate in the lexicon. Due to the repetitive character of the texts – administrative work involves many recurrent issues – there is also a lot of repetition in the vocabulary across the corpus. This increases the chance that a word misrecognized in one place has a correct occurrence in another.

The procedure of finding correction candidates is algorithmically complex, since the orthographical similarity of words is not easily described in a formal way. There is no linear ordering that would group together similar words. In the simplest approach to searching for similar words in a large list, every word has to be compared to every other word, which has quadratic complexity regarding the number of words. In our system we avoid this with two different approaches that are applied subsequently. In the first step, only a limited set of character substitutions is performed, whereas the second step allows for a broader range of deviations between an erroneous form and its correction.

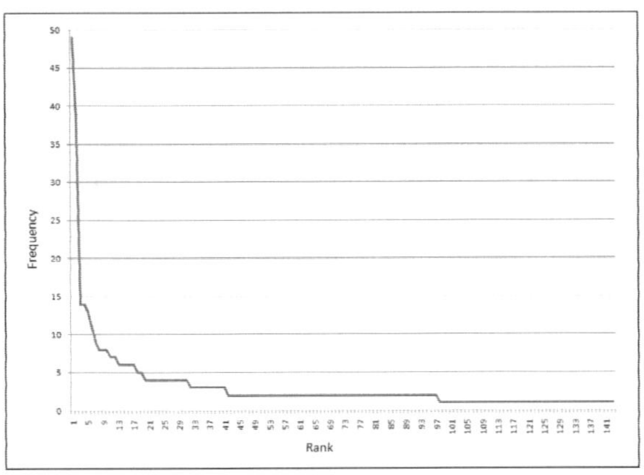

Figure 3: OCR errors ranked by their frequency, from a sample text of approx. 50,000 characters length.

3.2.1 Substitution of similar characters

In this approach we attempt to undo the most common OCR errors. When working with automatically recognized text, one will inevitably notice that a small set of errors accounts for the majority of misrecognized characters. At character level, OCR errors can be described as substitutions of single characters. Thus, by ranking these error types by their frequency, it can be shown that already a small sample of OCR errors resembles Zipfian distribution,[4] as is demonstrated in figure 3. For example, the 20 most frequent types of errors, which is less than 14 % of the 143 types encountered, sum up to 50 % of all occurrences of character errors. Table 1 shows the head of this error list as well as its tail. Among the top 6 we find pairs like *u* and *n* that are also often confounded when recognizing antiqua text as well as typical Gothic-script confusions like *d–b* or *s–f*. Figure 4 illustrates the optical similarity of certain characters that can also challenge the human eye. For example, due to its improper printing, the fifth letter cannot be determined clearly as *u* or *n*.

rank	frequency	{correct}–{recognized}
1	49	{u}–{n}
2	38	{n}–{u}
3	14	{a}–{ä}
4	14	{}–{.}
5	13	{d}–{b}
6	11	{s}–{f}
…	…	…
140	1	{o}–{p}
141	1	{r}–{?}
142	1	{§}–{8}
143	1	{ä}–{ö}

Table 1: Either ends of a ranked list, showing character errors and their frequency.

Figure 4: Gothic characters of the *Schwabacher Fraktur* that are frequently confused by the OCR system. From left to right, the characters are: *s* (in its long form), *f*, *u*, *n*, *u* or *n*, *B*, *V*, *R*, *N*.

For our correction system we use a manually edited substitution table that is based on these observations. The substitution pairs are inverted and used as replacement operations that are applied to the misspelled word forms. The spelling vari-

[4] Zipf's Law states that, given a large corpus of natural language data, the rank of each word is inversely proportional to its frequency.

ants produced are then searched for correct words that can be found in our dictionary. For example, given an erroneous token *sprechcn* and a substitution pair *e, c* stating that recognized *c* can represent actual *e*, the system produces the variants *spreehcn*, *sprechen* and *spreehen*. Consulting the dictionary finally uncovers *sprechen* (Engl.: "to speak") as a correct word, suggesting it as a correction for garbled *sprechcn*.

3.2.2 Searching shared trigrams

In a second step, we look for similar words more generally. This is applied to the erroneous words that could not be corrected by the method described above. There are various techniques to efficiently find similar words in large mounds of data, such as Reynaert's (2005) anagram hashing method, that treats words as multisets of words and models edit operations as arithmetic functions. Mihov and Schulz (2004) combine finite-state automata with filtering methods that include a-tergo dictionaries.

In our approach, we use character n-grams to find similar correct words for each of the erroneous words. Since many of the corrections with a close editing distance have already been found in the previous step, we have to look for corrections in a wider spectrum now. In order to reduce the search space, we create an index of trigrams that points to the lexicon entries. Every word in the lexicon is split into overlapping sequences of three characters, which are then stored in a hashed data structure. For example, from *ersten* (Engl.: "first") we get the four trigrams *ers*, *rst*, *ste* and *ten*. Each trigram is used as a key that points to a list of all words containing this three-letter sequence, so *ten* not only leads to *ersten*, but also to *warten* (Engl.: "wait") and many other words with the substring *ten*.

Likewise, all trigrams are derived from each erroneous word form. All lexicon entries that share at least one trigram with the word in question can thus be accessed by the trigram index. The lexicon entries found are now ranked by the number of trigrams shared with the error word. To stay with the previous example, a misrecognized word form *rrsten*[5] has three trigrams (*rst*, *ste*, *ten*) in common with *ersten*, but only one trigram (*ten*) is shared with *warten*.

The correction candidates found with this method are further challenged, e. g. by using the Levenshtein distance as a similarity measure and by rejecting corrections that affect the ending of a word.[6]

3.3 Evaluation

In order to measure the effect of the correction system, we manually corrected a random sample of 100 resolutions (approximately 35,000 word tokens). Using the ISRI OCR-Evaluation Frontiers Toolkit (Rice, 1996), we determined the recognition accuracy before and after the correction step. As can be seen in table 2, the text quality in terms of word accuracy could be improved from 96.72 % to 98.36 %, which means that the total number of misrecognized words was reduced by half.

4 Crowd Correction

Inspired by the Australian Newspaper Digitisation Program (Holley, 2009) and their online crowd-correction system, we are setting up an online application. We are working on a tool that allows for browsing through the corpus and reading the text in a synoptical view of both the recognized plain text and a scan image of the original printed page. Our online readers will have the possibility to immediately correct errors in the recognized text by clicking a word token for editing. The original word in the scan image is highlighted for convenience of the user, which permits fast comparison of image and text, so the intended spelling of a word can be verified quickly.

Crowd correction combines easy access of the historic documents with manual correcting. Similar to the concept of publicly maintained services as Wikipedia and its followers, information is provided free of charge. At the same time, the user has the possibility to give something back by im-

[5] The correction pair *ersten–rrsten* is not found in the first step although its editing distance is 1 and thus minimal. But since the error `{e}–{r}` has a low frequency, it is not contained in the substitution table, which makes this correction invisible for the common-error routine.

[6] Editing operations affecting a word's ending are a delicate issue in an inflecting language like German, since it is likely that we are dealing with morphological variation instead of an OCR error. Data sparseness of rare words can lead to unfortunate constellations. For example, the adjective form *innere* (Engl.: "inner") is present in the lexicon, while the inflectional variant *innern* is lacking. However, the latter form is indeed present in the corpus, but only in the misrecognized form *iunern*. As *innere* is the only valuable correction candidate in this situation, the option would be changing misspelled *iunern* into grammatically inapt *innere*. For the sake of legibility, an unorthographical word is preferred to an ungrammatical form.

	plain	(errors)	corrected	(errors)	improvement
character accuracy	99.09 %	(2428)	99.39 %	(1622)	33.2 %
word accuracy	96.72 %	(1165)	98.36 %	(584)	49.9 %

Table 2: Evaluation results of the automated correction system.

proving the quality of the corpus. It is important to keep the technical barrier low, so that new users can start correcting straight away without needing to learn a new formalism. With our click-and-type tool the access is easy and intuitive. However, in consequence, the scope of the editing operations is limited to word level, it does not, for example, allow for rewriting whole passages.

5 Conclusion

With this project we demonstrate how to build a highly specialized correction system for a specific text collection. We are using both general and specific resources, while the approach as a whole is widely generalizable. Of course, working with older texts with less standardized orthography than late 19thcentury governmental resolutions may lead to a lower improvement, but the techniques we applied are not bound to a certain epoch. In the crowd correction approach we see the possibility to further improve OCR output in combination with online access of the historic texts.

References

Rose Holley. 2009. *How Good Can It Get? Analysing and Improving OCR Accuracy in Large Scale Historic Newspaper Digitisation Programs.* D-Lib Magazine, 15(3/4).

Stoyan Mihov and Klaus U. Schulz. 2004. *Fast Approximate Search in Large Dictionaries.* Computational Linguistics 30(4):451–477.

Ulrich Reffle. 2011. *Efficiently generating correction suggestions for garbled tokens of historical language.* Natural Language Engineering 17(2):265–282.

Martin Reynaert. 2005. *Text-Induced Spelling Correction.* Ph. D. thesis, Tilburg Universtiy, Tilburg, NL.

Martin Reynaert. 2008. *Non-Interactive OCR Post-Correction for Giga-Scale Digitization Projects.* Proceedings of the Computational Linguistics and Intelligent Text Processing 9th International Conference, CICLing 2008 Berlin, 617–630.

Stephen V. Rice. 1996. *Measuring the Accuracy of Page-Reading Systems.* Ph. D. dissertation, University of Nevada, Las Vegas, NV.

Martin Volk, Torsten Marek, and Rico Sennrich. 2010. *Reducing OCR Errors by Combining Two OCR Systems.* ECAI 2010 Workshop on Language Technology for Cultural Heritage, Social Sciences, and Humanities (LaTeCH 2010), Lisbon, Portugal, 16 August 2010 – 16 August 2010, 61–65.

Author Index